IRENAEUS OF LYONS

Eric Osborn's book presents a major study of Irenaeus (125–200), bishop of Lyons, who attacked Gnostic theosophy with positive ideas as well as negative critiques. Irenaeus' combination of argument and imagery, logic and aesthetic, was directed to a new document, the Christian bible. Dominated by a Socratic love of truth and a classical love of beauty he was a founder of Western humanism. Erasmus, who edited the first printed edition of Irenaeus, praised him for his freshness and vigour. He is today valued for his splendid aphorisms, his optimism, love of the created world, evolutionary view of history, theology of beauty, and humour. Why have two millennia of European culture been so creative? Irenaeus points to the sources: Greek ways of thinking and the Christian bible. Irenaeus' thought is complex, yet infinitely rewarding to the critical reader, and this full study of it will be of interest to theologians, historians of ideas, classicists, scientists and students.

ERIC OSBORN is Honorary Professor at the Department of History, La Trobe University and Professorial Fellow at the Department of Fine Arts, Classical Studies and Archaeology, University of Melbourne. His books (some of which have been translated into French and German) include *The beginning of Christian philosophy* (Cambridge, 1981), *The emergence of Christian theology* (Cambridge, 1993) and *Tertullian, first theologian of the West* (Cambridge, 1997).

IRENAEUS OF LYONS

ERIC OSBORN

Honorary Professor, La Trobe University, Melbourne
and
Professorial Fellow, University of Melbourne

CAMBRIDGE
UNIVERSITY PRESS

CAMBRIDGE UNIVERSITY PRESS
Cambridge, New York, Melbourne, Madrid, Cape Town, Singapore, São Paulo

Cambridge University Press
The Edinburgh Building, Cambridge CB2 2RU, UK

Published in the United States of America by Cambridge University Press, New York

www.cambridge.org
Information on this title: www.cambridge.org/9780521800068

© Eric Osborn 2001

First published 2001
This digitally printed first paperback version 2005

A catalogue record for this publication is available from the British Library

Library of Congress Cataloguing in Publication data
Osborn, Eric Francis.
Irenaeus of Lyons / Eric Osborn.
p.   cm.
Includes bibliographical references and index.
ISBN 0 521 80006 4 (hardback)
1. Christian saints – France – Lyon – Biography.
2. Irenaeus, Saint, Bishop of Lyon. I. Title.
BR1720.17 083 2001
270.1´092 – dc21
[B]   2001 025635 CIP

ISBN-13 978-0-521-80006-8 hardback
ISBN-10 0-521-80006-4 hardback

ISBN-13 978-0-521-67572-7 paperback
ISBN-10 0-521-67572-3 paperback

To
Sophie and Genevieve

Contents

Preface

In Irenaeus, Athens and Jerusalem meet at Patmos. The visions of
the prophets, which point to Christ, take the place of Plato's forms
and from them he proves the truth of the apostolic preaching. Here
Irenaeus follows Justin but with wider vision, for he is the first
writer to have a Christian bible before him. To this text he applies
the classical criteria of logic (what is true) and aesthetics (what is
fitting) to draw out his four concepts of divine Intellect, economy,
recapitulation and participation. His two criteria, along with his
exuberant images, present his reader first with a jungle and then
with a clear synthesis. From one central point he moves through the
universe of biblical imagery, rubbing argument and image together
because each is necessary to the other.

Irenaeus is a difficult author because of conflict within a clear
general structure. Loofs identified multiple sources and wished
to prove incoherence. His analysis was reasonably rejected by
Hitchcock and others. His general claim for multiple sources stands,
but his procedure is regressive rather than progressive. An interpreter may note what a source meant in an earlier context, but his
chief interest is what the author or compiler makes of anything he
includes. A second objection to Irenaeus was more to the point:
Koch alleged conceptual bankruptcy or a general lack of coherent
ideas.

The first step out of the genuine despair, which every interpreter
of Irenaeus knows, is a recognition of Irenaeus' criteria. Alongside
his logical argument which pursues truth there is his perception
of fitness. This governs the apparently ridiculous claim that there
must be four Gospels because there are four winds and because
living things are tetramorphous. With prophetic visions as the final

xi

source of truth, aesthetic fitness governs exposition. Here the interpreter of Irenaeus needs a poet. I was fortunate to find Chris Wallace Crabbe's comic poem 'Why does a cauliflower so much resemble a brain?' and to discuss with him the way poetic association works. Prophetic imagery is born afresh in Irenaeus through poetic association. How argument and imagery fit together is an endless inquiry. Their presence as two criteria must be recognised in Irenaeus and the whole of Christian culture.

The other step for an interpreter is to identify the concepts, which govern his author's thought. For much of the twentieth century no one wrote a theology of Irenaeus. Many wrote on specific concepts of economy (divine plan) and recapitulation (summing-up of all things). These concepts do not explain, however, the immediacy of God whose glory is a living man. Following the useful rule that a thinker's ideas centre on the points where his interpreters disagree, the concept of participation emerged. Since participation is always participation of someone or something, the concept of the divine Intellect as the source of all goodness moved to the beginning of the analysis. Participation is only possible if God wills to share his goodness. The four concepts: divine Intellect, economy, recapitulation and participation govern the gospel, which Irenaeus declares. God and man are joined when God becomes what men are in order to bring them to be what he is. Economy and recapitulation join, as Irenaeus puts it, the end to the beginning, man to God. The four concepts are intelligible in succession: the divine Intellect plans the economy, which ends in recapitulation and the sharing of divine goodness. They must be kept together. The immediacy of God is known because God creates from nothing, never allows Adam to leave his hands, becomes man that man might share in God. If we ignore the first and last concepts (divine goodness and participation) we omit the point of the process, which is to join divine glory to human life. Economy and recapitulation lose point without their source (divine goodness) and end (participation).

To the logical exploration of these ideas Irenaeus adds his other criterion, an aesthetic of divine glory. The divine economy is a prolongation of God, which may be seen. Irenaeus is an empiricist whose vision of God is the source of life. This element of Irenaeus has constituted his appeal to Christians over the centuries. It may be noted in contrast to a modern writer whose language reflects many of the ideas of Irenaeus. T. S. Eliot speaks, as does Irenaeus, of the moment in which past and future are conquered and reconciled, and of the crowned knot of fire in which all is brought to a good end. Yet Eliot writes with the hostility of an Absolute Idealist to empiricism which is the folly of old men. Irenaeus is close to Hopkins who sees God's glory in the world.

How do we use the four concepts and the two criteria to combat the accusation of confusion against Irenaeus? First, we must identify the vocabulary which Irenaeus uses to express his concepts. We must learn his language. Because Irenaeus is drawing on different sources, we must show that his opinions are not confined to one part of his work. Secondly, vocabulary takes meaning within argument. Therefore we must trace his arguments which are of three kinds. There is straight logical argument as in the refutation of Gnosticism in Book 2. There is the accumulated imagery of lists of prophecy which prove the truth of the apostolic preaching. Finally there is the composite argument of Irenaeus where the logic leap-frogs through scripture which is its guarantee of truth. This is exemplified in the two arguments, which end in love of enemies as the essence of recapitulation. These different kinds of argument are to be expected from the two criteria of logic and aesthetics.

One point of possible confusion may be clarified. I have hesitantly (because of probable misunderstanding) pointed to the presence of a Platonic paradigm in Irenaeus. He explicitly opposes Platonism on fundamental points: the status of forms and the material world, the meaning of history and the nature of man. Yet willy-nilly he thinks in the framework of his time and shares with the opposing Platonic underworld an intellectual machinery which makes controversy and new thought possible.

Remarkably, the chief influence of Gnosticism on Irenaeus was that it forced him to take Athens seriously. Gnosticism had to be met near Plato. Reasoned argument had to guide a barrage of texts. As a result Gnosticism (theosophy) stimulated its opposite (philosophy) and exegesis to produce Christian theology. Argument and imagery presented to inquirers a better use of the Socratic tradition. Gnostics were strong on picture and myth but weak on argument. When we have seen this, we begin to understand the second century, that fertile period which formed Western thought.

Since my concern is to understand Irenaeus, his criteria and his concepts, I have taken the account of his Protean opponents at face value. By setting out the teachings to which he is opposed he has defined the indefinable Gnosticism in a way that seems no longer possible. Since the variety of groups called 'Gnostic' rivals the incoherence of contemporary Anglo-American Christianity, some scholars today challenge the usefulness of the term. Even the general assessment of Gnostics is uncertain. Once seen (by Irenaeus and Plotinus) as world-haters, many are now seen as world-lovers, who were concerned to lessen the tension between their religion and society. I have discussed these issues in an appendix; but they are marginal to my purpose. Fortunately, Irenaeus set out carefully the views, which he rejected; their importance for us is that they gave him a stimulus without which he might never have completed the first great synthesis of Christian thought. The exploration of that synthesis is my concern. His claim that the transcendence of divine love implies God's immediacy may be a rejection of the 'separate God' of Gnosticism; but it is much more besides. It is a profound interpretation of the Christian gospel.

Orbe's favoured epithet for Irenaeus was 'rich'. This prolixity has squeezed out many pages of secondary discussion and I cannot hope to indicate my debt to those who have written about him during the last two hundred years. What remains will demonstrate that Irenaeus not only said good things, but that he gave good reasons for saying these things. The general reader may bypass, on first reading, the multiplicity of references to the text, which the scholar needs in order to learn the language of Irenaeus, to prove that the four concepts are universal and to elucidate their meaning. Equally important is the analysis of argument, for it is here, not in the aphorisms, that the synthesis of Irenaeus is evident.

From conversations over the years with Jacques Fantino, E. P. Meijering and John Rist, each of whom read a first draft, and with Norbert Brox, Louis Doutreleau, Robert Grant, Christoph Markschies, Denis Minns, Antonio Orbe, Pierre Prigent, and Bernard Sesboüé, I have learnt more than I can say. The late André Benoit was my colleague in Strasbourg twenty years ago.

They all saw Irenaeus' richness of thought, imagery and humanity. I am profoundly grateful to them. John Behr and Bernard Sesboüé sent me, in advance, the proofs of their fine new books.

In Rome, the community and library of the Augustinianum have helped me greatly. In Cambridge, Wesley House and my own college (Queens') have always been hospitable, while at Tübingen the Stift has warmly received me. At the local level, I have gained much from colleagues in History at La Trobe University and in Classics at Melbourne. Margot Hyslop of the Borchardt Library, La Trobe, has been a constant help.

From John Honner (who edited first and final drafts), Clive Bloomfield (who checked all Irenaeus' references), Grantley McDonald (who checked other references) and Edward Morgan (who found books and typed) I have received indispensable aid through the generosity of the Australian Research Council.

Finally, my thanks go to Jan Chapman and Kevin Taylor of Cambridge University Press who thoughtfully and intelligently guided the manuscript into print.

The book is dedicated, with great affection, to my granddaughters, Sophie and Genevieve.

Abbreviations

ABR	*Australian Biblical Review*
AJPP	*Australasian Journal of Philosophy and Psychology*
AHAW.PH	Abhandlungen der Heidelberger Akademie der Wissenschaften – Philosophisch-historische Klasse
ANCL	Ante-Nicene Christian Library
AThR	*Anglican Theological Review*
Aug	*Augustinianum*
BJRL	*Bulletin of the John Rylands Library*
BLE	*Bulletin de littérature ecclésiastique*
ChH	*Church History*
CICL	Cahiers de l'institut catholique de Lyon
CNRS	Centre National de la Recherche Scientifique
CSCO	Corpus Scriptorum Christianorum Orientalium
DK	H. Diels and W. Kranz, *Die Fragmente der Vorsokratiker* (7th edn; Berlin, 1951–4)
DR	*Downside Review*
DS	*Dictionnaire de spiritualité*
DViv	*Dieu vivant*
EThL	*Ephemerides theologicae Lovanienses*
EThSt	Erfurter Theologische Studien
EvQ	*Evangelical Quarterly*
FZPhTh	*Freiburger Zeitschrift für Philosophie und Theologie*
GOTR	*Greek Orthodox Theological Review*
Greg	*Gregorianum*
H.E.	Eusebius, *Ecclesiastical History*
HTh	*History and Theory*
HThR	*Harvard Theological Review*
Irén	*Irénikon*

JThS	*Journal of Theological Studies*
KRS	G. S. Kirk, J. E. Raven and M. Schofield, *The Presocratic philosophers* (2nd edn; Cambridge, 1983)
LCL	Loeb Classical Library
LS	A. A. Long and D. N. Sedley, *The Hellenistic philosophers*, 2 vols. (Cambridge, 1987)
Miss	*Missionalia*
MThZ	*Münchener Theologische Zeitschrift*
Mus	*Muséon*
NAKG	*Nederlandsch archief voor kerkgeschiedenis*
NAWG.PH	Nachrichten der Akademie der Wissenschaften in Göttingen – Philologisch-historische Klasse
NedThT	*Nederlandsche Theologisch Tijdschrift*
NRTh	*Nouvelle revue théologique*
NT	*Novum Testamentum*
NTS	*New Testament Studies*
OrChrAn	Orientalia Christiana Analecta
PAS	*Proceedings of the Aristotelian Society*
PG	*Patrologia graeca* (Migne)
Ph	*Philologus*
Phron	*Phronesis*
REG	*Revue des études grecques*
RevBen	*Revue Benedictine*
RevSR	*Revue des sciences religieuses*
RFNS	*Revista di filosofia neo-scolastica*
RHPhR	*Revue d'histoire et de philosophie religieuses*
RSLR	*Revista di storia e letteratura religiosa*
RSPhTh	*Revue des sciences philosophiques et théologiques*
RSR	*Recherches de science religieuse*
RThAM	*Recherches de théologie ancienne et médiévale*
RThPh	*Revue de théologie et de philosophie*
RTR	*Reformed Theological Review*
SC	Sources chrétiennes
Schol	*Scholastik*
SecCent	*Second Century*
SJTh	*Scottish Journal of Theology*
StMiss	*Studia missionalia*

StTh	*Studia theologica*
StudAns	*Studia Anselmiana*
StudPatr	*Studia patristica*
SVF	*Stoicorum Veterum Fragmenta*
SVTQ	*St Vladimir's Theological Quarterly*
ThH	Théologie historique
ThLZ	*Theologische Literaturzeitung*
ThQ	*Theologische Quartalschrift*
ThR	*Theologische Rundschau*
ThStK	*Theologische Studien und Kritiken*
Trad	*Traditio*
TRE	*Theologische Realenzyklopädie*
TS	*Theological Studies*
TU	Texte und Untersuchungen
USQR	*Union Seminary Quarterly Review*
VigChr	*Vigiliae Christianae*
VetChr	*Vetera Christianorum*
ZAC	*Zeitschrift für antikes Christentum*
ZKG	*Zeitschrift für Kirchengeschichte*
ZKTh	*Zeitschrift für katholische Theologie*
ZNW	*Zeitschrift für die neutestamentliche Wissenschaft*
ZThK	*Zeitschrift für Theologie und Kirche*

Titles of Greek patristic writings follow the abbreviations of G. W. H. Lampe, *A dictionary of patristic Greek* (Oxford, 1961).

REFERENCES TO IRENAEUS

(3.3.1) refers to *Against heresies*, Book 3, chapter 3, paragraph 1 (SC); (4 pref. 4) refers to *Against heresies*, Book 4, preface, paragraph 4; (*dem.* 20) refers to *Demonstration of the apostolic preaching*, section 20 (SC); (frag. 4) refers to fragment 4 in the edition of W. Harvey (Cambridge, 1857).

CHAPTER I

Irenaeus: argument and imagery

1.1 LIFE AND WORK

The original Greek text of Irenaeus' *Against heresies* is found only in fragmentary form, while a complete Latin translation prepared about the year 380 has survived. There are three early manuscripts of the Latin translation, the oldest of which (Claromontanus) dates from the tenth or eleventh century. The others are later (Leydensis, Arundelianus). Erasmus' *editio princeps* of Irenaeus (1526) contains some readings not represented by any of these three manuscripts and the sources from which his variants may derive have since disappeared. Useful editions of *Against heresies* have subsequently been prepared by Massuet, Stieren and Harvey. The recent edition by Rousseau, Doutreleau and others (Sources Chrétiennes) supersedes earlier editions.

Eusebius mentions another work by Irenaeus, *The demonstration of the apostolic preaching*, known since 1907 in a sixth-century Armenian version. Lost works include the *Letter to Florinus* (also known as *Concerning the sole rule of God, or that God is not the author of evil*), *On the Ogdoad*, an attack on the Valentinian Ogdoad, which presents primitive apostolic tradition, *On schism*, addressed to Blastus and *On knowledge*, a refutation of paganism. Irenaeus intended (but did not produce) a work against Marcion (3.12.12). His writings all date from the last two decades of the second century.

Most early theologians were travellers, but their movements and teachers are not always certain. Justin tells us his Palestinian place of birth and philosophical pedigree, and sets his dialogue in Ephesus;[1] his apology and the report of his martyrdom establish that he taught

---

[1] According to Eusebius, *H.E.* 4.18.8.

and died at Rome. Tertullian illuminates his own native setting in
Carthage, but says nothing of time spent elsewhere. Clement of
Alexandria tells us where he went to learn (*stromateis* 1.1.11) but
does not name his teachers.

We know a little more of Irenaeus' personal life and history.
There are limits: despite attempts to prove his non-Hellenic origin, his birthplace remains uncertain. There is wide disagreement on the date of his birth, with estimates from those of
Dodwell (AD 98), Grabe (108), Tillémont and Lightfoot (120), Ropes
(126), Harvey (130), to those of Dupin, Massuet and Kling (140),
Böhringer, Ziegler and others (147). The most probable date lies
between 130 and 140.[2] The early estimates ignore the late development of his writing. The late estimates probably make him
too young for episcopacy in 177, when he succeeded the ninety-
year-old Pothinus. Irenaeus' claim (5.30.3) that the Apocalypse was
written towards the end of the reign of Domitian († 96) and near to
the time of his own generation makes a year of birth much after 130
improbable, since a generation was commonly reckoned as thirty
or forty years.

There is an uncertain tradition that Irenaeus died as a martyr
in 202 or 203 during the persecution of Septimius Severus.[3] This
claim is first found (410) in Jerome's commentary on Isaiah (ch. 64),
but not in his earlier (392) *De viris illustribus*, suggesting that the
story may be an interpolation from Gallic traditions concerning
the havoc of the persecution in Lyons.

The church at Lyons had begun about the middle of the second
century, since those arrested in 177 included its founders. The
community was originally Greek and Greek-speaking but included
Romans whose Latin names occur among those of the martyrs.
Irenaeus indicates a Celtic element in the church and it is clear
that, although small, the community represented all social ranks.
The churches of Lyons and nearby Vienne were closely related,
while connections with Rome and Asia Minor were strong; but the
church did not reflect the dominance of the city in the whole of

---

[2] A. Benoit, *Saint-Irénée, introduction à l'étude de sa théologie* (Paris, 1960), 50.
[3] See J. van der Straeten, 'Saint-Irénée fut-il martyre?', in *Les martyrs de Lyon (177)*, CNRS
(Paris, 1978), 145–52. The whole of this book is useful for the understanding of the
historical background to Irenaeus.

Gaul.[4] Lyons was the centre, indeed the 'recapitulation' where all Gaul came together: 'All the threads of Roman public service in this great region converged at Lugdunum and were gathered up at that centre.'[5]

Irenaeus was still young when, at the royal court in Smyrna, he heard and saw Polycarp († 155/6).[6] The reference to the 'royal court' does not establish that the emperor was there at the time, nor is the emperor to be identified certainly with Hadrian, who was resident at Smyrna for the second time between 127 and 129. The period in question could better refer to 136, when the future emperor Antoninus Pius was in Smyrna as Proconsul of Asia. Irenaeus' report of Polycarp's words on the decline of the times imply that Polycarp was an older man when Irenaeus heard him, and that he himself was young. A Moscow manuscript of the *Martyrdom of Polycarp* states that Irenaeus was teaching in Rome at the time of Polycarp's death.

Irenaeus names Polycarp as the dominant influence of his youth. As a bishop, Irenaeus was closer to the collegiate pattern of Polycarp than to the monarchical pattern of Ignatius.[7] We know from Irenaeus (3.3.4) that Polycarp visited Rome two years before his martyrdom to confer with Anicetus on controversy concerning the date of Easter (*H.E.* 5.24.12–17).

Irenaeus elegantly claims to have no rhetoric or excellence of style,[8] but shows some rhetorical skill and a knowledge of the works of Plato, Homer, Hesiod and Pindar. Although he does not confront the philosophical tradition as do Clement and Origen, his account of God reveals his awareness of the Middle Platonic and Stoic philosophies of the day. He may have gone to Rome to study rhetoric and then gone on to Lyons.[9] However, Smyrna was a centre of the Second Sophistic movement and his skills could have been learnt at home. His attack on Sophists may be seen as turning

---

[4] Benoit, *Introduction*, 52 5.
[5] James S. Reid, *The municipalities of the Roman empire* (Cambridge, 1913), 179.
[6] Irenaeus, *Letter to Florinus*, in Eusebius, *H.E.* 4.14.
[7] J. de Roulet, 'Saint Irénée évêque', *RHPhR* 73,3 (1993), 261 80.
[8] This does not mean, as Harvey argues, that he was of Syrian origin. See W. Harvey, *Against heresies*, text (Cambridge, 1857), vol. I, cliv.
[9] P. Nautin, *Lettres et écrivains chrétiens des IIe et IIIe siècles* (Paris, 1961), 93. See whole section 33 104.

sophistic weapons against their owners, although Benoit considered that he 'has not totally assimilated rhetoric'.[10] His dominat-
ing love of truth came through Justin, from Socrates, Plato and
Paul.

Irenaeus travelled (by way of Rome) to the great city of Lyons,
situated at the confluence of the Rhône and the Saône in the centre
of Celtic Gaul, which at that time stretched from the Seine to the
Garonne.[11] During the persecution of the church at Lyons in 177,
he carried a letter from the confessors in Lyons to Eleutherus,
bishop of Rome. It is possible that Irenaeus was already bishop
of Vienne and that he took over the care of both churches when
Pothinus died. This would explain why Irenaeus was not himself
in prison at the time.[12] Irenaeus' journey, 'for the peace of the
churches', was on behalf of the confessors at Lyons (*H.E.* 5.3.4).
In the same year Pothinus, bishop of Lyons, died in prison, and
Irenaeus succeeded to his office. Irenaeus' participation in current
controversies extended into Victor's tenure as bishop of Rome. His
Against heresies[13] was written at Lyons.

We have in a letter an extended account of the persecution at
Lyons. The servants of Christ in Vienne and Lyons send to Asian
and Phrygian brethren a greeting for 'peace, grace and glory' based
on a common faith and hope in redemption (*H.E.* 5.1.3). The
violent sufferings of the martyrs are contrasted with their moderation and humanity (*H.E.* 5.2.7). The churches of Vienne and
Lyons enjoy peace and concord because of the virtues of the
martyrs. Vettius Epagathas, for instance, 'possesses fullness of
love to God and neighbour', is fervent in the spirit and is the
comforter of Christians because he has within him the comforter, the spirit. The fullness of his love is seen in his defence
of his brothers, for whom he gives his life (*H.E.* 5.1.9–10).
The criterion of a true prophet is not asceticism but love of

---

[10] See Benoit, *Introduction* (58 9), who cites A. Boulanger, *Aelius Aristide et la sophistique dans les provinces d'Asie-Mineure au IIe siècle de notre ère* (Paris, 1923), 441 4. See also F. Sagnard, *La gnose valentinienne et le témoignage de saint Irénée* (Paris, 1947), 69 80 and R. M. Grant, 'Irenaeus and hellenistic culture', *HThR* 42 (1949), 41 51.

[11] L. Cracco Ruggini, 'Les structures de la société et de l'économie lyonnaises par rapport à la politique locale et impériale', in *Les martyrs (177)*, 65 97.

[12] Nautin, *Lettres et écrivains*, 94.

[13] The shorter title given to 'Unmasking and overthrow of so-called knowledge'.

God and neighbour.[14] The story of Blandina gives the same pre-eminence to love (*H.E.* 5.1.55–6). Pothinus was fortified by the power of the spirit with a burning desire to be a martyr (*H.E.* 5.1.29). The martyrs had the holy spirit as their counsellor (*H.E.* 5.3.3), and Irenaeus came with their commendation (*H.E.* 5.4).[15]

In the brief letter to Eleutherus, the martyrs commend Irenaeus as brother, companion and 'zealous for the covenant of Christ' (*H.E.* 5.4.2), a description reminiscent of Elijah, who was very zealous for the Lord God (1 Kings 19:14), and of Mattathias, who was zealous for the law (1 Macc. 2:27).[16] Eusebius' claim that Irenaeus was a peacemaker in name and nature (*H.E.* 5.24.18) is not simply a play on words but a fact borne out by Irenaeus' life and work (*H.E.* 5.23–5).

His irenic approach shows that his objection to heresies on matters of faith had little to do with a struggle for power. Peace was strengthened by disagreement on points which were not matters of faith (*H.E.* 5.24). Even on matters of faith, elsewhere he prays for his adversaries whom he loves more than they love themselves (3.25.7). Eusebius considers the Easter controversy to be very serious. The Roman church's authoritarian intervention in the controversy shocked the churches. Irenaeus stood in the middle of this debate; his theology of redemption, while close to the view of the Quartodecimans as expounded by Melito, was quite compatible with the Roman view of Easter. Irenaeus argued to Victor that both parties in the controversy should be free to celebrate Easter in the tradition of their own church, pointing out that no Roman predecessor had thought it necessary to excommunicate the churches of Asia Minor for their adherence to a primitive practice (*H.E.* 5.24).

Irenaeus explains the difference between the Quartodeciman practice of the Asian churches and other churches, who refused to end their fast on any other day than Sunday, the day of resurrection.

---

[14] 'Une telle présentation insistant sur l'amour et le Saint Esprit se pose discrètement en antithèse de Montan et de ses prophétesses', E. Lanne, 'Saint Irénée de Lyon, artisan de la paix entre les églises', *Irén* 69 (1996), 457.

[15] Lanne, 'Saint Irénée de Lyon', 458–9.

[16] Ibid., 460.

If the Quartodeciman practice could not claim ancient and apostolic tradition, Polycrates of Ephesus found a basis for this position in Philip and John, who kept the fourteenth day according to the gospel and the rule of faith (*H.E.* 5.24.6). He agrees that the mystery of resurrection should be celebrated only on the Lord's day, but urges Victor not to reject those churches which hold to an ancient custom. He goes on to talk of different traditions of fasting which had their origin in the past. Our predecessors (he argues), without precision, preserved and transmitted their custom in simplicity; despite their differences, they kept the peace. In striking words, he claims that 'disagreement on fasting validates the agreement on faith';[17] differences of practice had been tolerated because they did not compromise the essential unity of the faith. In the second passage which Eusebius cites, Irenaeus offers examples from history – Roman bishops before Soter had accepted the Quartodeciman practice. They did not observe this practice themselves, but maintained peace with those who did. Irenaeus gives the example of Polycarp and Anicetus. When Polycarp visited Rome, the bishop deferred to him in sacramental communion. Accordingly, peace should prevail rather than uniformity of practice. Matters of faith are different, because, as he points out (1.10.1, 2), there was one faith throughout the world.

In Irenaeus' explanation (4.33) of Paul's words that a truly spiritual disciple judges all and is himself judged by no one (1 Cor. 2:15), a reference to the Montanist controversy has been discerned: he who has received the spirit of God stands in succession to the prophets whose history of salvation he interprets. The truly spiritual disciple confronts the 'pneumatics', the heretics who reject the truth of the church. He also judges false prophets, those who cause schism, who lack the love of God, and who divide the great and glorious body of Christ; these strain at a gnat and swallow a camel (4.33.7). Irenaeus goes on to speak about the supreme gift of love that joins the martyr to the true prophet and to the truly spiritual disciple.

The name of Irenaeus as a peacemaker spread far and wide. A fragment of *Against heresies*, found at Oxyrhynchus, is contemporary

---

[17] καὶ ἡ διαφωνία τῆς νηστείας τὴν ὁμόνοιαν τῆς πίστεως συνίστησι.

with Irenaeus himself. This shows the speed with which his ideas concerning concord between different traditions influenced the whole church.

How close was the link between the churches of Asia and Lyons? Opinions differ. Bowersock denies all relation between the churches of Lyons and Asia. Kraft claims the church at Lyons to be pre-Montanist and closely linked with Asia. Mondésert sums up the controversy as 'not proven'. Frend claims that the church at Lyons, originally touched by Montanism, came to reject it because of its divisive tendencies.[18]

1.2 IRENAEUS PHILOSOPHUS?

The perennial appeal of Irenaeus springs, says Sagnard, from his sincerity and optimism.[19] In 1526 Erasmus wrote with enthusiasm of the freshness and vigour which he found in the work he edited. The writings of Irenaeus seemed fresh with the first force of the gospel and the dedication of one who is ready to die for his faith. Martyrs have a distinctive diction which is earnest, strong and bold. Irenaeus gained these qualities because of his proximity to the days of the apostles and the flowers of martyrdom. He had listened avidly to Polycarp, who had known apostles who had seen and heard the lord and who possessed a vivid and comprehensive memory. From such beginnings the writings of Irenaeus convey the heart of the gospel and the aspiration of martyrdom.

Irenaeus' strength of mind and strong digestive system (*patientis stomachi*) enabled him, said Erasmus, to handle the tedious monstrosities of the heretics. His opponent Valentinus was a most pompous Platonist who turned his gifts to the confusion of the church and the fabrication of intricate fables. Against the carping of impious philosophers, the philosophy of the gospel is established in strength. While Irenaeus is provoked by the censures of the heretics, his chief concern is positive; the response far exceeds the stimulus. He must use the whole armament of the divine scriptures to confirm the truth which has been attacked. The first Christian

---

[18] See *Les martyrs (177)*, where each of these views is stated.
[19] Sagnard, *La gnose valentinienne*, 78 9.

conflict had been against the Jews. The second was against philosophers and heretics. Philosophy which had caused the trouble, provided the cure. When Valentinus philosophus attacked the church,
Justin philosophus and Irenaeus philosophus defended it. Marcion
philosophus was answered by Tertullian philosophus and Celsus
philosophus by Origen philosophus. Erasmus concludes with the
hope that God will raise up peacemakers (Irenaei) to lead the church
of his day out of its troubles.

   Despite his physical revulsion against the theosophical maunder-
ings of Valentinus, Erasmus still calls him a philosopher. Here he
follows the convention of his time and brings out the point that the
contest was intellectual and not a struggle for power. Valentinus
may have lacked all the qualities which Erasmus looked for in a
human mind, but he had to be elevated to the status of philosopher in order to be attacked by argument.[20] Today questions of
genre ('Is X a philosopher?') are rightly considered less important than the identification of 'the people with poetic gifts, all
the original minds who had a talent for redescription'.[21] Gnostics cited philosophical opinions without argument, and philosophy without argument is like opera without music, ballet without movement and Shakespeare without words. Irenaeus shows
less knowledge of philosophy than he does of literature and
rhetoric. Philosophers' opinions (cited thirty-two times, chiefly
in Book 2), as distinct from the practice of argument, were of
little use.[22] They are never an indication of philosophy, which
may be found rather in Irenaeus' love of argument, subtlety of
reasoning, and sense of measure and harmony.[23] Nevertheless,
because of popular convention and inevitable misunderstanding, it is unwise to follow Erasmus in speaking of Irenaeus as
a philosopher.

[20] Today we might distinguish between a philosopher's philosopher and an historian's
    philosopher. A philosopher's philosopher argues about such subjects as God, freedom,
    immortality, logic, epistemology, aesthetics, ethics and such subjects as have been linked
    with them by philosophical convention. Clement of Alexandria, following Aristotle, in-
    sisted that philosophy was necessary, because if you argued that it was not you had already
    begun to philosophize. The historian's philosopher cites the opinions of philosophers, ar-
    guing very little if at all.
[21] R. Rorty, *Contingency, irony and solidarity* (Cambridge, 1989), 76.
[22] Benoit, *Introduction*, 73
[23] Ibid., 50 and Sagnard, *La gnose valentinienne*, 70–7.

1.3 THE UNEXPECTED JUNGLE

No one has presented a more unified account of God, the world and history than has Irenaeus. From the moment of his creation, Adam never left the hands of God. The entire universe, visible and invisible, has been brought together in Christ. 'There is one God the father . . . and one Christ our lord who comes through the whole economy to sum up the universe in himself . . . and as head of the church he draws all things to himself at the proper time' (3.16.6). 'There is nothing out of place' (3.16.7). This unbroken unity embraces opposites, as prophets and psalms declare that the man without beauty, humble and humiliated is holy lord, wonderful counsellor, beautiful, mighty God and coming judge (3.19.2). In contrast to this universal synthesis, the reader of Irenaeus is confronted by stark problems of incoherence, which provoked the conclusion by two great scholars that the thought of Irenaeus is a jungle (*Urwald, forêt vierge*).[24] No careful reader of Irenaeus can avoid the sense of confusion.

The nineteenth century produced many valuable expositions of Irenaeus. Duncker found a system in Irenaeus which cohered around his christology. Irenaeus had turned to John for theology, to Paul for anthropology, and his christology joined these two different tendencies. Later writers denied the systematic nature of the doctrine of Irenaeus, although they did not agree on the kind of system they were rejecting. Ziegler would not set out a coherent system which began from a central point and showed breaks within the system presented by Duncker. What we have in Irenaeus, according to Ziegler, is not so much his own system but rather the common doctrine of the ancient church. Irenaeus the bishop wishes to set out the main points of the doctrine of the universal church. Harnack adopted a fragmentary approach to Irenaeus: there was no synthesis, but many separate pieces of tradition which needed to be identified. The ruling principles were that the same God was creator and saviour and that Jesus Christ is saviour as God who has become man.

---

[24] Literally 'primeval forest', 'virgin forest': Koch and D'Alès respectively. The former describes Irenaeus as a confused compiler 'doctor constructivus et confusus'.

In the early twentieth century, Bonwetsch produced a lucid and concise account, then Koch claimed a limited coherence on the subject of Adam and evolution but could not credit Irenaeus with anything like general coherence. Beuzart did not see any conceptual scheme in Irenaeus, whose thought he deemed to be governed by polemic and practical needs. Consequently the difficulties and obscurities do not reward investigation. Lawson found nothing systematic in Irenaeus but believed that the many details of his thought had a common effect.

The scene remains confused. The distinguished major contributor, Orbe, has established a school of interpretation which follows his own voluminous work. Orbe takes the whole of Irenaeus seriously, understands him profoundly and explores him endlessly. Yet Orbe's success is almost a deterrent, because he refuses to abbreviate the rich complexity of Irenaeus and the mass of argument and imagery leaves readers overwhelmed.

In English there have been two recent short works, both written as part of a series based on a particular method. Grant set out the historical and cultural background of Irenaeus and selected passages which illuminate the background and the content of Irenaeus. While Minns is aware of complexity, a necessary brevity limits his exposition to Irenaeus' account of what become the main elements of Christian doctrine.[25] Fantino and Sesboüé offer extended treatments and other works may be expected, for there is interest in Irenaeus and appreciation of his worth. Much of the recent energy expended in Irenaean studies has gone into the preparation of an excellent text and translation, where the work of Rousseau and Doutreleau displays depth of understanding.

1.4 SOURCE CRITICISM AND CONCEPTUAL BANKRUPTCY

Early in the twentieth century, there appeared a remarkable work of source criticism which was to define the mood of scholarship for many years. Loofs analysed the writing of Irenaeus into four or five main sources which were mutually incoherent.[26] According to

---

[25] This is justified because Irenaeus claims that all thinking must be done in the context of the rule of faith.

[26] Loofs built on earlier work of Harnack and Bousset.

Loofs, Irenaeus was, if anything, a bad theologian, and perhaps not even a theologian at all. Loofs concluded, 'Irenaeus has become a much slighter figure as a theological writer than was previously supposed . . . As a theologian he has become even smaller.'[27] Irenaeus was so confused that he allowed the attribute of divinity not only to the father and the son but also to believers (it did not occur to Loofs that this was what anyone might find in the Fourth Gospel). Further, Irenaeus' favourite theme of recapitulation is a trivial flourish which has no real basis in his thought.[28] Theophilus had done a better job. Only, concludes Loofs, when one distinguishes his own meagre theological contribution from the priceless sources which he conveyed, is it possible to understand why Irenaeus was so prized in the ancient church.[29]

While negative response to this analysis came from several sides, such as that of Montgomery Hitchcock, and Loofs' argument was taken apart, the composite nature of Irenaeus was sufficiently accepted to make further exposition insecure. In the middle of the century, Benoit wrote his introduction to the study of Irenaeus, a lucid work in which he indicated that the theology of Irenaeus must wait for an expositor. There was too much incoherence, he believed, to write anything more than an introduction. From the beginning he rejected Loofs' conclusions as incomplete because it seemed that Loofs had made no attempt to understand the total thought of Irenaeus.[30] He pleaded, 'Is it not possible today, after these analytic studies and the many works of detail on Irenaeus to give a more synthetic account of his thought and his theology?'[31] Since then, there have been many works on particular themes of Irenaeus, and the secondary literature has not ceased to grow.

---

[27] F. Loofs, *Theophilus von Antiochien adversus Marcionem und die anderen theologischen Quellen bei Irenaeus*, TU 46,2 (Leipzig, 1930), 432.
[28] Ibid., 434: 'wenn man davon absieht, was er an Lesefrüchten in dies bunte Gefäss hineingesteckt hat'. In source analysis, incompatible strands may be assigned to different sources before a thorough search for conceptual coherence has been made.
[29] Yet Loofs was not content with a fragmentary view of Irenaeus but analysed the sources of the different sections and then looked for something which joined them all together.
[30] Benoit, *Introduction*, 35: 'il faut . . . achever le travail de Loofs . . . il faut reconstituer l'image d'ensemble . . . retrouver la vie intérieure et profonde qui a animé cet homme que fut Irénée'. He cites Marc Bloch, 'l'objet de l'histoire est par nature l'homme' and H-I. Marrou, 'c'est la complexité du réel, de l'homme qui est l'objet de l'histoire'.
[31] Benoit, *Introduction*, 40–1.

In contrast to the general trend, Wingren[32] found in Irenaeus the fusion of all previous Christian tradition into a harmonious whole. Without predecessors, Irenaeus unified the many strands of Christian thought. Dominant in this unification was the concept of God's historical dealing with man (1.10.3). The first two and a half books of *Against heresies* provide a straightforward view of saving history in opposition to the Gnostics. Here Irenaeus is concerned with the one creator God through whose economy 'the cosmos and history are embraced and held, given form and order and healed and redeemed'.[33]

A second criticism (conceptual bankruptcy) was far more serious than that of Loofs. Koch, after a successful analysis of Irenaeus' motif of education, nevertheless insisted that one should not look for concepts in Irenaeus whose mind works with intuitions and impressions, or even in verbal play. He was not a man of ideas, according to Koch, and we should not look for rational coherence in his writings. Houssiau, on the other hand, usefully looked for cohesion or harmony within the ideas of Irenaeus, an aesthetic rather than a logical consistency.[34] The key criterion for Irenaeus is what is appropriate or fitting, *to prepon* ($\tau\grave{o}$ $\pi\rho\acute{e}\pi ov$). Particular concepts of Irenaeus have drawn exploration from many scholars. The most recent example is the work by John Behr on Irenaeus' anthropology. Within the limits of these specific studies Irenaeus has been shown, time and again, to be a creative and consistent thinker. Finally, Fantino produced what Benoit happily welcomed as the 'theology of Irenaeus' for which he had waited and, most recently, Sesboüé has shown the coherence of Irenaeus' thought around the central issue of recapitulation.

1.5 CONTENT, CONTOUR AND CONFLICT

Five centrifugal factors – diversity of adversary, tradition, scripture, imagery and aphorism – diffuse the thought of Irenaeus. Firstly, the

[32] G. Wingren, *Man and the incarnation. A study in the biblical theology of Irenaeus* (Edinburgh, 1959).
[33] M. Widmann, 'Irenäus und seine theologischen Väter', *ZThK* 54 (1957), 160.
[34] But see the limitations of his work as indicated by Benoit and Daniélou at Benoit, *Introduction*, 40 f.

diverse opinions and the particularity of Gnostic schools oblige him
to wander into different paths. Secondly, Irenaeus does not want to
say anything new. The tradition of the gospel is clear; yet tradition
is never homogeneous, but always marked by particular insights.
Thirdly, scripture is the supreme source of apostolic and prophetic
tradition. The variety of biblical witness seems invincible. Fourthly,
a mixture of images and ideas is never tidy. The exuberant images
are not a cadenza, a flourish within the main work, but the origin
of ideas. Fifthly, Irenaeus is concerned to purify the language of
the church and has the gift of striking utterance. His aphorisms are
famous ('The glory of God is a living man and the life of man is the
vision of God', 4.20.7) but their meaning is never obvious. Just as
Tertullian's striking aphorisms concerning Athens and Jerusalem,
or concerning the paradox of God and man, led his interpreters
time and again to misunderstand, so Irenaeus' brilliant sayings may
further disrupt the coherence of his work.

When confronted by such confusion, it is wise to ask three questions concerning *content, contour and conflict*.

The first question concerns *content*. What does Irenaeus say?
The overall plan of his *Against heresies* is straightforward. In the
first book, he sets out systems of gnosis with many variants. He
gives a genealogy of the Gnostic schools and makes the claim that
to overcome gnosis one needs simply to reveal and unmask. In
Book 2, he sets out a refutation of the doctrines he has listed in
Book 1. He refutes the heretical account of pleroma and aeons,
the arithmetical and exegetical exercises, and the account of the
final consummation. Then comes a refutation of the doctrines
of those who are not Valentinian. He speaks of the magic of
Carpocrates and Simon, of moral licentiousness, of transmigration
of souls. The different heavens of Basilides and the plurality of gods
are all attacked. In Book 3, he begins from the authority and truth
of scriptures, and then goes on to argue for the unicity of God and
the unicity of Christ. This he does on the basis of scriptures.
Book 4 has two main parts – in the first, Irenaeus refutes Gnosticism on the grounds of the clear and unambiguous statements
of Jesus, and in the second he refutes their account on the basis of the parables of Jesus. There are two smaller sections, one
which deals with the prophecies and the prophets, and the other

which deals with human free will. Book 5 is even simpler in its outline. It deals first with the words of Paul on the resurrection of the flesh, moves on to an extended account of the recapitulation in Christ and concludes with an exegesis of the temptation and two treatises, one on the Antichrist and the other on the millennium. The content, therefore, of the books, can be set out and seen at a glance.

Further, unity of content may be noted in the way in which the rule of faith brings clarity. God the father is perfect, omnipresent, sovereign mind, and the source of all good. God creates all things out of nothing, and man is his creature. God's plan is fulfilled through his constant activity from the beginning. The hands of God, the son and spirit never leave man but accustom him to God as they accustom God to man. Another theme which holds Irenaeus' thought together is the doctrine of recapitulation. By his life, death and resurrection, Christ corrected what had gone wrong in Adam and perfected what was begun in Adam. He inaugurated a new humanity which would find its consummation in the future. Because gnosis began with epistemology Irenaeus has a constant concern for truth and argument. The bible stands in the centre and Irenaeus is the first witness to a Christian bible containing works from old and new testaments. His understanding of scripture is not literal and biblicist, but theological and analytic. His ideas are formed through an understanding of the theology of Paul and John rather than from an accumulation of texts.[35] He takes from John the theme of glory and presents an aesthetic theology. Anthropology is a central concern, because Gnostics present a distinctive account of captive man. Man is made in the image and likeness of God and consists of body and soul with a gift of the divine spirit by which eternal life is possible. The ethical questions which are important in his conflict with the Gnostics concern free will, the martyr's love of truth and the love of enemies, for it is on the cross where Jesus forgives his enemies that God is most perfectly seen.

The second question concerns *contour*. There is a remarkable unity of content in Irenaeus through the rule of faith and the

---

[35] Like Clement of Alexandria, he interprets *kata noun* as distinct from *kata lexin*.

sequence of his own ideas. This is reassuring, but does not indicate a comprehensive account. All these themes may be found elsewhere in early Christian literature and they do not indicate the originality which we can sense in Irenaeus. Therefore we ask whether there is a shape to be found in his thought. Complex authors have an intellectual physiognomy which offers a way forward. Irenaeus invites diagrams, and many useful diagrams of his doctrine of recapitulation have been produced.[36] How did he think, how did he prove, how did he understand the ways of God? A good image is that of the hourglass lying on its side so that it presents a movement from left to right. It begins with creation and ends with the consummation of all things. The first half of the hourglass bears on its sides the message of the prophets. The visions of the prophets represent the mind of God, and take the place for Irenaeus of the world of Platonic forms. Like the forms, they reach a first principle in Christ as the Christian equivalent of the form of the good. The narrow neck of the hourglass is the recapitulation of all things in Christ, and the second half of the hourglass bears on its side the message of the prophets and the words of Christ and the apostles. Within the hourglass the believer lives, looking to the prophets through Christ and looking to the Gospels and the writings of the apostles. These represent the mind of God and find their climax in a form of perfect goodness which is Christ who sums up all things.

Irenaeus presents a continuous history which has a distinctive shape, where sources of knowledge are given through prophets and apostles to provide knowledge of truth. Irenaeus displays a form of horizontal Platonism.[37] Christ the rising sun sheds his light over the world and brings light to those who receive it. The prophets, saints and apostles, and above all the words of Jesus, take the place of the Platonic forms. So we may understand Irenaeus and his exegesis, which bounces off the sides of the hourglass in ways which

---

[36] See, for example, B. Sesboüé, *Tout récapituler dans le Christ, christologie et sotériologie d'Irénée de Lyon* (Paris, 2000), 182.

[37] In attributing a Platonic paradigm I am describing the general structure which the culture has imposed on his thought and not a conscious allegiance. We are all members of a linguistic community, which shapes our language. 'For it is not words which refer but speakers using words' who refer to the reality we confront; J. M. Soskice, *Metaphor and religious language* (Oxford, 1985), 136, with acknowledgement to Hilary Putnam, 'Realism and reason', in *Meaning and the moral sciences* (London, 1978), 123.

are provocative. His cadenzas are important because they indicate
divine truth in the words of prophets, Christ and the apostles. The
prolixity of Irenaeus is not a problem when we see it as an attempt
to convey the richness of the mind of God as found in scripture.

Irenaeus was not conscious of this Platonic pattern in his thought;
he did not acknowledge the authority of any philosopher and his
accounts of body, physical world, incarnation and history were
opposite to those of Plato. This Platonic pattern was simply the
way in which most minds of his time functioned and, in order to
communicate and to think alongside them, he reflected a Platonic
structure. We may call this a Platonic paradigm, and it may increase
hostility towards Christians from professed Platonists (like Celsus),
who acknowledge a loyalty to Plato. It is remarkable when we
look at Celsus alongside Origen, or Marcus Aurelius alongside
Tertullian, to find how similar is the logic of thought in opposing
sides. Without this similar structure, there was no way in which
attack or communication could take place. Irenaeus had taken
many of his Platonic insights from Justin, who equally rejected any
philosophical school, and insisted that truth was above and beyond
particular allegiance.

The third method for tracking down an elusive thinker is to
look at the points where his interpreters have disagreed vigorously.
These points of *conflict* will show that he has given grounds for
opposing views, and that his own view must be one which allows
for interpretation in opposite directions.

Consider first the various interpretations of Irenaeus' use of image and likeness. Here it has been argued that Irenaeus makes no
distinction between image and likeness, or that for him the image
is distinct from likeness and permanent in face of the variable likeness. Many ways of identification have been followed because of the
later Christian use of this phrase. There is an answer to the puzzle
to be found in the Platonic relation of participation, assimilation or
communion. A particular participates in a form and draws from
the form its being and identity. It can never become the form, but
can only become like the form. Plato talks, in his simplest account,
about the bed, which the carpenter makes, as being a copy, image
or likeness of the form of the ideal bed in heaven. In Irenaeus the
image of God given in creation is the beginning of the process of

growing like God. Because it is part of creation it will remain in all humans; all will have the possibility of participation and assimilation to God. What Adam lost was the likeness to God, which sprang from his participation. The affinity which lay behind this assimilation remained. Participation means that which participates both is and is not the object or form in which it participates. So it is possible for man to participate in God and still fall far short of God. Likeness to God can grow in humans, but never cease to be likeness rather than identity.

Or again, consider the arguments that have raged about Irenaeus' thought on the nature of man. Is man body, soul and spirit, or is he body and soul to be enlivened by the spirit of God? Here again Irenaeus follows the tradition of Justin, that the soul is not life, but participates in life. Therefore, apart from the spirit of God, the soul cannot live. Man as a living being must be body, soul and spirit. But the spirit is not a part of man in the way in which his body and soul are parts. The spirit comes from God. How then, his interpreters have puzzled, is the spirit of man to be considered? Is it divine spirit or is it merely a part of a human being? For Irenaeus the relationship between man and the divine spirit is one of participation. Body and soul participate in the divine spirit. Their participation is not complete identity and therefore must be considered as a copy, a pledge, or a share. It is and it is not divine spirit; it is a participation.

These two examples show that Irenaeus used a Platonic move to explain the relation of man to God. Man's perception of God, by which he gained life, was his participation in God. No one would deny that the Platonic concept of participation is full of difficulties; however, Plato was aware of those difficulties and even after he had stated them in the *Parmenides* still used the notion of participation to govern the relation between particulars and forms. Irenaeus uses this relationship to express man's real but incomplete participation in the life of God.

It will become increasingly clear that Irenaeus draws from his Platonic paradigm not merely an outline which presents his ethics, metaphysics and logic as a dialectic which culminates in Christ as first principle, but also the notion of participation, which governs the second half of this book.

Irenaeus is an enthusiast, and an enthusiast betrays his motives by
the way in which he writes. The dominant values of Irenaeus may
be grasped when we stand back from the text. First, Irenaeus follows
Justin as a lover of truth. He is concerned to argue and to expose
error, just as Socrates was first interested in the love of truth, which
he set above life itself. Justin had taken this theme in his apology
to the emperor, just as Socrates had done in his apology.[38] The
passion for truth, which marked the Platonic tradition, governs
Irenaeus in his approach to heresy, following the aphorism 'amicus
Plato, magis amica veritas'. This is what moves Irenaeus from the
beginning to the end of his work. He is concerned to argue, expose,
illuminate and expound. Furthermore, he gives us his criterion for
truth and sets out a rule, which contains the test of any proposition.
Just as philosophers followed a rule, so Irenaeus has a rule which
he is prepared to state.

The freshness of Irenaeus is due first to his passion for truth and,
secondly, to his sense of beauty and proportion, which is needed
because his source of truth is prophetic vision, not Platonic argument. He has a theological aesthetic which culminates in the vision
of divine glory. The prophets speak as moved by the spirit and in
description of their prophetic vision. This gives them immediate access to the mind of God. Therefore the interpreter of the bible must
take the patterns of saving history and link them in a way that is
fitting. The recurring argument in Irenaeus' exegesis has been char-
acterised as *decet – fieri potest – ergo est* (it is fitting – it is possible – therefore it is).[39] Like the philosopher of Plato, the interpreter who sees
the divine dialectic, divides and joins the visions which come to him.

The standard of *to prepon*, what is fitting or appropriate, governs
the coherence of biblical imagery. It has a long history in classical
and Hellenistic thought.[40] The verb appears in Homer with the

---

[38] See my *Justin Martyr* (Tübingen, 1973), 77–86.

[39] J. Hoh, *Die Lehre des hl. Irenäus über das Neue Testament* (Münster, 1919), 112. Here Hoh says
that this method could not refute Gnostic interpretation, because it was arbitrary and
overdone. 'Das Prinzip von der Tiefe der Schrift wird zu Tode geritten mit der (latent
wirkenden) Schlussformel: decet – fieri potest – ergo est.'

[40] The following synopsis of a controversial and wide-ranging theme is indebted to Max
Pohlenz, 'τὸ πρέπον, ein Beitrag zur Geschichte des griechischen Geistes', NAWG.PH 1
(1933), 53–93.

elementary meaning of 'what appears or seems', but moves quickly to become a concept of value so that 'what seems' is 'what is seemly'. In Aeschylus, for example, certain behaviour is appropriate to grief, and victory is appropriate to mortals. The verb now occurs in the third person only, frequently impersonal, while the participle *prepon* continues to be used.

So it is common to speak of types of behaviour which are appropriate for the old, for the young, for man, for woman, for slave and for free. Plato especially develops this idea. Ion speaks of the essence of his art as enabling each to speak in an appropriate manner, whether man or woman, slave or free, ruler or ruled, and in the *Gorgias* Plato speaks of painters, architects and others as having the one concern to join different things together and to harmonise them in a way which is appropriate (*Gorg.* 503e–504a). In oratory, mere technical skill is not enough. The true orator also needs to combine a sense of time with what is fitting and what is new. Already by the year 400 BC aesthetic theory requires that poetry and prose follow proportion in arrangement of parts and in the adjustment to persons concerned and the object under discussion. For Plato *to prepon* must also be applied to music (*Republic* 399a), and Aristides Quintilianus later defines music as combining voices and movement in what is fitting (*On music* 4.1).

The Greek mind demands form, proportion and appropriateness between reality and appearance, between presentation and content, between parts and whole.[41] The important thing for the artist is not whether his working material is precious, but whether it is appropriate (*Hippias Major* 290f); beauty is defined in terms of *to prepon* (*Hippias Major* 293e). This is joined to what pleases ear and eye. An intellectual investigation for Plato is also governed by what is fitting. There is no mathematical or chronological limit to an inquiry, but only what is appropriate (*Statesman* 284e).

Aristotle uses the notion of what is fitting in his *Ethics*, and especially in his *Rhetoric* (3.1403b–4b; 1408ab). Good prose must steer a fitting course between poetry and common speech. In both prose and poetry, each topic is dealt with in an appropriate way. Rhetoric

[41] Ibid., 55.

must reflect the moral character and the feelings of the speakers and be appropriate to the object which is described. Theophrastus and Dionysius of Halicarnassus (*De compositione verborum* 10–13, 20) wrote similarly. Cicero also (*Orator ad M. Brutum* 71) speaks of *decorum*, by which subject matter, speaker and hearer are joined in an appropriate way. The one kind of oratory cannot be used to different persons at different times on different subjects.

Horace begins his *Ars poetica* with the demand that each element should have its appropriate place. A thing may be beautiful only in its place. Quintilian insists that in rhetoric every excellence requires its appropriate place. Only in relation to the whole can an individual excellence be exhibited (*Institutio oratoria* 11.1.2). Similarly in architecture, Vitruvius begins (*De architectura* 1.2) with order, disposition, rhythm, symmetry, decor and economy as the six excellences of design.

Fitness/appropriateness became a central value of classical culture. Beginning from what is appropriate to certain human groups, it moves to what is appropriate to personal identity, art and ethics. The end of this development does not emerge until the Hellenistic time. Only here does aesthetic perception gain a stature beside reason and intellect.

1.7   THE FOUR CONCEPTS

At the end of a penetrating essay,[42] Hugo Koch acknowledged a coherence in Irenaeus' soteriology, which had been regarded as contradictory. Koch insisted, however, that this did not cancel all the contradictions of Irenaeus' intellectual jungle, for Irenaeus is not a man of concepts but of words and images. He brings his interpreters to despair, for no sooner have they clarified his ideas on a particular point, than he leads them out of sunlight into fog. 'He has precisely no concepts, but images, visions, impressions, moods and often nothing but words. Life, death, resurrection, immortality, incorruptibility, image and likeness, spirit – these words do not express consistently the same ideas, but are used sometimes in a

---

[42] Hugo Koch, 'Zur Lehre vom Urstand und von der Erlösung bei Irenaeus', *ThStK* 96–7 (1925), 183–214.

natural and sometimes in a supernatural sense, while often their real meaning remains uncertain.'[43]

Against this conclusion, I wish to show that Irenaeus has four concepts which govern all that he says. The confusion of his interpreters springs primarily from their failure to identify these four concepts and to appreciate his two standards of truth and beauty, logic and aesthetics. The 'images, visions, impressions, moods' point to his second standard. Taken together, his logical and aesthetic criteria illuminate four massive concepts: Intellect, economy, recapitulation and participation. It is common to ignore the first and last of these concepts. Divine Intellect is needed because, as Irenaeus and Vitruvius indicated, economy belongs to a wise architect. Participation is needed because human response is part of economy and recapitulation; the glory of God is a living man.

Intellect: God is universal Intellect, embracing all things in knowledge and vision, indivisible and simultaneous, entire and identical, the source of all good things.

Economy: from the order of God's saving activity his plan may be discerned. The change and movement of divine activity and presence (Ps. 139), rather than transcendent, unchanging forms or numbers furnish the content of the divine mind. They, not the mighty acts of God (Pss. 135, 136), make sense of history as a mass of divine economies brought together in one inclusive economy. They are all devices by which the good shepherd brings mankind home to his fold. They belong within history but are not identified with every course of events. They give meaning to the story of mankind. They point to God and are seen only through God who moves directly in the world.

Recapitulation: change, not changelessness, is the sign of divine activity. All finds meaning in the person and work of Jesus Christ who is first principle of truth, goodness and being. So far from transcendent simplicity, his work involves joining the end to the beginning and changing reality in a radical way, so that the word becomes flesh, Alpha is joined to Omega, and death becomes life.

[43] Ibid., 213: 'er hat eben keine Begriffe, sondern Bilder, Schauungen, Eindrücke, Stimmungen, manchmal auch nur Worte ...'

Participation: as God has ever been a presence from which man could not escape, now that presence is an intricate immediacy apart from which neither God nor man can be understood. God has become man. The purpose of the divine exchange is that man might become what God is. God's light or glory shines not in supernal heights but in a living man. From the vision of God who is light comes the life of man, and the end of all things is the participation of God in man and of man in God.

These four concepts determine the structure of this book. Beginning from the ever-present God as intellect and love (ch. 2), we move to his economy in creation (ch. 3) and saving history (ch. 4). This leads to recapitulation, the summing up of all things in Christ, first as correction and perfection (ch. 5) and next as inauguration and consummation (ch. 6). Human participation in God follows. First, participation in truth is through the rule of faith (ch. 7) and through scripture (ch. 8). Participation in divine glory elucidates the aesthetic criterion (ch. 9). Participation in being or life moves through the contested area of Irenaeus' anthropology (ch. 10). Finally, ethics show how love which rejoices in truth can participate in divine goodness (ch. 11). A conclusion sketches the results of the investigation and notes some contemporary consequences (ch. 12).

1.8   ARGUMENT AND IMAGES

Irenaeus was driven to use aesthetics as well as logic. His practical problem was the chameleon quality of Gnosticism, which could assimilate philosophical theorems and polytheistic tendencies, so infiltrating the Christian community that Jewish and pagan critics made no distinction between Gnostics and Christians. This fluidity may perhaps be explained by the aesthetic orientation of Gnosticism,[44] according to which Valentinus is a powerful poet who induces aesthetic awareness.[45] The divine is interesting because it

---

[44] H. U. von Balthasar, *Herrlichkeit. Eine theologische Ästhetik*, vol. II (Einsiedeln, 1962), 38 40, quoted in H. Verweyen, 'Frühchristliche Theologie in der Herausforderung durch die antike Welt', *ZKTh* 109 (1987), 394: 'das Ganze schimmert von einer seltsam unstofflichen, zugleich leidenschaftlichen und leidenschaftslosen Schönheit'.

[45] Ibid.: 'dieselbe tragische und manichäische Zerrissenheit und vor allem dieselbe ästhetische Indifferenz und Zweideutigkeit, die mit allen Positionen nur musikalisch

so closely resembles the human whose little passing patterns are elevated to the Gnostic absolute. With such a Protean antagonist, no
rational discussion (as with Jews and philosophers) was adequate,
and any attempt at common ground would dissolve the substance
of Jewish-Christian belief in a sea of fantasy.

Irenaeus turns to aesthetic from the beginning. He uses three
metaphors: Gnostics are wolves in sheep's clothing; they have
claimed the mosaic of a little fox to be the portrayal of a king;
they hide like a dangerous beast in a wood by day and need
to be brought into the open so that *detectio* (unmasking) may
lead to their *eversio* (overthrow) (1.31.3, 4). In argument, Irenaeus
turns to tradition (rule of faith and apostolic succession) and to
scripture. He contrasts the universal spread of the rule with the local sectarian Gnostic phenomena. He challenges the Gnostic claim
to secret exegetical practice by reference to the visible unbroken
succession of the apostles and the eminence of Rome. The centre
of Irenaeus' case against the Gnostics is his lively interpretation
of scripture, through argument and images. No one had done this
before him.[46] Here he found his four concepts: Intellect, economy,
recapitulation and participation.

Irenaeus' four concepts were guided by his two criteria: logic and
aesthetics. Loofs' criticism may be put aside,[47] but Koch's criticism
may stand firm until we comprehend Irenaeus' second criterion.
The 'images, visions, impressions, moods' fulfil Irenaeus' aesthetic
criterion. In all the confusion of controversy about Irenaeus there
is one illuminating question: how does he combine logic and aesthetic, argument and image? This question highlights the perennial richness and vulnerability of Western thought. Especially since
Plato, logic and aesthetic have been contrapuntally present. People
with strict criteria of truth, like Milton and Bunyan, have produced
aesthetic masterpieces. Wittgenstein's *Tractatus*, with all its logic,
presents a powerful picture. Acceptable argument changes and acceptable art changes too; but argument needs imagery to hold it
together.

spielt, ohne sich je einer einzigen zu verpflichten, und deshalb das ästhetische Blendwerk
schlechthin erzeugt'.
[46] Verweyen, 'Frühchristliche Theologie', 397 *et passim*.
[47] G. Ruiz, 'L'enfance d'Adam selon Saint Irénée de Lyon', *BLE* 89 (1988), 97.

The combination of argument and imagery presents a special problem to interpreters of Irenaeus. For the imagery is often backed by aphorism, which conflates imagery or argument. The best known aphorism ('The glory of God is a living man and the life of man is the vision of God') conflates John 1:4 and Matthew 5:16. There is an impressive popular work, which consists of compelling quotations from Irenaeus.[48] Why cannot an exposition of Irenaeus have the same translucent simplicity and fulfil the demands of a secular world for an unsubtle theology (*theologia blytoniensis*)?[49] First, because the careful reader finds, with Koch, that the images and aphorisms do not provide consistent concepts.[50] They are too exuberant. To understand Irenaeus, the interpreter must turn also to his arguments, which may be spread contrapuntally (with images) over many chapters of text.[51] Second, the practice of argument is where Irenaeus outstrips his opposition. In Gnosticism, which thought in pictures, transcendence and exclusiveness implied remoteness; in the argument of Irenaeus, transcendent love implied nearness and the exclusiveness of Christ brought all things together. Fortunately for us, the accepted method in the history of ideas after the last fifty years is analysis of argument[52] with elucidation of problems and learning an author's vocabulary. If we follow this path, we shall find an Irenaeus whose thought is consistent and whose concepts make the aphorisms and images coherent.

---

[48] P. Ferlay, *Saint Irénée de Lyon, La symphonie du salut* (Paris, 1982).

[49] The subtlety and length (1559 pages) of Hans Küng's two great books of apologetic (*On being a Christian* and *Does God exist?*) brought dismay despite international success.

[50] See Koch above, note 43, 'Bilder, Schauungen, Eindrücke, Stimmungen'.

[51] This is the case, for example, with his two arguments in Books 3 and 4, which find the apex of recapitulation in the words, 'Father, forgive them'. See my 'Love of enemies and recapitulation', *VigChr* 54,1 (2000), 12 31.

[52] Ibid., 14: 'An analysis is neither a summary nor a paraphrase. It does not list information, but indicates a movement, which logically links a series of propositions and a succession of images. This movement is clearer in Tertullian where argument pleads a case than in Irenaeus where the images can be excessive.'

PART I

Divine Intellect

God is the universal, omnipotent intelligence, from whom nothing is hidden, who knows our needs before we ask him and who shows his goodness and love on every side.

He is all thought, all will, all Intellect, all light, all seeing, all hearing, the fount of all good things. (1.12.2)

For God excels nature, having in himself the will because he is good, the power because he is powerful, and the perfecting because he is rich and perfect. (2.29.2)

One God and father of all who is over all, through all and in all. (Eph. 4:6)

Absolute causality, which for Irenaeus as a Christian must be good, sums up Irenaeus' idea of God.

J. Kunze,
Die Gotteslehre des Irenaeus (Leipzig 1891), 32

Thy ceaseless, unexhausted love, Unmerited and free . . .
Throughout the universe it reigns, Unalterably sure;
And while the truth of God remains, The goodness must endure. Hymn of Charles Wesley

CHAPTER 2

One God: Intellect and love

Irenaeus presents an immediate, infinite God whose presence streams through his creation in goodness and beauty. This immediacy comes because unity and universality are ruled by transcendent love. While transcendence commonly implies separation, transcendent love implies immediacy. The unknowable God has become knowable as universal Intellect in his good economy for all creation.[1] Irenaeus describes himself (3.6.3, 4) as standing like Elijah before the prophets of Baal on Mount Carmel (1 Kings 18:36) to pray to the God of all creation, the father of Jesus Christ and the God of the patriarchs:

Therefore I also call upon you, Lord God of Abraham, and God of Isaac and God of Jacob and Israel, you who are the father of our Lord Jesus Christ, the God who, through the greatness of your mercy have shown favour to us, that we should know you, who have made heaven and earth, who exercise rule over all, you who are the only and true God, above whom there is no other God.

The Mount Carmel prayer is the motif of Irenaeus' theology. It is part of God's economy and is anticipatory of Christ. Irenaeus' account of God is rich because it rejects diverse errors and draws on diverse strands of intellectual tradition; yet, whatever the complexity, God remains one and universal.

God is the intimate, ultimate, personal and transcendent first cause of all things. 'His greatness lacks nothing but contains all things, comes close to us and is with us' (4.19.3). Irenaeus' account of God is a blend of three parts: the God of the bible, the classical

---

[1] As Tertullian later put it, the sight and hearing of the only God extended into every secret place (*De oratione* 1).

tradition of metaphysical mind and the God of popular piety. Remarkably, he moves from the biblical to the popular God by means
of the universal Intellect of the classical tradition.

2.1 ATTRIBUTES OF GOD: FROM OPULENCE TO OMNIPRESENCE

God is one, universal cause, creator, omnipotent, free and rich. His
opulence is universal as ever-present Intellect. Irenaeus' various
accounts of God show a clear and consistent awareness of God's
attributes.[2]

God is one, as even the heretics admit (1.22.1). He is unmade
and unbegotten, without beginning and without end (2.34.2; 3.8.3;
4.38.1). Herein lies his perfection (4.38.3), eternity and immutabil-
ity (2.34.2; 4.11.2; 4.38.1). He contains all things in his vastness
and is contained by none (4.6.2; 4.19.3). The Gnostics go wrong
when they put God within a larger whole (4.3.1). God holds all
things and is held by none (2.30.9). To borrow Gnostic language,
God is the pleroma ('fullness') of all things (2.1.2).

'He is the cause of being to all things' (4.38.3). As universal
cause, God contains all things. [3] For the Johannine prologue insists
that there is nothing beyond what he has made (1.22.1). Only he
who made all things is rightly called 'God' and 'lord' (3.8.3). His
immanence matches his transcendence: 'God is he who works all
things in all' (4.20.6). Indeed he leaves nothing for anyone else to
do; look where we will, we shall find nothing created by the devil;
God has made it all (4.41.1) to conform with his providence and to
be governed by his command (4.36.6).

Creation defines the difference between God and man: God
makes, man is made. God's goodness, too, is defined by his creative
acts, while man's nature is defined by his creaturely status (4.39).
This was to be the mystery of the universe revealed to Augustine
at Ostia: 'We did not make ourselves, he who made us is he who
abides forever' (*Confessions* 9.10; cf. Ps. 99:3).

No external compulsion lies on God. Above all things he is
free and sovereign; he can never be the slave of necessity (5.4.2)

---

[2] For a general introduction see J. Kunze, *Die Gotteslehre des Irenaeus* (Leipzig, 1891).

[3] *solus continens omnia et omnibus ut sint ipse praestans* (2.1.1; 2.35.3; 3.8.3; 3.20.2; 4.20.6; 4.36.6).

as was Homer's Zeus (2.5.4). His will has universal precedence and dominion; all must submit to it (2.34.4). He takes precedence because he alone is unbegotten and first cause of all that exists (4.38.3). All things are subject to his will. His common titles – most high, omnipotent, God over all[4] – declare his supreme power. No human mind can penetrate beyond him; indeed, it would be foolish to try (2.25.4). Any such attempt leads to the fallacy and futility of infinite regress (2.16.3; 4.19.1). It is safer and better to take the creator as the only God than to exhaust one's mind in irreligious wandering (2.16.3).

The oneness of God implies the omnipotence of his free and powerful will.[5] Irenaeus begins his critique of Gnostic ideas: 'unmoved by another, freely of his own decision he made all things, since he alone is God, alone lord, alone creator, alone father, alone containing all things, and giving existence to all things' (2.1.1). Such a God must be free and self-determining, subject to no external necessity. The Gnostic aeons were, in Irenaeus' opinion, derived from Plato's forms, which served as a model for the creator. Irenaeus agrees with the Middle Platonic tradition of his own day in not allowing such entities to exist outside the divine mind.[6] Further, Irenaeus agrees with Plato when he makes the goodness of the creator, his power and wisdom, the source of creation (4.38.3; cf. Plato, *Timaeus* 29d–30a). While God's will is identical with his thought and infinitely powerful, it bears some similarity to the human will whose freedom reflects a divine likeness (4.37.4). In all of this Irenaeus not only argues philosophically, but uses arguments which philosophers had used.[7]

God is 'rich'.[8] Irenaeus stresses the attributes of power (which has no limit), goodness (which guides his every act), wisdom (which

---

4 *altissimus, omnipotens, super omnia Deus* (2.6.1–3).
5 E. P. Meijering, 'Irenaeus' relation to philosophy in the light of his concept of free will', in *God, being, history* (Amsterdam, Oxford and New York, 1975), 19.
6 See A. H. Armstrong, 'The background of the doctrine "that the intelligibles are not outside the intellect"', in *Les sources de Plotin* (Geneva, 1960), 391–413.
7 Some other philosophical arguments used by Irenaeus are examined by Meijering in his essay, 'Some observations on Irenaeus' polemics against the Gnostics', in *God, being, history*, 31–8.
8 *dives.* Found in Paul's account of the great exchange where he who is rich becomes poor so that we through his poverty might become rich (2 Cor. 8:9), and in Ephesians 2:4 where the opulence of love is the source of salvation.

orders his acts). In one place the three are joined (4.38.3). Elsewhere
he speaks of love, power and wisdom (5.17.1), of kindness and
power (4.38.4), of power and wisdom (2.30.3). All this points to the
opulence of God, especially evident in his raising of the dead. 'For
God excels nature, having in himself the will because he is good,
the power because he is powerful, and the perfecting because he is
rich and perfect' (2.29.2). His generosity and richness are evident
in the varied splendour of creation (2.10.3; cf. 3.16.7 and 5.33.4).
Here Irenaeus finds proof, against Marcion, of the goodness of
the creator (3.25.2, 3). Further he argues that justice, goodness and
wisdom are inseparable in the God who demonstrated these virtues
in creation and history (2.30.9; cf. 4.36.6).

God's opulence exceeds our grasp. Irenaeus, like the philosophers of his time, insists that finite cannot know infinite and creature cannot speak of creator. The names which we rightly give to
God (light, mind) never carry a literal meaning. Only love can give
access to him who transcends all our words (2.13.4). To overcome
his inaccessibility, some men stupidly break him up into parts and
present him as a composite being (1.15.5; 2.17.7; 2.28.4). This
Gnostic error expands human psychological distinctions into divisions and applies them to God (2.13.10; 1.15.5). But the undivided
God is simple (2.13.3; 2.28.4; 4.11.2) and is all good things at once
(2.13.9). The Gnostic aeons are the names of powers which are
ever within God. Intellect and life are inseparable (2.13.9). God is
entire Intellect, spirit, sense, idea, reason, hearing, eye, light and
source of every good thing (2.13.3).

The greatness of God lies beyond human knowledge. He cannot
be measured (4.20.1). While he came to be known by men, this
knowledge did not cover his magnitude or his substance, which no
one has measured or touched (3.24.2). To all his creatures he remains an unknown God who transcends their investigation (4.20.4;
cf. 4.19.3; 4.20.6). He is beyond human sight, definition, measure,
understanding and speech (1.10.3; 4.6.3; 4.19.2; 4.20.4, 5). This
transcendence means that no matter how much a man learns of
God there is always something beyond (4.20.7).

On the other hand, through his word, his creatures learn that
the invisible and ineffable father is the one God 'who encloses all

things and grants their being' (4.20.6).[9] Through his own love and immeasurable goodness he became known as the one true God who made and formed all things (3.24.2; 4.20.1). He who directs and governs is known through his providence (3.25.1; 2.6.1).

Irenaeus is precluded by his loyalty to Christian tradition from saying new things about God. What he does is to select one element from the Christian tradition and present it in a way which reflects a philosophical as well as a biblical ancestry. This Christian claim is one already accepted, he believes, by all men. His unique contribution is to exaggerate the common human awareness of a divine being into the striking claim: *that God is a universal, intelligent being, from whom nothing is hidden, who knows our needs before we ask him and who shows his love and glory on every side, especially through his prophets and supremely in his son.*

The opulence of divine Intellect comprises unity, immediacy, universality, goodness, beauty and love. The more love transcends, the closer it comes. The immediacy of God, shown in history, finds a climax in incarnation; but incarnation is the tip of a visible iceberg. God's love and presence are everywhere. This theme is dominant in the bible, especially in the Wisdom literature (Psalms, Proverbs, Wisdom, Ecclesiasticus and Baruch). For good reasons Irenaeus takes his argument here from philosophical tradition more than the bible. (He will set out the full range of the biblical witness in the *Demonstration*.) His adversaries had shown such dexterity in rearranging and twisting texts that, like Tertullian, he knew such argument would bring at best uncertain victory (*de praescriptione haereticorum* 19.1) and that conflict of this kind brought only a pain to belly and to brain (*de praescr.* 16.2). Further, pre-Christian scripture was little help against those who rejected the creator and his scriptures. Finally Irenaeus has adopted philosophy because of his universal God, who is Intellect. The divine mind speaks to human minds.

God has implanted in all humans an intuition of his eminence. All things know by rational instinct that there is one God and universal lord (2.6.1). To this awareness is added the evidence

---

[9] See below, 3.1–3.2.2.

of the world's design, which points to the existence and rational nature of the creator (2.9.1). From all that he has made,
his power and wisdom shine; only wilful insensibility can blind
men to this rich revelation (2.30.3; 2.27.2). All who were not
sunk in depravity and superstition recognized God in creation
and providence (3.25.1), and from the beginning God has been
known to his creatures (2.30.9; 4.6.7; 4.20.7; 4.28.2). Yet the vision of God is something more, for while man cannot of himself see God, 'yet God is willingly seen by men, by whom he
wills, when he wills, and how he wills' (4.20.5). Only when instructed by God (*deo docente*) can a human know God; only with
God can God be known (4.6.4). Knowledge gained by love in
nearness to God gives to the simple-minded a gift which far
outstrips the blasphemies of the pretentious (2.26.1). Within this
intimacy, unnecessary questions (like the nature of God's activity before creation) are rightly left to God himself (2.28.3,
6, 7).[10]

2.2 METAPHYSIC OF MIND

Despite his occasional hostility to philosophy, Irenaeus is happy to
use without acknowledgment Xenophanes' account of the cosmic
mind. He uses this text frequently without once acknowledging
his source. Unacknowledged citation was common in the second
century[11] and a commonplace could be used without indicating any philosophical allegiance. Philosophical elements in
early Christian thought[12] may be directly borrowed, either

---

[10] 2.28 brings up a number of questions about Irenaeus' epistemology. Does he lean towards
scepticism or empiricism? His scepticism is qualified because he distinguishes between
what can be known by humans and what cannot, and between knowing 'that' and
knowing 'how' (2.28.7); we should give up causal investigations and stick to knowledge
of facts. A similar distinction is made by Galen: nature is not comprehensible when it
comes to searching out causes. See discussion in W. R. Schoedel, 'Theological method in
Irenaeus (*Adversus haereses* 2.25–28)', *JThS*, 35 (1984), 31–49 who cites. R. Walzer, *Galen
on medical experience* (London, 1944), 113–14.
[11] The *Deipnosophistai* of Athenaeus provide the clearest example. See my 'Philo and
Clement: citation and influence', in *Lebendige Überlieferung*. FS for H. J. Vogt, ed. N. el
Khoury et al. (Beirut and Ostfildern, 1992), 231.
[12] See my 'Was Tertullian a philosopher?', *StudPatr* 31 (1997), 328.

acknowledged or unacknowledged, part of a current paradigm, already used by a Christian writer, selected eclectically from 'whatever has been well said',[13] or simply absorbed from the language of the day. The use of the Xenophanes fragment varies enormously.[14] Irenaeus, we shall see, draws a wide range of meaning together. The meaning of a commonplace lies not in its common presence but in the use each writer makes of it.

Irenaeus, like Tertullian, says negative things about philosophers (2.14.3, 4) but then goes on to use, with discernment, the philosophers and the traditions which derive from them.[15] These continue to attract interest, but do not indicate an engagement with contemporary philosophy such as we find in Clement of Alexandria and Origen. He accepts unambiguously the Socratic love of truth and the classical value of fitness or beauty as his criteria. This discriminating approach, as Meijering has shown, confirms Harnack's verdict on Irenaeus, that his dogma is conceived and constructed by a Greek mind on an evangelical foundation.[16] His account of cosmic Intellect, for example, is part of a long philosophical tradition.[17]

Irenaeus rejects those unargued elements of philosophy which Gnostics used.[18] Heretics have collected what has been said by philosophers who do not know God, and have composed a pastiche which deceives by its novelty, a concoction of old doctrines

---

[13] Justin (*2 apology* 13.4) and Clement (*str.* 1.7.37) insist that whatever has been well said belongs to Christians because it comes from the logos sown far and wide by the perfect Logos.

[14] Unacknowledged use of the fragment in question is found in the philosophers Sextus Empiricus (*adversus Mathematicos* 9.144), Diogenes Laertius (9.19) and Pliny the Elder (*Naturalis historia* 2.14), in Christian writers Clement of Alexandria (*str.* 7.2.5.5; 7.7.37.6), Cyril of Jerusalem (*catecheses illuminandorum* 6.7) and Theodoret of Cyr (*commentarii in Psalmos* 129.2). Closer to Irenaeus in the Western tradition, the text is found in Novatian (*de trinitate* 6) and, within Gaul, Hilary of Poitiers (*Tractatus super Psalmos* 129,3), Vitricius from Rouen (*Praise of saints* 8) and Claudianus Mamertus from Vienne (*de statu animae* 1.21). See R. M. Grant, *Irenaeus of Lyons* (London and New York, 1997), 44 5, 193.

[15] See J. Birrer, *Der Mensch als Medium und Adressat der Schöpfungsoffenbarung* (Bern, 1989), 47 65 ('Philosophische Elemente in *Adversus haereses*'), 65 7 ('Logik und Metaphysik als Waffen irenäischer Polemik').

[16] A. von Harnack, *Lehrbuch der Dogmengeschichte*, 4th edn (1909), vol. 1, 24, cited in Meijering, 'Irenaeus' polemics', in *God, being, history*, 37.

[17] See H. J. Krämer, *Der Ursprung der Geistmetaphysik* (Amsterdam, 1964), for a magisterial treatment of the theme.

[18] Meijering, 'Irenaeus ... his concept of free will', in *God, being, history*. 24 5.

without religious or intellectual value. Irenaeus lists the conclusions of Presocratic philosophers and shows their presence in the Gnostic myth (2.14.2). Traces of Democritus, Epicurus, Plato and the Stoics are also found in Gnostic writings (2.14.3, 4).[19] The philosophers disagreed with one another and were wrong on many points, claiming knowledge of things which men cannot know (2.28.2).[20]

Irenaeus attacked Gnostics for their lack of consistent argument. The one all-embracing God provided a rational first principle. Irenaeus required that any argument, about man or God, should not contradict itself. Since God is the highest and all-embracing reality, there can be no other God beside God (2.1.2), and beyond God there can be no higher necessity, for God is all-embracing and all-powerful. Unless God were rational first principle of all, there would be no limit to thought. Unending worlds and gods would follow (2.1.4). Thinking must have clear limits and a clear orientation; these are lost when one goes in search of a God higher than God. As in Anselm: God is that being than which nothing greater can be thought, the final ground and measure of thought. This idea sprang from Christian belief in the one God over, through, and in all (Eph. 4:6).[21]

The first Greek steps towards a Christian idea of God were unwittingly indicated by Xenophanes of Colophon (570–475 BC). He denounced the moral deficiency of the gods with their comic anthropomorphism and proposed one god, a universal mind (KRS, 166–72). There was one god, who excelled all gods and men, and who did not resemble men 'in body or in thought' (KRS, 170), and '*all of him sees, all thinks, all hears*' (KRS, 172). Equally daring is the claim that this one intellectual god directly and drastically affects the physical world; 'without toil he shakes all things by the thought of his mind' (KRS, 171). Aristotle saw Xenophanes as the first

---

[19] See Grant, *Irenaeus of Lyons*, 43.

[20] Seneca (*De beneficiis* 7.1.5) speaks similarly of things which are unknowable or useless.

[21] The omnipotence of God cannot be handled without the acceptance of rational principles; yet this produces difficulties at two points: firstly, how can God embrace all things without contradictions?; secondly, how can the apparent contradictions between the old and new testament texts be reconciled with the idea of a consistent God? R. Schwager, 'Der Gott des Alten Testaments und der Gott des Gekreuzigten. Eine Untersuchung zur Erlösungslehre bei Markion und Irenäus', *ZKTh* 102 (1980), 289–313.

monist or henist[22] who, when referring to the whole world, 'said the One was god'.[23] The metaphysic of mind continued through Heraclitus, Parmenides and Anaxagoras to Plato and to Aristotle whose first cause is mind or thought, a thinking of thinking (Met. 12.1074b).

It is astonishing how much of what Irenaeus says about the creator, who excels nature, has Stoic overtones, despite the fact that the Stoic creator, in contrast with the Christian God, is so immanent as to be identical with the world.[24] As in Irenaeus, Stoic theology of cosmic mind builds on a universal natural awareness of God, who is an immortal, rational, animate being. Divine providence precludes evil. Creator and father of all, he pervades his creation and his powers give rise to the many names of the gods (Diogenes Laertius 7.147; LS, 54A).[25] What wicked men do wrong, he sets right, making the crooked straight and turning chaos into order, so welding into one 'all things good and bad that they all share in a single everlasting reason' (Cleanthes, *Hymn to Zeus*; LS, 54I).

God must be proved and providence defended. The order of the universe, the temperate climate and the movement of the heavenly bodies cannot be accidental (Cicero, *De Natura Deorum* 2.12–15; LS, 54C). Our preconception joins to divine immortality the characteristics of benevolence, caring and beneficence (Plutarch, *De communibus notitiis* 1075E: LS, 54K). The teleological proof, frequently repeated (Cicero, *ND* 2.88; LS, 54L), springs from the beauty of the world (Cicero, *ND* 2.93; LS, 54M) and is supported by forms of the ontological argument (Sextus Empiricus, *adv. Math.* 9.133–6, Cicero, *ND* 2.16; LS, 54D–E). Three proofs of providence point to universal government by the gods: the gods exist and they must govern the world; the surpassing beauty of the world proves that things are under the control of a sentient, animate nature; finally,

---

[22] Aristotle, *Metaphysics* 1.986b21.
[23] Aristotle, *Met.* 1.986b24. This linked him historically with the Eleatics whom Plato (*Theaetetus* 181a6) had described as 'partisans of the whole'.
[24] This Stoic element has been widely ignored, despite the outstanding work of Michel Spanneut, *Le stoïcisme des pères de l'église* (Paris, 1957).
[25] LS refers to A. A. Long and D. N. Sedley, *The Hellenistic Philosophers*, 2 vols. (Cambridge, 1987).

the wonder which we feel before marvels of heaven and earth se-
cures belief in providence (Cicero, *ND* 2.75–6; LS, 54J).

Yet God works from within more than from above. Divine power
is found in universal reason, mind, intellect. More concretely,
fire and all changing things like water, earth, air, sun, moon and
stars, the totality of things and men who have gained immortality,
embody god (Cicero, *ND* 1.39; LS, 54B). Governed by its intellect
and reason, the world is perfect and complete in all the parts which
fit together for human benefit. Man is made to contemplate this perfection of which he is a tiny part (Cicero, *ND* 2.37–9; LS, 54H). The
beauty and variety of nature are full of surprises, such as the pea-
cock, which was created for the sake of its tail (Plutarch, *De Stoicorum
repugnantiis* 1044D; LS, 54O). The harmony of good and evil is no
great problem since they can only exist in 'a kind of opposed interde-
pendence. And there is no such opposite without its matching opposite.' Justice, courage, moderation, prudence and truth all depend
on their opposites. Good and evil, fortune and misfortune, pain
and pleasure 'are tied to each other in polar opposition'. Nature
did not intend evils but they followed as concomitant with certain
goods. The thinness of the skull, needed for thinking, promoted
the inconvenience of fragility. As soon as nature produced virtues,
vices also emerged, 'thanks to their relationship of oppositeness'
(Chrysippus, *On providence* 4, at Aulus Gellius 7.1.1–13; LS, 54Q).

Xenocrates has been identified as the founder of the metaphysic
of mind, which dominates later ancient philosophy.[26] The monad
is mind (frag. 16) which contemplates the ideas. Here we find the
theme that is later found in Irenaeus, in Christian and later Platonism, that the ideas exist in the divine mind.[27] Alcinous placed Intellect above the Soul in a threefold hierarchy which Irenaeus would
have rejected (*Didaskalikos* 10). First-principle was the first unmoved
Intellect; then came the ever-active Intellect of the entire heaven
which thought all things together, and finally came the potential
Intellect which was a power of the world – soul. The first Intellect
thinks of itself as did the first mover of Aristotle, and resembles
the sun, which gives sight and the desired object which promotes

---

[26] Krämer, *Der Ursprung der Geistmetaphysik*, 126.
[27] See above at note 3.

the movement of desire. Immobile, it moves the second Intellect of the whole heaven.[28] Now the first God is eternal, ineffable, complete in itself, that is without needs, eternally complete, that is perfect at every point. It is deity, substantiality, truth, symmetry, Good. 'I do not name these terms as a list of separate attributes but with the idea that they all are conceived in the same unity.' God is Good because as far as possible, he spreads his benefits on all things, and is the cause of everything good. He is Beauty because he is himself by nature perfect and proportioned. He is Truth because he is the principle of all truth as the sun is the principle of all light. He is Father, because he is the cause of all things and because he sets in order (*kosmein*) the Intellect of the heavens and the world-soul in accord with himself and his thoughts. For it is by his will that he has filled all things with himself, having awoken the world-soul and having turned it to himself because he is the cause of the Intellect which is in it (*Did.* 10).

So the metaphysic of mind moves through Plato, Aristotle and the Stoics to the Middle Platonic philosophy of Irenaeus' day. This development has been traced in more detail elsewhere.[29] Its effect on Irenaeus is crucial for his biblical sources alone cannot explain his use of Intellect as a designation of God. He moves into the philosophical paradigm in order to demolish his opponents and to claim popular piety.

Irenaeus holds as compatible the cosmic Intellect, which is 'the way religious and pious people may speak of God' (2.13.3), and a recognition of God as ineffable, 'above all these things and therefore beyond description' (2.13.4).[30] For God's Intellect and light are

---

[28] Why does it think of itself? It is the highest beauty and must think the most beautiful thought possible. Since there is nothing more beautiful than itself it thinks perpetually of itself.

[29] See my *The emergence of Christian theology* (Cambridge, 1993), chapter 2.

[30] Irenaeus does not explicitly engage with Middle Platonism, but there is an interesting parallel where both use the Xenophanes tradition in two ways: to avoid clashes between positive and negative theology and between the inclusiveness or exclusiveness of the divine fullness. The conflict between negative and positive theology emerges in the incompatibility of the three ways of knowing God (negation, analogy, eminence). If nothing can be predicated of God, how can analogy or eminence be applicable? A solution is found when Middle Platonism turns back to Xenophanes and claims ambiguity. Pseudo-Aristotle describes God as eternal, one, homogeneous, spherical, neither unlimited nor limited, neither still nor moving in *de Melisso Xenophane Gorgia* 3.977a37 to 977b21

not at all like our intellect and light (2.13.4), which means that negation and eminence are necessary to each other. Irenaeus does not separate the account of God as total vision and total hearing from a higher account of the ineffable universal father. They are ways of speaking (or not speaking) about the same being.[31]

2.3   DIVINE INTELLECT IN IRENAEUS

The richness of Irenaeus' account of God is displayed in his varied use of the theme of Xenophanes' cosmic mind. From this short statement he develops an argued theology: *God as Intellect is indivisible and simultaneous, sovereign and homogeneous, entire and identical, the source of all good things.*[32]

('Aristotelis qui fertur de Melisso Xenophane Gorgia libellus', ed. H. Diels, Philosophische und historische Abhandlungen der königlichen Akademie der Wissenschaften zu Berlin. Aus den Jahren 1899 und 1900 (Berlin, 1900). See translation in Aristotle, *Complete works*, ed. J. Barnes (Princeton, 1995).) Simplicius explains that God is at rest 'according to the abiding that is beyond motion and rest' (*On Aristotle's Physics* 23.13 14). God is spherical only in the sense of being 'everywhere homogeneous' (*Phys.* 23.17 19) and simple. These ways of speaking about an ineffable transcendent God resemble the account of Irenaeus.

For Irenaeus as for Platonists the divine fullness must be reconciled with transcendence. Eudorus described Pythagorean monism and dualism *as alternate ways of viewing the same realities*. Eudorus' account of the Pythagoreans (at Simpl. *Phys.* 181.17) and Xenophanes place the supreme God above the opposites which arise from him. The Platonisation of Pythagoreanism tried to reconcile monism with dualism. In Eudorus the polarities, although derived from the One are not present in it. Monism was indicated by the higher way and dualism by the second way (*Phys.* 181.10 12). Before Eudorus there seems no evidence of his view that the One is the highest God and beyond the opposites. The Pythagoreanism of Xenophanes (*Phys.* 29.12ff.) is best explained on the assumption that originally it was Eudorus who interpreted Xenophanes in this way. Conversely, the positioning by Eudorus of a One that is a most high God beyond the Pythagorean opposites is best explained on the assumption that his interpretation of Xenophanes played a decisive part (J. Mansfeld, 'Compatible alternatives', in *Knowledge of God in the Graeco-Roman World*, ed. R. van den Broek, T. Baarda and J. Mansfeld (Leiden, 1988), 104). Again in Alcinous, the three ways (negation, analogy, eminence) may be seen as alternative ways of conceiving the First God, ranked in order of value. This points back to Eudorus' distinction between two accounts (logoi) or ways (tropoi) which are ranked in order of preference. I am indebted to Mansfeld's excellent essay.

[31] A distinction between the two might be found in Clement's account of the ineffable One (*str.* 5.12.81.4 82.4) and his extended account (*str.* 4.25.156 7) of the logos, son or Intellect as the circle of one thing as all things. The first is infinite because the limits of the One have come together; the second is infinite through its inclusion of all things, but the son is in the father and the father in the son.

[32] Commonplaces are clues to uncommon ideas. For in the different way a thinker uses a commonplace we learn the newness of his thought. Clement of Alexandria uses Xenophanes' cosmic Intellect in another two ways: to describe the universality of saving

Indivisibility and simultaneity

The cosmic Intellect is indivisible and simultaneous. The complicated mentality of Bythos, who produces Ennoia, Thelesis, followed by Aletheia and Monogenes (or Intellect), recalls the dithering of Homer's Zeus. How different is the universal God whose thought is his will and his perfected act: for he is 'all thought, all will, all intellect, all light, all eye, all hearing, entire source of all good things' (1.12.2).

The divine mind has universal knowledge and power. Acts of thought and perception which are separate in mortals are united in divine simplicity which fulfils perfectly and simultaneously the act which it conceives. The divine mind of the Gnostics is not like that; it is divided and confused like fabled Zeus.

Sovereignty and homogeneity

A more extended account of the sovereign Intellect is found at 2.13. Intellect cannot be derived, as it is by the Valentinians from Bythos (depth) and Ennoia (thought), for it is prior to these, being 'principal and supreme ... and source of all mental activity' (*principale et summum ... et fons universi sensus*) (2.13.1). Idea (*ennoia*) cannot be the mother of intellect as the Gnostic hierarchy claims. The intellect produces thoughts; thought cannot produce the intellect. Intellect is the father of idea/thought (*ennoia*). Within Intellect is that hidden and invisible mental state (*adfectio*) from which all intellectual activity derives.

From this mental state are generated mind (*sensus*, which the Latin translator sometimes uses as the equivalent of *nous* or Intellect), idea/thought (*ennoia*), and consideration (*enthymesis*). Intellect includes all these which are not entities outside the intellect. In all mental activities *sensus* (i.e. mind/intellect) remains within, creating and administering. It governs all freely by its own power and will.

The sequence of mental process may be set out: idea/thought (*ennoia*) to consideration (*enthymesis*) to reflection (*sensatio*) to

providence (*str.* 7.2.5); and to describe the universal spiritual presence which makes the whole of life a festival of praise, and where 'the thoughts of the saints cut through not only the air but the whole world, and God's power with the speed of light sees through the whole soul' (*str.* 7.7.35 7).

deliberation (*consilium*) to judgement (*cogitationis examinatio*) to word (*verbum*) which may be inner or uttered (2.13.2).[33] All these are one and the same for they take their beginning from Intellect, and are governed by Intellect which is invisible, yet like light emits a ray but cannot be reduced to its emissions. Still more, God the father of all cannot be reduced to a series of mental acts for his thoughts are not like our thoughts (Isa. 55:8). He is 'simple, not compounded, without different members, entirely alike and equal to himself, for he is wholly intellect, wholly spirit and wholly intellection, wholly thought, wholly reason, wholly hearing, wholly seeing, wholly light and entire source of all good things, which is the way devout and faithful people speak of God' (2.13.3). This account of God is not restricted to Christians; it is the way in which all religious and pious people speak of him.

For all his universality, this God is ineffable. He could be rightly described as 'the mind which embraces all', but he is not like the human intellect. He may be called light but he is different from our kind of light. Whatever terms we apply to him are used in love, but we know that our thoughts of him go far beyond them. This points to the transcendence of our intellect as well as of his. For if human understanding is not caused by or reducible to its inseparable emissions, much more is God (*totus sensus*) not separable or reducible.

Either the universal father (Intellect) is void or everything is in him and remains in him (2.13.7). Just as shapes (circles, squares) drawn in the water still share in the water, so every mental act continues to participate in the father. Much that the Valentinians have said about the emissions of the pleroma could be affirmed of human minds; but they simply commit the anthropomorphic fallacy which Xenophanes attacked. The timetable of the Valentinian emissions cannot be applied to the God who is over all and who, in a simultaneous, equal, similar and homogeneous manner, is total Intellect, logos, vision, hearing, mind, word.

[33] See A. Rousseau and L. Doutreleau, *Irénée de Lyon, Contre les hérésies*, Book II, vol. II, SC 294 (Paris, 1982): 'pensée', 'considération', 'réflexion', 'délibération', 'discours intérieur', 'verbe immanent', 'verbe proféré'.

Similarly life, incorruption and truth are perfections which exist always in God and are not separable phenomena (2.13.9). We may plausibly pile together all intellectual acts and verbal utterances when we consider the human mind; but such a procedure is entirely implausible in any account of God (2.13.10). The rejection of all anthropomorphism stands firm.

Entirety and identity

Irenaeus returns to the theme of Intellect in *Against heresies* 2.28. He sets the question in a wider setting and shows positively that the divisions which he disallows between the aeons or emissions cannot apply to the relation between God and the word.

All thinking must be done in the context of the rule of truth (2.28.1). For the rule is truth itself and saves us from being diverted in every direction. Rather we should inquire into the mystery and economy of the living God[34] and, as we learn what great things he has done for us, we should increase in our love for him. The rule of faith provides the belief from which we should never fall: one God created the world and gave man the power to grow.

If the scriptures still leave us with many puzzles, we should not try to solve them by finding other gods (2.28.2). The scriptures are the perfect work of the logos and the spirit, to whom we are inferior. There is nothing wrong in leaving things unexplained. We do not know why the Nile rises, why birds migrate, why tides change, not to mention the weather. These things have their causes; but only God knows what they are.

We are forever learning and God is forever teaching us (2.28.3). Only three things will remain the same: faith, hope and love, all directed to one God. In hope we receive more and more as we learn of God's inexhaustible riches. Holding to our faith we find in scripture one harmonious truth. We know that at a fixed time God produced the world and do not ask what he was doing before this. To claim that he was derived from defect and ignorance is blasphemy (2.28.4).

---

[34] *inquisitionem mysterii et dispositionis exsistentis Dei.*

Anthropomorphism reserves nothing for the uniqueness of God. The plurality in God which divides his thought from his logos, life and Christ is drawn from human psychology.[35] But (as Xenophanes also went on to say) these things cannot be applied to God. The scriptures tell us that God is all entire intellect, logos, active spirit, always the same. Therefore these divisions and processes cannot exist in him.

God, who is all intellect and logos[36] speaks what he thinks and thinks what he speaks (2.28.5). His thought is logos, and logos is intellect, and universal Intellect which includes all things in its comprehension is the father himself. The division of this unity projects human processes on to the logos whose generation cannot be described (Isa. 53:8).

Such anthropomorphic subdivision is irrational and presumptuous (2.28.6). Even the son does not know all that the father knows. How was the son produced from the father? No one knows but the father and the son. Valentinus, Marcion, even principalities and powers have no access to this knowledge. We do not know how God produced material substance, or why some of his creatures sinned and rebelled against him (2.28.7).

Finality and generosity of the divine economy

We come now to Irenaeus' last move. He has argued at length for the indivisible integrity of Intellect as the source of all good things. How is this good dispersed? The answer is the divine economy, which unites the many economies of God as the Platonic forms are united within the divine Intellect.

In *Against heresies* 4.11, Irenaeus begins from the longing of prophets and just men to see the future advent and perfection of their lord (cf. Matt. 13:17). This is only possible because the coming lord of both testaments disclosed the future as part of God's continuous plan from creation to law, and then from reproof to adoption, to incorruptible inheritance and perfection. All progress

---

[35] Such a move is as foolish as the snub-nosed Ethiopian gods and the red-haired Thracian deities whom Xenophanes ridiculed.

[36] *totus exsistens mens, totus exsistens logos.*

springs from the command to man that he should increase and multiply (4.11.1); all points to the divine economy and shows how different God is from man (4.11.2). God is, man becomes; God makes, man is made; God is always the same, but man grows from beginning through middle to end; God makes well, and man is well made; God's perfection is shown in his glory which depends on man's enrichment.

Here the theme of divine perfection serves a more positive purpose than that found in Books 1 and 2, for man is the receptacle for God's goodness, the instrument whereby God is glorified. Those who bear fruit, those who use the talents he has given, are the great receivers, the faithful servants who enter into the joy of their lord.

And while God indeed does good, good is done to man. And while God is indeed perfect in all things, equal and like to himself, since he is all light, all mind, all substance and source of all good things, man receives progress and increase towards God. For while God is always the same, man when found in God will always advance towards God.[37]

The divine perfection is a contrast to human contingency. Yet it is not aloof from that contingency but active to bring it from small things to great, from creation to glorification; all of which points to the goodness of God who does good to a man who receives good. Against dualist detractors of creator and creation, Irenaeus shows how divine perfection needs a contingent creature capable of consummation. The God who pours out his goodness in changing ways is a greater God than a perfection which exists in stagnant isolation.[38] The pattern of his out-pouring, his economy whereby man is embraced and brought to God, now becomes the centre of interest.[39]

To sum up this section: *God as Intellect is indivisible and simultaneous, sovereign and homogeneous, entire and identical, the source of all good things to man.* In face of Gnostic myth, Irenaeus develops an intricate argument, the influence of which cannot be exaggerated. For, without a refined theism, christology is a keystone without an arch.

---

[37] *homo in deo inventus semper proficiet ad deum.*
[38] Cf. Plutarch, *Moralia* 1129, *de latenter vivendo*, 4.
[39] See following chapters 3 and 4.

2.4 PLOTINUS

When we come to Plotinus, however, we find someone who is profoundly useful for the study of Irenaeus. Historically there is no
connection; but we shall find that, philosophically, there is near
identity in their response to Gnosticism. The objections which
Plotinus raises against Gnostics are the same as those which
Irenaeus had raised: proliferation of first principles and denigration of the physical world.[40] Against them he sets, as does Irenaeus,
the vision of a divine Intellect where all things are joined in beauty
and contemplation; the Gnostic subdivision of Intellect leads to infinite regress. Between the two accounts there is neither an historical dependence nor a similar social setting. Irenaeus and Plotinus
thought that Gnostics were logically wrong and set out argument
accordingly.

Plotinus sees the objections in a wider context, for the
Pythagorean tendency to elemental division, proliferation and hierarchy had begun in Middle Platonism and was to take off in later
Platonism. Plotinus sets out his own three principles of One, Intellect and Soul and asks whether it could be possible to add to them
and if so, in what way. Intellect is what it is, 'always the same, resting
in a static activity'. There is no duality (thinking of thinking), for
the 'intellect that thinks that it thinks will be altogether the same as
the intellect which did the thinking'. A separation of these elements
would be absurd, since even in human minds it would be blamed
as folly. To proliferate further would be still more absurd because
of infinite regress.[41] 'But if one even introduced another, third, distinction ... one which says that it thinks that it thinks that it thinks,
the absurdity would become even clearer' (*Enneads* 2.9.1).[42] One

[40] This does not mean that there is total identity between the complex ideas of Plotinus and
    Irenaeus. It means, as in the following chapter, that they used similar arguments against
    Gnostics on the proliferation of first principles and denigration of the physical world.
    For differences on other points see R. A. Norris, Jr, 'Irenaeus and Plotinus answer the
    Gnostics: a note on the relation between Christian thought and Platonism', *USQR* 36,1
    (1980), 13–24.

[41] I have referred elsewhere to the multiplication of intermediaries as the 'bureaucratic
    fallacy'. Its devotional value is indicated by T. S. Eliot in his poem, 'The naming of cats',
    where the ultimate name is described as 'the thought, of the thought, of the thought of
    the name'.

[42] Here and elsewhere I have followed the translation of A. H. Armstrong, LCL (London,
    1979).

must not 'make superfluous distinctions in the realities of the intelligible world which the nature of these realities does not admit: we
must lay down that there is one intellect, unchangeably the same,
without any sort of decline, imitating the Father as far as is possible
to it' (*Enn.* 2.9.2).

Even soul retains a unity through the light which it receives and
gives, just as all things 'must exist for ever in ordered dependence
upon each other; those other than the First have come into being in
the sense that they are derived from other, higher, principles' (*Enn.*
2.9.3). It is wrong to claim that the soul produced the world through
a defect or moral decline, for the universal soul is complete. The
direction is not down but upwards, inspired by intelligible realities
which elevate. Despite all the unpleasant things in it, the world
is the best imaginable likeness of the intelligible world. For 'what
sphere could be more exact or more dignified or better ordered in
its circuit (than the sphere of this universe) after the self-enclosed
circle there of the intelligible universe?' (*Enn.* 2.9.4). Incredibly, the
Gnostics think that they themselves possess a divine soul, while the
whole heaven and the stars, far superior in order and design, lack
immortal soul (*Enn.* 2.9.5). With meretricious pomposity, they try to
improve on Plato's account of how things were made, but succeed
only in dragging the unity of Intellect down to the plurality of the
world of sense:

And by giving names to a multitude of intelligible realities they think
they will appear to have discovered the exact truth, though by this very
multiplicity they bring the intelligible nature into the likeness of the sense-
world, the inferior world, when one ought there in the intelligible to aim
at the smallest possible number, and attribute everything to the reality
which comes after the First and so be quit of multiplicity, since it is all
things and the first intellect and substance and all the other excellences
that come after the first nature. (*Enn.* 2.9.6)

When they stay with Plato, they are all right; but when they 'wish
to oppose the ancient teachings they introduce all sorts of comings
into being and passings away, and disapprove of this universe'.

Intellect contains all intelligible things within itself. 'We have
here, then, one nature, Intellect, all realities, and truth: if so, it
is a great god; or better, not just a god, but it demands as of

right that this which it is is universal god' (*Enn.* 5.5.3). As such it sees all things being itself pure light like the light of the sun (*Enn.* 5.5.7).

Intellect unites the universe and all the gods within itself, so that it, the one god, is all. For

> they are all together and each one again apart in a position without separation, possessing no perceptible shape … But this, the (intelligible) All, is universal power, extending to infinity and powerful to infinity; and that god is so great that his parts have become infinite. For what place can we speak of where he is not there before us? (*Enn.* 5.8.9)

Zeus leads other gods, spirits and souls through sight.

> But he appears to them from some invisible place and dawning upon them from on high illuminates everything and fills it with his rays, and dazzles those of them who are below, and they turn away unable to see him, as if he was the sun. Some endure him and gaze upon him, but others are troubled in proportion to their distance from him.

Those who see may not have the same vision, some seeing archetypal justice, others the source of integrity. Yet in the end some see the totality of the intellectual world from beginning to end.

> Zeus then sees these things, and with him any one of us who is his fellow-lover, and finally he sees, abiding over all, beauty as a whole, by his participation in the intelligible beauty; for it shines bright upon all and fills those who have come to be there so that they too become beautiful. (*Enn.* 5.8.10)

2.5　KNOWLEDGE, LOVE AND UNITY OF THE DIVINE INTELLECT

Irenaeus' empiricist tendency and openness to learn the economies of God (2.25.3) mark a new stage in the development of theological method. Yet much about God cannot be known. The account of the divine Intellect ends with the prophets and the economy by which God brought man to perfection (4.11). They are stupid who believe that they can transcend God and know him from above (4.19.2). The God who holds the earth, from the heights of heaven to the depths of the abyss, in his fist, is beyond the human mind. His hand surrounds the vastness of the physical universe and penetrates the secrets of the human thought. Yet knowledge of God is possible through the love which leads us to him by his word, who contains the pattern of the world he made. God's word and wisdom, son and spirit were always with him (4.20.1). The one God and father who is above all and in us all, has delivered knowledge without limit to his son (Matt. 11:27) who has the key of David to open and shut the book of the father (Rev. 3:7) (4.20.2). The word and wisdom of the father were present with him to create and to witness his joy when the world and humanity were made (Prov. 3:19, 20; 8:22–5 and 27–31) (4.20.3). The great God is known through love which is focussed in his word, who by his incarnation has joined end to beginning, man to God. He in turn is known through the prophets who told of his coming and our salvation (4.20.4)

As the word unites the economies of glory by which man, found in God, ever advances to God, we return to the first divine attribute which we noted – his unity. Irenaeus' account of God as universal Intellect is reflected in a consistent rejection of dualism. In response to the divisive tendency of Gnosis in so many conceptual fields, Irenaeus argues for the unity of God,[43] the unity of man, and the unity of the history of salvation, the scriptures and the church. When any one of these points of unity is denied the others are also affected.[44] All heresies deny creation and the salvation of the flesh (4 pref. 4). God is separated from the world (2.31.1), goodness is separated from justice. [45] The old testament is either incompatible with or, at best (as in the Letter to Flora; Epiphanius, *Panarion haereses* 33.3–7) an image of, the new testament. The higher God of Gnostics is incompatible with Plato's good creator who is always joined to justice (3.25.5) and close to the Epicurean god who does nothing for himself or for others (3.24.2).

The unity of God and man in the incarnate Christ hinges on the reality of the flesh of Christ, without which there could be no recapitulation of Adam (3.22.1). His ineffable generation from the father is one with his generation from the virgin, through the

---

43 M. A. Donovan, *One right reading?* (Minnesota, 1997), 55: 'there is one God who is alone Lord, Creator, Father and container of all'.

44 Ysabel de Andía, 'Irénée, théologien de l'unité', *NRTh* 109 (1987), 31.

45 S. Petrement, *Le Dieu séparé. Les origines du gnosticisme* (Paris, 1984).

sign of Immanuel (3.19.2). The unity of the spirit, who spoke by the prophets and who makes men sons by adoption, is claimed (3.21.4). The economy of salvation, governed by a rhythm or movement of father, son and spirit, is mirrored in the unity of the old and new testaments (4.10.1; 4.23.1). One God, through his spirit, unites his church, 'for where the church is, there is God's spirit and where God's spirit is, there is the church and all grace' (3.24.1). Only the one spirit can impart truth and incorruption to the church, which is one in its catholic extension and its apostolic tradition.[46] Mankind, divided into three classes by the heretics, is united by the image and likeness of God. No man is consubstantial with God but all may participate in him.[47] The unity of mankind is central to the Gnostic debate.[48]

We return to Elijah who is no longer on Mount Carmel but emerging distraught from the cave. The prophets, says Irenaeus, did not see the face of God openly but they saw the economies and mysteries which would lead man to the open vision of God (4.20.10). Elijah stands in the presence of the lord who is not in the wind, the earthquake or the fire but in the murmur of a soft breeze. Here is indicated to Elijah, indignant at the sin and slaughter on Mount Carmel, the ultimacy of the peace to which the name of Irenaeus pointed. The gentleness and tranquillity of God's incarnation pointed to the mildness and peace of his kingdom. 'For, after the wind which shatters the mountains, the earthquake and the fire, will come the calm and peaceful times of his kingdom, when, in utter tranquillity, the spirit of God will bring life and growth to mankind' (4.20.10). To this life and growth we turn as we consider the divine economy.

[46] de Andía, 'Irénée, théologien de l'unité', 46.
[47] Ibid., 40.
[48] See A. Orbe, 'La definición del hombre en la teología del s. II', *Greg* 48 (1967), 522–76.

PART II

Economy

God makes, man is made. As wise architect and sovereign king, God creates from nothing all that is, ordering opposites by his artistry. His plan unites disparate elements from creation to Christ.

> So it is that a metrical line is beautiful in its own kind although two syllables of that line cannot be pronounced simultaneously . . . a line which is not simultaneously possessed of all its virtues but which produces them in order.
>
> Augustine, *On true religion*, 22,42

> For just as God spoke then to Adam in the evening, as he searched for him, so in the last days, with the same voice, he has visited the race of Adam, searching for it.
>
> (5.15.4)

> The world in fact discerned by modern science has an openness in its becoming which is consonant, not only with its being a world of which we are actually inhabitants, but also a world which is the creation of the true and living God, continually at work within the process.
>
> J. C. Polkinghorne,
> *Science and providence* (Boston, 1989), 99

CHAPTER 3

One creator: ut sapiens architectus et maximus rex

Irenaeus' account of the divine Intellect declares God's undivided unity and universal goodness. It ends with the distinction between God who makes and man who is made, between God who does good and man to whom good is done. Man, found in God, will always be advancing to God. This movement defines the economy of salvation which begins with creation.

Creation is a difficult concept, for it uses the notion of causation outside the process of the world whence that notion derives and wherein it makes sense. We speak of causes in order to understand the relation between parts of the world; to lift the idea outside the world and apply it to the undifferentiated whole is a strange move, rather like asking, 'Is this man a foot?' Yet the question 'Why does anything exist?' has long been taken seriously. Monotheism, especially in its Judaeo-Christian form, declares God to be sole cause of all that is.

How can sense be made of this kind of causation?

3.1 TWO ANALOGIES – WISE ARCHITECT AND SOVEREIGN KING

The making of a universe differs from the making of a cake, yet accounts of creation commonly set out steps which are more culinary than conceptual. Irenaeus begins with two images which have been used to relate the world to one first cause. The architect/builder produces order from disorder. The monarch/magician produces by word, will and power. The two images may conflict – one presupposes matter and the other does not. Both are found in the final form of the Genesis narrative. The formless void is brought into order by the commands which begin 'let there be light!' Yet too many cooks have taken these analogies as alternative recipes and accuse early Christian thinkers of not seeing a problem. In Theophilus and Irenaeus what begins as a precaution, to prevent analogies from clashing, ends as a breakthrough.

God as architect/master-builder bestows the order which displays his agency, and God as king gives the command which is the cause of all that is. The first analogy depends on the order and beauty of the universe which inspire belief, but implies the existence of unformed matter and conflicts with belief in one first-principle. God can deliver us from infinite regress only if there is no second ultimate entity beside him. Even if he created the unformed matter first, and then brought order from chaos, could he allow the existence of unformed chaotic stuff which was unworthy of his creative wisdom? Simultaneity is the only option for monotheism, and that is supplied by the second analogy of royal command: God spoke and it was so.

Irenaeus uses the royal command analogy against Gnostic dualism, drawing on scripture and philosophy. In scripture this analogy takes over in the Psalms, and John insists, 'apart from him nothing came into being'. 'Creation from nothing' has for Paul a place which is more than cosmological. The great antitheses of Romans 4:5, 17, *justificatio impii, resurrectio mortuorum, creatio ex nihilo*, point to the heart of the gospel and of monotheism.[1]

3.2.1 SOVEREIGN KING

The one God creates by sovereign will and word. Either the supreme being who contains all things formed all creation by his will, or an unlimited number of creators and gods must be posited, none of whom is God because they are all contained within a larger whole (2.1.5).

God's will, not any angelic action, is the cause of the world (2.2.3). He does not need external instruments; his own word is suitable and efficient for the formation of all things. The Gospel tells us (Jn 1:3) that all things were made by his word. Genesis and the

---

[1] They suggest that Christian faith begins in the middle with justification, then goes back to creation and on to resurrection.

Psalms of David make the same point (2.2.5). 'He spoke and it was; he commanded and it stood firm' (Ps. 33:9). 'He spoke the word and they (the heavens) were created' (Ps. 148:5). Alone he did this for there are no lesser gods or angels mentioned at the beginning (Gen. 1:1) (2.2.6). It is he who gave life and length of days (Ps. 21:4); we live, not of ourselves, but by the grace of God (2.34.3).

For early Christian writers there is one omnipotent God, alone unbegotten and first cause of all things (4.38.3). Everything owes its existence to him (4.20.6).[2] He is the sole source of all good things (1.12.2; 4.11.2). Himself uncreated, without beginning or end and in need of nothing, entirely sufficient to himself, he is to *all* other things, the cause of their being (3.8.3).

God is omnipotent, first, in the sense that all other things depend on him for being (3.20.2).[3] His containing of all things is the source of their being (4.20.6).[4] Secondly, God is omnipotent in that what he does is dependent on his will alone. Because he is the sole source of being[5] he makes things of his own free will (2.1.1). He makes, disposes and perfects all things freely, by himself and of his own power, so that the substance of all things is not matter but is his will. He who alone made all things is alone omnipotent. The pronoun 'himself' makes the same point.[6] We have here not merely the primitive Christian determination to understand God as the 'living lord of the world',[7] but an appropriation of philosophical terms to exclude other possible causes from the making of the world.

Thirdly, God does not need matter as human makers need it. He calls into existence the matter with which he works, when it previously did not exist (2.10.4). Fourthly, he did not need angelic helpers for he had his own hands, the son and the spirit through whom and in whom he made all things freely and of his own accord (4.7.4; 5.1.3).

---

2 *Omnibus praestat esse.*

3 *potentissimus omnium deus, quique omnibus ut sint praestitit.*

4 *qui continet omnia et omnibus esse praestat.*

5 'He is alone God, lord, founder, father and container of all things.' The adjective 'alone' is applied to God five times in this sentence.

6 *Ipse fabricator, ipse conditor, ipse inventor, ipse factor, ipse dominus omnium.*

7 Bonwetsch quotes Seeberg to this effect; G. N. Bonwetsch, *Die Theologie des Irenäus* (Gütersloh, 1925), 55.

For the Gnostics, creation is troublesome because a good God seems to have created a world in which there is evil. Therefore they set God at a distance from the world by creating a hierarchy and generally distinguishing between the creator and the highest God. Marcion, as Tertullian reports, claims that since evil is bad, the god who uses it cannot be good. The true god works through his word alone (Marc. 4.9.7).

The first objection to Gnostic/Marcionite teaching lay in its attribution of the work of creation to an inferior angel or god. Irenaeus pointed to the testimony of all scripture that the one and only God had made all things by his word (2.27.2; 1.10.3), and that this God is both just and good (3.25.2). God must have the power to judge in order to be God (3.25.2). It is he who has given power to earthly authorities (5.24.2) who ensure peace in the world (4.30.3). In the end his justice will reward the righteous in a renewed creation.

Creation begins God's economy of salvation. It has a beginning in time but is not confined to the past. God fulfils his continuous plan of salvation with the help of his creation, not in spite of it (5.18.1), and receives of his own in the bread and wine of the eucharist (4.17.5), which gives to our bodies the hope of resurrection (4.18.5). All creation serves the end of human salvation, when tribulation kneads us into bread fit for the banquet of the king (5.28.4). Pagan persecutors are useful to the righteous, just as the stalk is needed for wheat to grow and straw is useful to the refinement of gold (5.29.1). The shape of the world must pass away so that the wheat may be gathered into the granary and the straw thrown into the fire (4.4.3). Irenaeus' constant refrain is that God has made all things for man so that man might reach fullness of stature and length of days (5.5.1).

Millennial hope is part of Irenaeus' defence of creation. In the first stage the world restored to its original excellence will be placed at the service of the righteous (5.32.1). It is the shape of this world, not the substance of creation, which will pass away, so that a renewed humanity may converse in a way which is forever new (5.36.1). This renewed earth is something which man has never known because paradise was in the fourth heaven (2.30.7). It will produce in great abundance. The promise will be realised and will confirm God's visible control of all creation.[8]

3.2.2   ENCLOSING, NOT ENCLOSED

This formula expresses the ultimacy of God as first cause and his immediacy as he holds creation in his grasp. Against the Gnostic position Irenaeus argues philosophically for the necessity of a first cause and the universal simultaneity of his action. Irenaeus applies against Gnostic dualism, the formula 'enclosing, not enclosed'. His argument runs as follows:

God who has nothing above or after him is the only God, only lord, only creator, only father. His oneness implies that he contains all things and that all things were created by his command (2.1.1).

It is necessary that the Pleroma (fullness) should contain all things in his vastness and that he should not be contained.

There cannot be anything beyond him for three reasons:
- (a) that would mean that the Pleroma lacked something which is a contradiction;
- (b) God's alleged relation to the thing beyond him would imply that he had a beginning, middle and end;
- (c) he would be limited and enclosed by what is outside him.

The Gnostic father/pleroma is enclosed by another mighty being which is greater than he because the container is greater than the contained. The greater is stronger, more sovereign and therefore God.

Either the greater Pleroma/2, which is beyond the lesser Pleroma/1, contains Pleroma/1 and is contained by Pleroma/1, or there is an infinite distance between Pleroma/1 and Pleroma/2. If the second alternative is true, there is a third immensity Pleroma/3 which is greater than and contains Pleroma/1 and Pleroma/2.

This fails because of infinite regress. If Pleroma/3 has its beginning above, and its end below what it contains, then it must have limits at the sides where new existences begin. The endless proliferation leads away from God to the non-existent.

For Marcion, as for the Valentinians, the same argument for a higher good is infinitely repeatable.

To sum up, either one being contains and creates all according to his own will, or there is a limitless plurality of creators and gods who begin and

---

[8] E. Norelli, 'Paix, justice, intégrité de la création: Irénée de Lyon et ses adversaires', *Irén* 64,1 (1991), 40.

end from each other on every side, are contained and therefore not God.[9]

Creation must occur within God's territory, otherwise God will be enclosed by what is beyond him (2.2.2).[10]

Gnostics would have understood the kind of argument which Irenaeus uses for they were prepared to claim that God encloses all.[11] Their monism was explicit. This was not consistent, claimed Irenaeus, with their assertion that creation is like a stain on the garment of the All. A pictorial simile cannot evade the well-constructed argument which Irenaeus brings (2.4.2).

Book 2 of *Against heresies* contains the most condensed argument of the whole work. In 2.31 Irenaeus returns to sum up his arguments against the Gnostics: his first concern has been to argue for a creator God who is not shut up and restricted by something beyond him and who is one and one only, not a member of a series.

3.2.3   ONE CREATOR, NO REGRESS

Irenaeus says that he has proved in Book 1 that there is one God, a creator who is not the fruit of any defect but prior to all things.

[9] On the bureaucratic fallacy see above, section 2.4 and note 41.

[10] A similar argument is found in the contemporary Platonism of Pseudo-Aristotle's *de Melisso Xenophane Gorgia* ('Aristotelis qui fertur de Melisso Xenophane Gorgia libellus', ed. H. Diels; translation in Aristotle, *Complete works*, ed. J. Barnes (Princeton, 1995)). Also see discussion, W. R. Schoedel, 'Enclosing, not enclosed: the early Christian doctrine of God', in *Early Christian literature and the classical intellectual tradition*, FS for R. M. Grant, ed. W. R. Schoedel and R. L. Wilken (Paris, 1979), 78–80. God must rule and not be ruled (*de Melisso Xenophane Gorgia* 3.977a27), for if there were two or more he would cease to be 'mightiest and best of all' (3.977a24). Both Melissus (1.947a11) and Xenophanes (3.977b6) argue, it is claimed, against any limits on the One (cf. Melissus fr. 5–6). Nor can the One be finite in the sense of having a beginning, middle and end (3.977b4; cf. Melissus fr. 2–4).

Melissus also uses the argument for oneness which rejects the possibility of a void between the One and the Many. Zeno's paradox (frag. 3) that the many would have to be both limited and unlimited, depends on the need for something between entities which could be multiplied endlessly. Irenaeus seems closer to the infinite One of Melissus than to either the limited sphere of Parmenides or the One of Xenophanes, which is neither limited nor unlimited (cf. *de Melisso Xenophane Gorgia* 3.977b3).

[11] The Gospel of Truth speaks of him who encloses every place, but is not enclosed by anything. In this writing, Sophia and Demiurge, who are pivotal for Valentinian dualism, are nowhere to be found. See Schoedel, 'Enclosing', 80-1, where there is extended reference to the work of S. Arai, *Die Christologie des Evangelium Veritatis* (Leiden, 1964).

There is nothing above him and nothing after him (2.1.1). Indeed this is the first and most important axiom of true belief. One God is creator of heaven and earth and all things in them. The creator is not an unhappy accident in a plan which went astray.

His will is supreme and he freely created all that is. His oneness and his universality go together, for the only God, lord, creator, father, alone contains all things. Oneness further implies that he alone commands all things into existence (2.1.1).

Oneness implies fullness. We have seen that God, as fullness or pleroma, contains all things in his immensity which has no beginning, middle or end to its infinity (2.1.2). Here Irenaeus is formed by the theology of *Ephesians*, which derives from the principle, 'One God and father of all, who is above all, in all and through all' (Eph. 4:6). Creation by one creator is a precondition of recapitulation within the body of Christ and recapitulation is a precondition of salvation (2.2.6). Those in error do not believe that God is powerful or bountiful enough to create matter because they are ignorant of the power of a divine essence. Absurdly, they believe that their mother produced matter from her tears and perspiration, her passions and her sorrow (2.10.3). Irenaeus uses four strong adjectives to repudiate the theory that the intention of errant aeons produced the matter of creation: such a belief is incredible, fatuous, impossible, inconsistent (2.10.4).

Omnipotence implies oneness. The chief objection to multiple creators is that they lead to an infinite regress. If the Valentinians introduce a third kind of existence to separate the pleroma from what is beyond it, infinite regress follows (2.1.3). The same objection applies to Marcion's second god. Moving beyond one God (or pleroma) necessitates further gods (or pleromata) (2.1.4). Similar problems arise from belief in a void beyond the pleroma (2.3 and 2.4) or from the demiurge's need for a pattern from which to work. For if the demiurge needed a pattern and took it from things above as formed by Bythos, from what pattern did Bythos shape the pleroma, and so on?

Either the creator God used his own internal 'intention' as a pattern for creation, or we must go on asking for the origin of the higher pattern (2.16.1). Typically, Basilides has 365 successive heavens (2.16.2).

3.3.1   WISE ARCHITECT – WORD AND PLAN

Irenaeus perceives that the word of the king and the rational plan of the architect are joined because word is reason. God caused all things by his word and needed no assistance from angels. He himself in himself, in a way which we cannot describe, predestinated all things, formed them as he pleased, giving harmony to all things, assigning them their own place. He gave different natures to beings spiritual, celestial, angelic, animal, aquatic and terrestrial, because he endowed a nature suitable to the kind of life assigned to them (2.2.4).

The word within humans joins word and plan. The view that angels and creator were ignorant of the supreme God is absurd when all rational creatures know of him. For his invisible essence is mighty and confers on all a profound mental intuition and perception of his most powerful, omnipotent greatness. Although no one knows father but son, all know one fact at least because reason, implanted in their minds, moves them and reveals to them that there is one God, lord of all (2.6.1).

Even the demons know of the over-arching existence of God and, like every creature, they tremble when his name is invoked, just as all the subjects of the Roman emperor, however distant and unseen he may be, live in awareness of his rule (2.6.2). Moreover, those outside the community of Christian faith join in the universal consent to a belief that God is creator. Men of ancient times praise the one God who is maker of heaven and earth: the prophets remind us of this truth and heathen learn it from the creation which reveals him who formed it (2.9.1).

Creation is not foreign to the God above all, for he formed things various and diversified by his own word, in his own territory and as he pleased, since he was maker of all things, as a wise architect and sovereign king (2.11.1).

In contrast to the rationality of the divine plan the Gnostic myth shows no place for reason. The Valentinians put 'idea' before 'mind' when it is obvious that this cannot be the logical order.[12] Their drama is reminiscent of Antiphanes, a comic poet, whose

---

[12] The *stoicheia* doctrine of some Pythagoreans and Platonists showed a rational procession from the One and the Two.

Theogony is nearer to truth. This is the genre into which they fit. Gnostics merely change names in what is everywhere performed in theatres (2.14.1). They also produce an irrational patchwork of philosophers' opinions, mixing Thales, Anaximander and irreligious Anaxagoras (2.14.2).[13] Yet it is acknowledged that Gnostics, for all their use of 'philosophical concepts and schemes', claimed a higher source of truth than argued reason. Being super-rational, they did not use philosophers' concepts but words. They sought to 'learn up all the germs of the transcendental terms, and plant them everywhere', for, as ever, 'The meaning doesn't matter if it's only idle chatter of a transcendental kind.'[14] Consequently it is right to conclude that 'A rational approach . . . was not to be achieved on the basis of gnostic presuppositions.'[15]

Irenaeus believes he has shown, so his summary claims (2.30.9), by numerous and very clear arguments, that God made all things freely of his own power, that he arranged and finished them, so that his will is the substance of all things. One only God who created all things, alone omnipotent, the only father who founded and formed all things 'by word of his power' (Heb. 1:3), he fitted and arranged all things by his wisdom. He who cannot be contained, himself contains all things.

The plan of creation flows into the plan of the divine economy in history. The same God who is just and good formed man, planted paradise and made the world; then he sent the flood and saved Noah, chose Abraham and Isaac and Jacob, gave the law, spoke to the prophets, sent Christ and the apostles, called the church (2.30.9).

All sources of truth are united in declaring the creator's glory. Whether the source be apostles, the teaching of the lord, prophets, dictation of apostles or ministration of law, all praise one and the same being, God and father of all (2.35.4). For all things were made by one and the same father who adapts things visible and invisible to the natures and tendencies of the material. In short, all

---

[13] As noted above in chapter 2, Irenaeus has inherited a tradition which comes through Anaxagoras.

[14] W. S. Gilbert, 'Patience', *The Savoy Operas* (London, 1932), 164.

[15] G. May, *Schöpfung aus dem Nichts* (Berlin, 1978), 120; ET, *creatio ex nihilo* (Edinburgh, 1994), 118.

things have been made neither by angels, nor by any other power, but by God the father alone.

3.3.2 WISE ARCHITECT — THE CONFIGURATION OF CREATED THINGS

It is safer and more accurate to confess the truth: the creator who formed the world is the only God and there is none besides him who received from himself the model and figure of things which have been made. Weary with impious and circuitous description, we are compelled at some point or other, to fix our minds on some one and to confess that from him came the configuration of created things. From himself God found the model and form (*exemplum et figurationem*) of created things. (2.16.3)

In the divine plan, all things are made and fitted by God for a purpose, not connected by fanciful numbers like thirty (as Gnostics claim), but with existence and reason. Doctrine does not come from numbers, but numbers come from the system of doctrine. Created things derive their being from the one underived God, not vice versa (2.25.1).

Created things are opposite and inharmonious in themselves. As a modern poet says:

> All things counter, original, spare, strange;
> Whatever is fickle, freckled (who knows how?)
> With swift, slow; sweet, sour; adazzle, dim,
> He fathers-forth whose beauty is past change:
> Praise him.[16]

As the lyre has many and opposite notes but one unbroken melody arises from the intervals (i.e. differences) between notes, we do not divide the world but, says Irenaeus, we prove the judgement, goodness and skill shown in the whole work. We listen to the melody, praise the artist, admire the tension of some notes, attend to softness of others and discern sounds between these extremes, the special character and purpose of each, and the cause of variety; at the same time we hold to our rule that there is one artist and one God (2.25.2).

---

[16] Gerard Manley Hopkins, 'Pied Beauty'. *Poems and prose of G. M. Hopkins*, ed. W. H. Gardner (Penguin Books, 1953), 30.

Man is infinitely inferior to God, for he cannot have a plan of all things as God does. The limits of the human mind contrast with the infinity of the divine Intellect. Man is not uncreated, not coexistent with God as is the divine word; but he may now, through God's supreme goodness, receive the beginning of creation, and gradually learn from the word, the dispensations of God who made him (2.25.3). Therefore man should not try to go beyond God. Rather, he should come near to God through love not knowledge. It is better not to know why a single part of creation was made, but to believe in God and to continue in his love, for his love is the life of man (2.26.1).

There are some who always want to discover more than their masters. An analogy to Gnostic inquiry may be proposed. One could count human hairs and search for the reason why each human has a different number, a different size of head, and so on, and then found a sect on the achievement. Or one could count the sparrows which are caught (because God knows why so many were caught today, so many yesterday) and thus delude oneself and form a sect with others of like mind (2.26.2).

God's providence gives each thing its nature, rank and number. There is nothing accidental, but everything is appropriate to the divine way of thinking, which produces the proper causes of each kind (2.26.3). Gnostics who claim to be above the 'psychic' creator should prove superiority by their deeds not by mere words (2.30.2). For what have they achieved which is comparable to the heavens, earth, stars, lights of heaven, confining circles, rains, frosts and snows in their suitable season and special climate? How have they ordered the opposition of heat or dryness or formed rivers, fountains, flowers, trees, the variety of animals, rational and irrational, 'all adorned with beauty'? We see innumerable objects governed by the power, wisdom and greatness of the God who made them as well as the existences above heavens (2.30.3).

The Gnostic supreme god is above the creator. Yet how can an unproductive god be higher than one who is productive? If one has two tools, one in constant use and the other idle and useless, how can one claim the second to be superior (2.30.5)?

3.4   PLOTINUS' ARGUMENT FOR A GOOD CREATOR

The same arguments which Irenaeus uses are found in Plotinus, who had no interest in Christian authority; this proves that they spring not from authoritarian discipline but from independent concern for truth. They show that the challenge of Gnosticism was against a culture, not a church.[17] It is wrong to claim, as Gnostics do, that the soul produced the world through a defect or moral failure, for these terms cannot apply to the perfection of universal soul (*Enn.* 2.9.4).

Plotinus attacks the Gnostic negative account of the world and its maker (*Enn.* 2.9.3–5). He insists that the universal soul and the universe are good (*Enn.* 2.9.7, 8), that providence overrules the injustice of the world, and that Gnostics do not transcend the heavens (*Enn.* 2.9.9). Fallen Sophia and the demiurge are simply part of an absurd drama:

> Then they form an image of the image somewhere here below, through matter or materiality . . . and produce what they call the Maker, and make him revolt from his mother and drag the universe which proceeds from him down to the ultimate limit of images. The man who wrote this just meant to be blasphemous! (*Enn.* 2.9.10)

To begin with, if Wisdom did not descend but merely shone into darkness, she did not decline (*Enn.* 2.9.11). Nor can the relation of soul and matter through images make sense. 'Then how did matter, when it was illumined, make images of the soul kind, instead of bodily nature?' (*Enn.* 2.9.11). A maker of the universe who is derived from matter and image is a nonsense; 'but, over and above the fact that this is pure fiction, how does the making work? They say this comes first, and another after that, but they speak quite arbitrarily' (*Enn.* 2.9.11). Through ignorance of the nature of things they neglect the first things and indulge in 'the melodrama of the

---

[17] This does not mean that there is total identity between the complex ideas of Plotinus and Irenaeus. It means, as in the previous chapter (2.4), that they used similar argument against Gnostics on this point. They shared also a belief that the creator could never abandon his material creature and a predilection for the metaphor of light. However, their preoccupation, against Gnosticism, with truth and argument is confirmed by the disparity between their views on other matters and between the circumstances in which they were placed. See J. M. Rist, 'Plotinus on matter and evil', *Phron* 6 (1961), 154–66; D. O'Brien, *Théodicée plotinienne et théodicée gnostique* (Leiden, 1993).

terrors, as they think, in the cosmic spheres, which in reality "make all things sweet and lovely" (cf. Pindar, *Olympians* 1.48) for them' (*Enn.* 2.9.13). They tried to subject the cosmic powers by spells and incantations and did not acknowledge that diseases come from physical causes (*Enn.* 2.9.14).

Gnostic otherworldliness leads to immorality whereas Platonic otherworldliness leads to good morals. For the end of Gnostic fantasy is the despising of the world and moral values: 'this doctrine censures the lord of providence and providence itself still more crudely (than Epicurus) and despises all the laws of this world and the virtue whose winning extends back through all time' (*Enn.* 2.9.15).

Those who claim higher knowledge should display the first signs of knowledge by correcting their conduct to conform to the divine nature, which they claim, 'for that nature is aware of nobility (*kalon*) and despises the pleasure of the body' (*Enn.* 2.9.15). It is remarkable that Gnostics have never produced a moral treatise and indicate a persistent indifference to virtue. They may claim to 'look to God' but they are able at the same time to indulge in pluriform, pleasurable passions (*Enn.* 2.9.15). However, there is no way to God without virtue: 'God, if you talk about him without true virtue, is only a name' (*Enn.* 2.9.15).

Goodness does not fit with despising the universe and the gods. How does God care providentially for the Gnostics alone? He is present to all and to the universe in some way. If he is absent from the universe he will be absent from the Gnostics so that they cannot speak of him.

For providential care is much more of wholes than of parts, and the participation in God of that universal soul, too, is much greater. Its existence, and its intelligent existence, make this clear. For who of those who are so mindlessly highminded in looking down on it is as well ordered or has as intelligent a mind as the All? (*Enn.* 2.9.16)

There is no way in which a rational man can grasp the intelligible universe and not grasp its reflection in this world. 'For how could there be a musician who sees the melody in the intelligible world and will not be stirred when he hears the melody in sensible sounds? Or how could there be anyone skilled in geometry and numbers

who will not be pleased when he sees right relation, proportion
and order with his eyes?' He who sees the beauties of this world
will wonder at them and at their source (*Enn.* 2.9.16). The similarity
with Irenaeus is here uncanny and points to a perennial challenge.[18]
Beyond the bulk of the visible universe we grasp the force of the
intelligible archetype, where the force of God holds the beginning,
middle and end of the whole in his power.

The presence of God in the world is marked by beauty in physical and in ethical forms. Those who cannot see these things are
intellectually blind: 'they have no contemplation, then, and hence
no God. For the beauties here exist because of the first beauties.'
(*Enn.* 2.9.17). To go on to higher beauty does not imply insult to
lower beauties. For anything that is wholly beautiful is dominated
by beauty within. Gnostics are like people who criticise the house
they live in and denigrate its builder. The philosopher speaks well of
the builder and of the house which he will not always need. 'While
we have bodies we must stay in our houses, which have been built
for us by a good sister soul which has great power to work without
any toil or trouble' (*Enn.* 2.9.18). Instead of clashing or yielding to
pleasures and sights 'as we draw near to the completely untroubled
state we can imitate the soul of the universe and of the stars, and,
coming to a closeness of resemblance to them hasten on to the same
goal and have the same objects of contemplation' (*Enn.* 2.9.18).

3.5 GOD NEEDS NOTHING[19]

The attribute 'in need of nothing' ($\mathring{\alpha}\delta\acute{\epsilon}\eta\tau o\varsigma$) is widely affirmed of
God in the ancient world.[20] Irenaeus includes the same claim in
his rule of faith. The creator of all needed no help from any angels
or powers outside him, for God has no need 'but through his word
and spirit he makes, disposes, governs all things and grants them
their existence' (1.22.1ff.). Only God is free from need (3.8.3).

---

[18] A challenge which is posed, by the success of the deaf musician, in the recent novel,
Vikram Seth, *An equal music* (London, 1999).

[19] A. Orbe, *Espiritualidad de san Ireneo* (Rome, 1989), 45 89.

[20] From the Sophist Antiphon (*Aletheia* 98), Plato (*Tim.* 33d, 34d), Plutarch (*Lives*, Aristides
and Cato 4), Stoics (ap. Stobaeum 1.1.39), Lucretius (*De rerum natura* 2.646 50), Philo,
Plotinus, *Corpus Hermeticum*, Alcinoos, Apuleius, Sallustius, to 2 Maccabees 14:35, Acts
17:24 and Clement of Alexandria (*str.* 5.11.75.2 4), God's transcendence above all need
is declared. Orbe, *Espiritualidad*, 45 6.

On the other hand, Irenaeus attacks the common claim of heretics that God needs help in the work of creation,[21] that spirit can have no dealing with matter, and that therefore intermediaries are needed in creation. On the contrary, Irenaeus claims that God has his own hands (son and spirit) and attacks opponents who deny that God the spirit (as distinct from the psychic demiurge) can create the world and form man. The contrary claim that God needs intermediaries may spring from two different grounds: either he is too exalted to reach the world or he is too inadequate to produce a world.[22] If the God of the old testament is separated from the God of the new, then the creator will appear inferior. He is limited, needs man and the world, is a blind instrument, psychic, subject to human passions. He makes and conserves the material world subjecting it through law and prophets. He remains ignorant of the dispensation which he serves, of the economy of the spirit, of the true God. He is as far distant from the true God as he is from humans.

Irenaeus insists on one first principle, on the identity of creator and maker with the father, the God of spirit, the true transcendent God who needs nothing and depends on no one. In creating and fashioning the world God shows a free and positive disposition, which leads to the deification of the creature (*homo/plasma*). The creator establishes the dispensation wherein 'everything is directed to raise man to the condition of "god" in communion with life itself'.[23] The God of the old testament is declared to be free from need. Yahweh never wants for anything, while man wants perpetually.[24]

3.6.1 *CREATIO EX NIHILO*: CONCEPT WITHOUT FORMULA (JUSTIN)

Some have thought that *creatio ex nihilo* is not to be found in the old testament, in Judaism or in earliest Christian thought, where

---

[21] Orbe, *Espiritualidad.* 48.
[22] Ibid., 49.
[23] Ibid., 88-9.
[24] Ibid., 89. Orbe continues (91-123) with an excellent exposition of 'God makes, man is made' which links creation and anthropology.

creation is the production of things from unformed matter.[25]
This notion, it is claimed, is found as late as Justin (*1 apol.* 10.2;
59.1–5; 67.7).[26] Such a claim rests on the failure to recognise the
two models of king and architect and the failure to distinguish between words and concepts (5.13.2). The concept of creation from
nothing can be found without the formula and the formula can
be found without the concept. Accounts of creation can only be
understood in the context of their total argument, in a conceptual
not a culinary manner.[27]

Justin's account has been misunderstood through the failure to
distinguish words and concepts.[28] The cosmos (*dialogue with Trypho*
5,4; Plato, *Tim.* 41 ab) is transitory but kept in being by the will
of God. Justin's axiom (*dial.* 5.4–6) is that there can be only one
unoriginated or unbegotten (*agenneton*) being, from which it follows
that the soul is originate and transitory. *A fortiori* the same argument
would have to apply to matter. 'For what is unoriginated is similar to,
equal to, the same with, what is unoriginated . . . and consequently
there are not many things which are unoriginated'; wearied by
unending regress, the mind fixes on one unoriginated cause of
all (*dial.* 5). Yet we find the claim concerning Justin: 'in his explicit
statements about matter he *seems to* consider it an eternal, uncreated
substratum of the cosmos. *One gets the impression* that for Justin the
idea that the creation of the world must have resulted from matter
given in advance was so self-evident that he saw no problem in
it.'[29]

---

[25] In this brief account I have drawn on the excellent essay of J. Fantino, 'L'origine de la
doctrine de la création *ex nihilo*. A propos de l'ouvrage de G. May', *RSPhTh* 80,4 (1996),
589–602. The work of G. May, *Schöpfung aus dem Nichts*, ET *Creatio ex nihilo*, remains of
fundamental value because he has shown the fascination of the problem and the advance
made by Basilides.

[26] This does not mean, as we shall see, that Justin could have believed in a dualism of
God and matter. He insisted that there was only one unbegotten first-principle of all
things. See discussion in Osborn, *Justin Martyr*, 46–9.

[27] From Paul (Rom. 4) and the whole of scripture, early Christian writers took their doctrine
of *creatio ex nihilo*. There was one God, unique in power. Cf. Clement of Alexandria,
'Everything takes place at the same time as he commands it. It follows from his bare
intention to give a gift that the gift is fully made' (*paedagogus* 1.6.26). 'What he wills is
thereby real and the name for this reality is the world' (*paed.* 1.6.27). See E. Osborn, *The
philosophy of Clement of Alexandria* (Cambridge, 1957), 32–3.

[28] May, *Schöpfung*, 125, ET 123.

[29] Ibid., 126, ET 124. My italics.

If one looks to concepts rather than to words, one receives a different impression; it is clear that Justin would never have considered the concept of unoriginated matter because it contradicted his central belief about God, the sole unoriginated. One cannot get around this point by isolating the account of matter from the rest of Justin's thought. 'So when Justin *presupposes* an *eternal* material as the stuff of creation, this conception[30] simply has the function of explaining how the creation of the world was possible; Justin obviously cannot but represent it as only the formation of a material substratum. Beyond that the doctrine of uncreated matter plays no part in his thinking.'[31]

Justin's use of the architect/builder model includes an apologetic move (*1 apol.* 10). He is anxious to show his pagan readers that they have common beliefs with Christians. Our teachers, the prophets, gave to Plato the claim that God, having changed formless matter, made the world. Moses the first prophet, older than any Greek writer, tells how in the beginning, the spirit moved on the water and God said 'Let there be light.' From this, Plato, and those who agree with Plato, and we ourselves have learned that the whole world was made out of the substance of which Moses spoke and which the poets call Erebus. The agent of creation was the word of God. Plato also learnt that the creator made the sign of χ (*chi*) on the universe (*1 apol.* 60). In baptism we are born again through the name of God, the father and lord of the universe (*1 apol.* 61); on Sunday we celebrate the first day on which God changed darkness and matter to make the world. We acknowledge too the day when our saviour rose from the dead.

Justin here merely adumbrates (through resurrection and baptism) the image of the monarch who has no need beyond himself[32] and who acts directly and without process. However, matter does not imply dualism, especially when Irenaeus joins the king with the master builder. Matter is produced and ordered without interval. Unformed matter is part of a series which has been swept into one

---

[30] Note the fatal confusion of concepts with words and the slide from 'seems to' and 'gets the impression' to 'presupposes'. May shows great integrity by leaving enough clues to challenge his argument and display the vitality of the problem. My italics.

[31] May, *Schöpfung*, 127, ET 125.

[32] As Justin says in *1 apol.* 10 in the immediate context of a reference to creation from matter, and elsewhere.

by the power of God. Why does Justin not make this point?: first,
because none of his parallels between pagan and Christian beliefs – from necromancy to the ascension of the sons of Jupiter,
or the healing miracles of Aesculapius or Perseus' virgin birth
(*1 apol.* 18–22) – suggests an identity between pagan and Christian
accounts; second, because it was wrong to talk about what God did
before creation.

3.6.2   *CREATIO EX NIHILO*: FORMULA WITHOUT CONCEPT (BASILIDES)

Basilides,[33] it has been claimed, is the first Christian theologian who
teaches *creatio ex nihilo*: 'God is non-being because he is above being,
the cosmos pre-existing in the world seed is non-being because it
has still to be realised in time and space (cf. Hippolytus, *Refutatio*
VII 22.1.6; X 14.2), and the world seed is created out of non–
being in the absolute sense, out of nothing.'[34] What distinguishes
Basilides from other Gnostics is that he 'looks on the supreme God,
exalted over being and over all plurality, as being also the creator
of the world and ascribes to the archons merely the function of
under-demiurges. From this statement *he has to reach the conclusion*
that God can only have created the cosmos out of nothing.'[35] But
does he reach this conclusion? It is more probable that he has used
the phrase 'out of nothing' without conceptual awareness. Yet the
claim is put strongly. Basilides is credited with the traditional concept of *creatio ex nihilo*, that the supreme God is the sole creator
and that negative theology requires that there are no analogies to
God's acts. 'Is it any more than a curious accident of history, that
the doctrine of *creatio ex nihilo* first meets us in unambiguous form
in the work of a gnostic theologian?'[36]

First, there is ambiguity. 'Not x creates not z from not y' is consistent with many claims, including, 'Anything which is not x creates

---

[33] We digress to discuss Basilides for three reasons: first, to examine the competitive claim
that he (not Irenaeus and Theophilus) invented creation *ex nihilo*; second, because the
difference between formulas and concepts needs to be asserted; and third, because the
contemporary discussion illuminates the problem.

[34] May, *Schöpfung*, 78, ET 76.

[35] Ibid., 77, ET 76. My italics.   [36] Ibid., 85, ET 83.

anything which is not z from anything which is not y' or 'Nothing creates nothing from nothing.' Secondly, if we distinguish three kinds of non-being – as above being, not-yet being and absolute not-being – the picture is more promising. The above-existent God creates from the non-existent the not-yet existent. This is the best case we can make for him; but there has been no creation for world seed is not yet being. Politicians commonly produce what is not yet out of what is absolutely not. Nothing comes of nothing. Being has not been produced. Thirdly, if we take the world seed as a stage in the process of creation, then creation takes place through an intermediate entity. Creation *ex nihilo* should be marked by immediacy and the absence of intermediaries. Here there is an intermediary and once again the bureaucratic fallacy has taken its toll; it cannot be the case that 'God makes the cosmos on the ground of the decisions of his will alone through his mighty word out of nothing' (21.4 and 22.3).[37] Fourthly, Basilides' claim to reject all analogies is inconsistent with his concept of world seed, which is analogous to growth within the world.

3.6.3 *CREATIO EX NIHILO*: FORMULA AND CONCEPT (IRENAEUS)

Theophilus of Antioch and Irenaeus change the scene by enunciating a strict account of *creatio ex nihilo*, the former engaging with Plato's *Timaeus*, perhaps the most heavily interpreted passage in classical literature,[38] the latter exercising argument against theosophy. Irenaeus attributes basic matter to the power and will of God. Men need material to make things. God provides his own material (2.10.4). Theophilus similarly points to the power of God demonstrated in *creatio ex nihilo* (*ad Autolycum* 2.4, 13). There is a difference in definition. Theophilus sees *creatio ex nihilo* in the creation of formless matter (*ad Aut.* 2.10) as the first stage of creation, but Irenaeus does not talk of formless matter: *creation of matter and the shaping of the world are two aspects of a single act by God who is both supreme king and wise architect.* This act is part of the divine economy and is the work

---

[37] Ibid., 74, ET 73.
[38] See M. Baltes, *Die Weltentstehung des platonischen Timaeus nach den antiken Interpreten*, 2 vols. (Leiden, 1976–8).

of the father through the son and spirit. Theophilus denies that matter could be uncreated (*ad Aut.* 2.4, 6). Irenaeus will not divide creation of matter from the formation of creatures since they are two aspects of one act.

For Plato demiurge, matter and forms present the move from one to many. For the Stoics God and matter coexist eternally and from these two principles the world is produced (*SVF* 1.85, 24). Neo-Pythagoreans and Middle Platonists argued for one or two first principles, the second principle being matter. Middle Platonists faced the problem posed by *Timaeus* 28b (the world has come into being [γέγονεν] from a first principle) and *Timaeus* 30a (God brought all that was visible from disorder to order). A monist interpretation taught that matter was coeternally dependent on God. A dualist interpretation saw unformed matter as independent of God until, at a point of time, God brought it into order. This view, held by Plutarch, Atticus, and Maximus Tyrius, was strongly opposed by Plotinus as well as by Alexander of Lycopolis in his rejection of Manicheism. Pythagoreans were either monists (Eudorus, Nicomachus of Gerasa, Moderatus of Gades) who derived the One/Dyad from the transcendent One (God took some of his own substance, deprived it of all qualities so that it was pure potentiality),[39] or dualists like Numenius (for whom both the One and the Dyad were ultimate).

In this debate the origin of matter became a crucial question. All agreed that the world came into being by the imposition of form on unformed matter. Did matter come from God or not? Gnostics linked this debate to the biblical account of creation. The primeval chaos of unformed matter derived from Sophia through the action of the Logos. Theophilus and Irenaeus, looking to the king rather than to the architect, insisted that the eternal uncreated God freely created all things out of nothing.[40]

Genesis 2:17b was taken by Gnostics to be proof of the impotence and inferiority of the demiurge, for Adam and Eve did not die

---

[39] See A. J. Festugière, *La révélation d'Hermès Trismégiste*, vol. IV: *Le dieu inconnu et la gnose* (Paris, 1954), 32–40.

[40] Theophilus attacks Platonists because they claim that matter is eternal (*ad Aut.* 2.4). Like Tertullian, he wrote against Hermogenes, but his work has not survived. Like Platonic monists, he claimed that God created matter; but he did not line up against dualists by deriving matter from the substance of God.

when they ate of the forbidden fruit. Their disobedience opened their eyes to true gnosis. Wisdom had spoken through the serpent and defeated the demiurge. Irenaeus offered five solutions to the problem: Adam and Eve died the death of the soul at the moment of their disobedience; when they took the forbidden fruit they became mortal; they died on the one day of creation; they died on the sixth day as did the second Adam; the day of the lord is a thousand years and Adam died at the age of 930. The second of the solutions (instant mortality) is most consistent with Irenaeus' thought.

Irenaeus differed from Theophilus because he did not divide *creatio ex nihilo* from the formation of creatures. Against Gnostics he affirmed that creation was one act of architect and king. Theophilus on the other hand distinguished creation of matter from production of creatures; he thereby confronted the widely held philosophical thesis of the eternity of matter. He put forward a general objection to the thesis: myths and philosophical accounts trace the origin of the world to an ultimate divine cause from which, through intermediaries, the world emanates; this impairs the divine transcendence and the freedom of the creative act.[41]

Creation from matter and creation from nothing point to our ruling themes of architect and king. It would be wrong to see this distinction as purely a second-century novelty. The whole of the old testament anticipates these two themes. The Genesis creation story resounds to the royal command: 'God said' (Gen. 1:3, 6, 9, 11, 14). In the Psalms, his throne is in the heavens (Ps. 11:4), when the lord thunders and the most high gave his voice (Ps. 18:13). The mighty God, even the lord has spoken and called the earth from the rising of the sun unto its going down (Ps. 50:1). God is our king of old, working salvation in the midst of the earth (Ps. 74:12).[42] He rules the raging of the sea. The architect/master-builder forms man out of dust (Gen. 2:7) and sets lights in the heavens (Gen. 1:16–17). In the Psalms the heavens are the work of his fingers (Ps. 8:3), the heavens declare his glory and the firmament shows his handiwork

---

[41] Fantino, 'L'origine de la doctrine', 601. 'C'est précisément ce point que veut exprimer la notion de création *ex nihilo*. Elle manifeste la transcendance de Dieu par rapport au créé et donc sa liberté dans l'action créatrice.'

[42] The voice of the lord thunders on the waters, powerful and full of majesty (Ps. 29:4–5), for God is king of all the earth (Ps. 47:7).

(Ps. 19:1). The earth is the lord's for he founded it on the seas and established it on the floods (Ps. 24:1–2). Before the mountains brought forth or ever God formed the earth and the world, even from everlasting to everlasting he is God (Ps. 90:2).

All this is supported by Irenaeus' account of Plato (3.25.5), whom he declares to be more religious than the Gnostics for three reasons: Plato declares that the same god is both just and good, is omnipotent, and himself executes judgement. God is the ancient word who possesses the beginning, middle and end of all that exists, who does everything rightly, moving around things according to their nature, and is followed by retributive justice for those who transgress the divine law. Elsewhere Plato says that the maker and framer of the universe is good; because he has no envy his goodness takes effect in the beginning and the course of the creation of the world. For Irenaeus, the Gnostic account of creation is false and inferior to Plato when it speaks of causes of the world such as ignorance, wandering, consequences of defect, the weeping mother or another god and father.

The will of the creator is the efficient cause of the world. God acts freely and of his own will (2.1.1; 3.8.3). The creative will of God expresses his goodness (4.38.3; 2.25.3; 2.29.2; 5.4.2). While Plato speaks of the will of the demiurge, the Valentinians fragment God with their account of 'thought' and 'will'; but for Irenaeus God is all will and all mind (1.12.2). The belief that God's will and its realisation go together is a common philosophical idea.[43] God created the world through himself (4.20.1) and from himself, freely and of his own choice, so that his will is the substance of all things (2.30.9).

To sum up the question of creation from nothing in Justin and Irenaeus, we can do no better than to quote Irenaeus concerning matter.

Moreover we shall not go wrong if we affirm the same thing concerning the origin of matter, namely that God produced it, for we have learned from the scriptures that God holds primacy over all things. But whence did he produce it and how? That, scripture nowhere explains, and we have

---

[43] A. J. Festugière, *La révélation d'Hermès Trismégiste*, vol. III: *Les doctrines de l'âme* (Paris, 1953), 159. Galen (*De usu partium* 11.14) claims against Moses that there are things impossible by nature and God chooses what is best from what is possible at the time.

no right, with our own opinions, to launch ourselves into an unending sea of fantasy concerning God; we must leave such knowledge to God. (2.28.7)

3.7   IMMEDIACY

Irenaeus analysed the concepts behind the two models with which he worked. So long as they were kept together there was no problem. When one was given culinary status and taken without conceptual awareness, trouble occurred. Those who claimed to be above reason showed that they were below it.

How did Irenaeus hold the two models together? *His concept of God as universal mind, indivisible, homogeneous and simultaneous, who thinks, wills, speaks and acts inseparably, makes the two models compatible and creation thinkable. Creatio ex nihilo* leads to an awareness of the immediacy[44] of God whose right hand will hold us, even when we take the wings of the morning and dwell in the uttermost parts of the sea. This is the exact opposite of the meaning of *ex nihilo* in Basilides, who separates God from creation by an intermediary. Remarkably, a recent study speaks of *creatio ex nihilo* and concludes in the same way:

Finally the collective effect of all the above should be to affirm, in the most radical way, that the Christian faith knows no doctrine of creation that is not a doctrine of *creatio ex nihilo* and that this doctrine demands to be articulated and interpreted in irreducibly trinitarian ways ... That is, it speaks not of some cosmological process but of the dynamic presence of the divine communion in the created order. God's presence is a free and ecstatic presence in, for and with the created order and God's purpose in this (discerned by the Spirit in and through the incarnate Son) is to bring to perfection the created order within his own life.[45]

---

[44] 'the immediacy (used in its literal, non-temporal sense!) of the totality of the created order's contingency upon God's creativity', A. J. Torrance, '*Creatio ex nihilo* and the Spatio-Temporal dimension with special reference to Jürgen Moltmann and D. C. Williams', in *The doctrine of creation*, ed. Colin E. Gunton (Edinburgh, 1997), 99.

[45] Ibid., 102.

CHAPTER 4

Economy: God as architect of time

The divine economy is not an abstract composition. It is the way in which the wise architect and sovereign king disposed the salvation of mankind. This disposition reflects a firmer reality within the events which are scattered around and within it. This reality is nothing less than the mind of God, seen by the prophets, and Irenaeus' answer to Platonic forms or geometry.[1] The pattern of the supreme disposer is not found in abstraction, but in the artistry of certain events woven together in time and place. It must not be confused with the narrower and less subtle concept of salvation as the mighty acts of God.

In Greek literature, the use of *oikonomia* ($o\grave{i}\kappa ovo\mu\acute{i}\alpha$) moved from domestic to political economy, from the management of a household to the management of a city (Aristotle, *Politics* 3.1285b). It became a common Hellenistic word for good administration or purposeful arrangement. Ephesians links it with the hidden divine purpose for the salvation of man (Eph. 1:9–12) and the realisation and revelation of that purpose (Eph. 3:2–11). Paul speaks of stewards, *oikonomoi*, who administered the mysteries of God (1 Cor. 4:1–2). The Stoics are the first to use *oikonomia* for God and the universe (*SVF* 2.945,273). For them everything has purpose and place within a world of conflict and contradictions. *Oikonomia* produces *sympatheia* to facilitate life according to nature (*SVF* 3.582). Beyond theology and philosophy, *oikonomia* is an important word for architecture (Vitruvius, *De arch.* 1.2.1). Rhetoricians also give importance to *dispositio* in the arrangement of discourse. Both of these uses of the word point to Irenaeus' aesthetic criterion of fitness.

[1] God is active in the lower half of Plato's Divided Line (*Rep.* 510) in the shapes and the shadows.

In patristic writers before Irenaeus the word *oikonomia* covers four main meanings: the plan of God and its fulfilment in the incarnation,[2] a particular work prophesied of Christ,[3] the office of a bishop,[4] and disposition or arrangement in general.[5] Justin develops the notion of multiple economies, such as events in the lives of patriarchs, within one grand economy. In this way he systematizes typology and anticipates Irenaeus.

This chapter, however, begins with a confession of defeat, for the keyword οἰκονομία has no direct equivalent in modern English. The present convention is to translate it as 'economy' in the sense of a system or plan. For Irenaeus' sense of economy, fortunately, we have a clue from the previous chapter where creation, the first step in the plan, was attributed to the 'wise architect and sovereign king' (2.11.1).

4.1 ECONOMY AND DIVINE ARCHITECT

To understand Irenaeus on the divine economy, we may begin with the classic writings of Vitruvius on architecture. Irenaeus speaks of God 'drawing up the plans for the edifice of salvation' (4.14.2)[6] and goes on to speak of God's provision for what is 'most apt', 'worthy' and 'in many modes adapted to the harmony (*consonantia*) of salvation'. Vitruvius (*De arch.* 1.2.1–9) links *oikonomia* with order, disposition, shapeliness, symmetry and correctness/aptness, as the six values of architecture.

All these values are important for Irenaeus, although he does not copy Vitruvius. Vitruvius analyses and separates where Irenaeus is deeply concerned for unity of process.[7] Order (*ordinatio, taxis*) is for Vitruvius the initial commitment to a geometrical pattern which remains in control. Design/disposition (*dispositio, diathesis*)

[2] Ignatius, *epistula ad Ephesios* 18.2; 20.1; Aristides, *ap.* 15.1; Justin, *dial.* 30.3; 31.1; 45; 87.5; 103.3; 120.1; Athenagoras, *presbeia* 22.4.
[3] Justin, *dial.* 67.6, 107.3; 134.2; 141.4.
[4] Ignatius, *Eph.* 6.1.
[5] *Martyrdom of Polycarp* 2.2; Tatian, *oratio ad Graecos* 5.1; 12.2; 12.3; 18.2; 19.4; 21.3; Theophilus of Antioch, *ad Autol.* 2.12, 29; *Epistula ad Diognetum* 4.5.
[6] *et his qui ei complacebant fabricationem salutis ut architectus delinians.*
[7] Vitruvius, *Ten books on architecture*, translation and commentary, I. D. Rowland, T. N. Howe and M. J. Drewe (Cambridge, 1999), 149–51. See also the text and translation by Frank Granger, LCL (2 vols. 1931, 1934).

places the various elements of the building on a grid. Shapeliness (*eurythmia*) is pleasing appearance and aesthetic value. Symmetry (*symmetria*) means that all parts of a building should be proportionate to one another and to the whole. Correctness/aptness (*decor*) is a control of licence by function, tradition and nature, which renders appropriate each part. What is fitting is determined by the formal rules of a culture, the culture itself and nature.

Economy/allocation (*distributio*) begins with a practical reference to costs and material but goes on to consider the needs of the client. Buildings must be variously disposed for the use of the owner, for town or country, for financiers or men of taste and for the powerful. 'And generally the *distributio* of buildings is to be adapted to the vocations of their owners' (*De arch.* 1.2.9).[8] Economy of salvation is adapted to the vocation of mankind; nothing human is alien to it.

Irenaeus uses the notion of economy with all the other values as supplementary.[9] They are all important to him, with first place going to aptness (*decor*), what is correct and fitting in contrast to the licence of Gnostics.[10] The economy of salvation must be fitting, apt, appropriate to man and God. Aptness stands beside truth in importance, as one of the two criteria. It is also the value where personal decision, of God or man, plays a dominant role. 'Given its orientation, *decor* stands somewhat alone among Vitruvius's fundamentals, for elsewhere his architect is not given much opportunity for making personal choices.'[11] By what he chooses as fitting, God tells us about himself.

For Irenaeus, the wise architect of creation continued his design in the history of man's salvation. In this he showed proportion, order, and just distribution between the parts. The beauty and disposition of God's saving work reflected his artistry in time.[12]

---

[8] A. A. Payne, *The architectural treatise in the Renaissance* (Cambridge, 1999), 40.

[9] Something of the same mobility is found in rhetoric. 'In rhetoric, *oikonomia* is active in realms that Vitruvius splits between *dispositio* and *distributio* – that is, it controls the ordering of the thoughts and of the appropriate means of expression', Payne, *The architectural treatise*, 255.

[10] See Payne, ibid., 15–21, on good and bad licence.

[11] Ibid., 36.

[12] 'Gottes zeithafte Kunst', H. U. von Balthasar, *Herrlichkeit*, II, 76. See below, chapter 9.

God's exuberance is economical in the sense that nothing is super-fluous in a great work of art. The Sistine Chapel is overwhelming but its plan is such that every part is necessary. That is what Irenaeus is trying to say about the economy.

God's saving work, which began with creation, was not limited to a particular event. Certainly it belonged within events and history. God became man that man might become God. God achieves this exchange in Christ as second Adam, who is both human creature and divine being. The incarnation thus fixes the economy of God within history. 'How can they be saved unless it be God who has worked their salvation on earth? And how can man pass into God if God has not passed into man?' (4.33.4).[13]

This exchange is not restricted to the incarnation, however, but works through all salvation history. 'Christ died for all' is not an isolated incident but the 'divine eternal history', said Hegel. The divine economy follows from creation as it negates the negations of creatureliness and sin. Hegel saw this divine im-pulse (*Moment*) in terms of dialectic. The return of the reconciled world to God is, for Hegel, a return to God himself as spirit, through the resurrection of Christ. 'Negation is thereby overcome and the negation of negation is thus the impulse of the divine nature.'[14] Negation, in Hegel's logic, is a productive force. He sees the negation of the separation between God and man, in Irenaean words to which he gives his own meaning: 'Unity of the divine and human nature: God is become man.'[15] Irenaeus does better than Hegel when he sees human history as the return of the jubilant divine shepherd with the lost sheep on his shoul-ders, but the reasoning around the metaphor is illuminated by Hegel.

The economy is the whole plan of God. One divine economy belongs to the one God, one plan to the one wise architect. The universal economy is made up of smaller diverse economies of events which form the different saving dispositions which God has

---

[13] J. T. Nielsen, *Adam and Christ in the theology of Irenaeus of Lyons* (Assen, 1968), 60.

[14] G. W. F. Hegel, *Vorlesungen über die Philosophie der Religion, Theorie — Werke — Ausgabe*, vol. XVII (Frankfurt, 1969), 294–5; cited in Ulrich Wilckens, *Der Brief an die Römer*, vol. I (Röm. 1–5), (Zurich, Einsiedeln and Cologne, 1978), 334. Negation, in Hegel's logic, is a productive force.

[15] Hegel, *Vorlesungen*, 203–4.

granted (3.12.13).[16] The old and new testaments display God's universal plan to bring salvation and blessing. Economy is central to Irenaeus, for the task of theology is to present the activity (*pragmateia*) and the economy of God in his relationship to man (1.10.3). The Gnostics, on the other hand, are ignorant of the scriptures and of the economy of God.

What does the word mean for Irenaeus? οἰκονομία is generally translated by *dispositio* (twenty-seven times).[17] It has four interlocking meanings:[18]

(A1) ordering or productive act (most commonly in Irenaeus);
(A2) a structured entity;
(B1) disposition, arrangement of things or events, the structure of an entity;
(B2) underlying purpose or plan behind things or events.

In general, early Christian writers join *B2* to *A1* (the disposition is never separate from the supreme disposer), defining the economy by the incarnation, and omitting the link with creation as found in the new testament. However, in Irenaeus, *oikonomia* becomes central, unifying creation and recapitulation. In the singular it refers chiefly to the incarnation and in the plural to the old testament manifestations of the word. In contrast, Gnosticism keeps *oikonomia* within the divine pleroma and allows it to be reflected in the lower world. The monad or dyad emits a primordial pair from which follows the deployment of the pleroma; outside the pleroma a second phase introduces the creation of the world.

Too large for exact definition, *oikonomia* can be taken as the ruling metaphor which holds Irenaeus' theology together.[19] One writer shows how such a synthesis could be established.[20] In God's plan the creation is made for man not man for the creation (5.29.1).

---

[16] Widmann, 'Irenäus und seine theologischen Väter', 156-73.
[17] It is translated once only by each of *dispensatio, creatio, ex omnibus factus*.
[18] J. Fantino, *La théologie d'Irénée* (Paris, 1994), 94-9. See whole chapter, 85-126.
[19] 'bildhafte Verdeutlichung', A. Bengsch, *Heilsgeschichte und Heilswissen*, EThSt 3 (Leipzig, 1957), 105-6.
[20] See Fantino's chapter, 'La structure trinitaire de l'economie chez Irénée', *La théologie*, 203-64.

Man's glory is to persevere in the service of God (4.14.1). God wishes to share his life with man.[21] Economy is presented in 'different tonalities': glory, incorruptibility and immortality, vision and knowledge of God, adoption as sons of God, image and likeness. These themes variously indicate the purpose of the economy and summarize the theology of Irenaeus.[22]

The economy is the history of humanity. Adam, as a collective figure, stands for the human race, which stems from him (4.33.15). He is the first or psychic/animal man (1 Cor. 15:45–6) (3.22.3; 5.12.2). Christ who is spiritual man is also collective (3.18.1). The church is the new humanity, the place of the spirit (3.24.1). Adam, as Paul wrote (Rom. 5:14), was a sketch of the future man, 'the shape of the coming one' (3.22.3), and at the same time the cause of continuing sin. The contrast between the old Adam born of the virgin earth and the new Adam born of the virgin Mary (3.21.10) is overcome in Jesus who unites in himself the created and the uncreated. He bestows the spirit on the church and all the earth (3.17.3), completing the threefold plan: creation, incarnation and the fullness of the spirit.

The economy is the history of salvation, a succession of times or seasons where man participates in God. In the first stage, faith in God and his purpose is governed by natural precepts (4.13.4), the second stage is the law (4.13.1) and the third stage is the gospel (4.16.4, 5). When the natural precepts were not obeyed, the law came both in response to sin (hardness of heart, failure of love) and to prophesy Christ. In the old testament, patriarchs and prophets prepared the way for Christ. In the new testament, law and prophets disappear, there is a return to natural law accompanied by the gift of the spirit and adoption as sons (4.16.5). The gift of the spirit is partial in the church but total in the kingdom of the father.[23]

Typology is integral to the economy, where it implies both a progression from Old to New and an equivalence because the New

[21] Ibid., 205.
[22] 'tonalités différentes', ibid., 219. The five themes are identified by Fantino, ibid., 207–18.
[23] Justin and other earlier writers had seen the testaments as part of the *oikonomia* which was linked with the Stoic and popular notion of the administration of the universe.

is the realization of the Old.[24] The spirit for which David prayed (Ps. 50:14), for example, is given at Pentecost for all nations (3.17.2). There are parallels between Irenaeus and Gnosticism, where perfection of knowledge is also given in the last days (2.4.2). Some forms of Gnosticism even allow for temporal progression[25] but it was the genius of Irenaeus 'to insert recapitulation into the *oikonomia*'.[26]

4.2.1 ECONOMY AS ACCUSTOMING

The first purpose of the economy was to accustom man to God and to accustom God to man.[27] This theme of accustoming or habituation runs throughout Irenaeus' writings. In Abraham, the first fellow-citizen of the word of God, man became accustomed to follow the word of God. In his sacrifice of his son he was a prophet who saw the economy of the Lord's passion, by which he and all who believed would be saved. Abraham's faith looked back to the creator and forward to the promise of posterity (4.21.1).

Between creation and incarnation God accustoms himself to man and man is accustomed to God. Abraham, Isaac and Jacob prefigure what is to come, and the economies of God accustom his people to live as strangers in the world and to follow the guidance of his word. Scripture prescribes a life which is alien to the world and obedient to God (4.21.3).

---

[24] J. Daniélou, *Gospel message and hellenistic culture* (ET; London, 1973), 207–9, 212–13. Fantino, *La théologie*, 236.

[25] H. I. Marrou, 'La théologie de L'histoire dans la gnose Valentinienne', in U. Bianchi (ed.), *Le origini dello gnosticismo* (Leiden, 1967), 220–4.

[26] Fantino, *La théologie*, 241. But is the parousia part of recapitulation? Wingren, Houssiau and Lassiat give an affirmative answer, and are criticised for doing so by Orbe and Rousseau (Wingren, *Man and the incarnation*, 192; A. Houssiau, *La christologie de saint Irénée* (Louvain and Gembloux, 1955), 219–20; H. Lassiat, *Promotion de l'homme en Jésus Christ d'après Irénée de Lyon* (Tours, 1974), 311–14). Incarnation and *parousia* are the time of the spirit, which is 'poured out in a new way on our humanity' (*dem.* 6). Fantino distinguishes recapitulation (incarnation) from the second coming (3.16.6). At the incarnation Jesus came in visible form, so as to be received and to accustom us to his presence (4.38.1). One text only (1.10.1) suggests this distinction; elsewhere recapitulation and incarnation are the same. Recapitulation is where the incarnate son passes on the spirit to humans. Incarnation joins the preparation which precedes it with the realisation which comes after it. See Fantino, *La théologie*, 256. Wingren, *Man and the incarnation*, 195–7.

[27] P. Evieux, 'Théologie de l'accoutumance chez saint Irénée', *RSR* 55 (1967), 5–54.

The incarnation marks a new stage in the process of accustoming. The spirit descends on the son of God, who has become man so that the spirit may be accustomed to live in a human being. He works, among men, the will of the father and replaces their oldness with the newness of Christ (3.17.1). In fulfilment of Isaiah's prophecy, God's spirit rests on men, indwelling the work of God's hands, regenerating and renewing man in soul and body.

In Christ, man is able to see God, to contain God, to accustom himself to participate in God while God is accustomed to live in man (3.20.2). The metaphor of light describes this movement. Just as those who see the light are in the light and participate in it, so those who see God are in God and participate in his glory. At the same time, the splendour of God gives life,[28] and those who see God participate in life (4.20.5). The progress from receiving God (*percipere/ accipere*) to containing God (*capere*), to holding on to God (*continere*), is set out (4.38.1, 2). The son of God, despite his perfection, takes the form of a child so that man might be able to contain him (4.38.2). Men are able to carry his glory within them because the perfect bread of the father is given to them in the form of milk. In this gentle way men become accustomed to eat and drink the word of God and to retain in themselves the bread of immortality which is the spirit of the father (4.38.1).

The notion of containing God is linked with that of carrying and retaining God in a life of liberty (4.13.2). God, through his spirit, gives life to the flesh on earth and the flesh, having been accustomed to that gift, can receive life eternal (5.3.3). To participate in God, man must simply turn his face towards God and become accustomed to the life of God within him.

Yet accustoming is intricate.[29] For A to become accustomed to B, there must be difference and reciprocity. A participates in B, is accustomed to and appropriates B; but B transforms A into something like himself by a process of assimilation. A, who accustoms himself, becomes accustomed because the good in which he participates increases his capacity to possess that good;

---

[28] Cf. 'In him was life and the life was the light of men', Jn 1:4.
[29] Evieux, 'L'accoutumance', 38.

reciprocally, the object of the accustoming becomes the subject, because he accustoms himself and models himself on him who apprehends.

Between men and God the process of accustoming moves towards a goal which is never fully achieved in time and space. The end seems unwilling to be possessed. There is also tension when A is participated by B but maintains his transcendence and raises B towards him. All this has to be worked out. Incarnation is a first step in accustoming man to God and God to man.

The concept of accustoming is turned to defend the resurrection of the flesh. God's hands are already accustomed to handle flesh because they formed and shaped Adam (5.5.1). The initiative lies always with God who brings life to our flesh, until in the resurrection we carry God within ourselves. We accustom ourselves little by little to contain and to carry God (5.8.1). The first perfect living man is Jesus Christ (5.1.3) and we shall be like him in the resurrection (5.8.1).

There is a place for accustoming right to the end, says Irenaeus. The just are raised to their place in the kingdom and are accustomed gradually to see God (5.32.1). The righteous will reign on earth and they will accustom themselves to grasp the glory of God (5.35.1). Even the kingdom of Christ is not yet the time nor the place to contain God (*capere Deum*). Rather it is the final preparation for man to receive the gift of incorruption and the vision of God. The entire creation is transformed and man is made one with Christ. Then in the kingdom of the son man will become perfectly like the son and be made incorporate in the son (5.36.3).

Accustoming shows the personal immediacy of the economy of salvation,[30] and the subtlety of Irenaeus' thought.

4.2.2   ECONOMY AS PROGRESSIVE REVELATION

Revelation is always personal. Our knowledge of God progresses as does our knowledge of other persons. 'No one knows the son but the father and no one knows the father but the son and he to

[30] Ibid., 53.

whom the son has willed to reveal him' (Matt. 11:27; Lk. 10:22).
The Gnostics wrongly record the saying as 'no one *knew* the father
but the son' (4.6.1). This would imply that:

> no one knew the true God before the coming of Christ;
> the prophets did not announce the true God;
> Christ only came into existence at his incarnation;
> the father only remembered to care for men in the time of
> Tiberius Caesar;
> the word of God has not always been present to creation;
> therefore a charge of culpable neglect against God should be
> considered.

The Gnostics are wrong, Irenaeus contends, because these propositions destroy faith in God, our maker.[31] Irenaeus adds a remarkable
citation from Justin's lost work against Marcion, to the effect that
he would not have believed the lord himself if he had declared another God beside the creator. However, says Justin, since the only
begotten son came to us from the only God who sums up the work
of his own hands in himself (*suum plasma in semetipsum recapitulans*),
faith and love towards him do not waver (4.6.2).[32]

Irenaeus sets out an extended argument (4.6.3–7) to show that
an unchanging God was revealed in new ways.

Revelation comes from father and son. The knowledge of the
father and son is mutual and only accessible if humans hold father
and son together. Revelation is active and personal. The son per-
forms what the father wills, while the father sends and the son is
sent.

Revelation is through manifestation of the son, who makes all
things manifest. The son is a revealing, enlightening word, not a
secretive, exclusive word. Therefore the son imparts to believers a
knowledge of the father. He does this through his incarnation.

---

[31] *ut et deum quidem mutet et eam quae est erga fabricatorem, qui nos alit per suam conditionem, fidem
nostram evacuet* (4.6.2).

[32] The citation is remarkable because it makes belief in one God the first axiom of the
Christian faith, because it elevates truth above highest tradition (as does Justin in the
Dialogue when he insists, 'I do not care whether Plato or Pythagoras or any other man
held such views, for this is what the truth is' (*dial.* 6)), and because it anticipates Irenaeus'
account of recapitulation. Its authenticity has been discussed. See J. A. Robinson, 'On a
quotation from Justin Martyr in Irenaeus', *JThS*, 31 (1930), 374–8.

Only those taught by God can know God; but God wants to be known. Therefore the manifestation of the father came through the son as a light shining in darkness. The father reveals himself to all, making the word visible to all. By becoming visible, the word declared the father and son to all. Because this revelation is for all, those who have seen but have not believed, will be judged.

Revelation began with creation and continued through law and prophets. In the whole of creation, especially humanity, the word reveals the lord who is maker (*fabricator*) of the world and the artificer (*artifex*) of man. This revelation is addressed to all, as were the law and the prophets, in which the word proclaimed himself and the father.

The final revelation was complex. When the invisible word manifested the father by becoming visible and tangible, 'the invisible reality which was seen in the son was the father, and the visible reality in which the father was seen was the son' (4.6.6).[33] All spoke with Christ and called him God; but not all believed.

The final revelation was accessible to all. A universal revelation was needed, if all were to receive a just judgement at the end. The death of Christ received universal testimony. Everyone declared him to be truly human; testimony that he was truly God came from father, spirit, angels, creation, men, rebel spirits and demons, the devil and finally from death itself.

Revelation is one continuous history. From the eternal universal work of revelation we grasp the continuity of history under the hand of the son, who for the father administers and perfects all things from beginning to end, for without him no one could know God (4.6.7).[34] The revelation of the father by the son is not a future but a past and present event which goes on through all time. The son is present to his creation from the beginning, revealing the father to all whom the father wills, as and how the father wills. Unity and universality mark the godhead and the salvation given to all believers (4.6.7). 'All the history of the world appears in this synthesis, so vast and yet so closely integrated; the

---

[33] *invisibile etenim filii pater, visibile autem patris filius.*

[34] *Omnia autem filius administrans patri perficit ab initio usque ad finem, et sine illo nemo potest cognoscere deum.*

divine plan reveals itself, wonderful in its unity and its progressive development.'[35]

The unity of history derives from the unity of the trinity, which preceded both history and creation. Not merely before Adam, but also before creation, the word and the father gave each other glory (4.14.1; cf. Jn 17:5). Universality of revelation extends to angels, archangels, principality and powers (2.30.9), but it is to man that God looks. The son shows God to men and presents man to God. God's glory is man made alive and man is alive when he sees God (4.20.7).

The spirit plays a continuing role as he reveals the word (*dem.* 5, 7). He inspires the prophets so that they declare God's plans (1.10.1) and make known the economies of father and the son (4.33.7). There is a progression from the spirit-given vision of the prophets to the 'adoptive' vision in the son and to the 'paternal' vision in the coming kingdom (4.20.5).

4.2.3   ECONOMY AS THE ASCENT OF MAN

In Irenaeus, divine plan and human development go together, for humanity never stands still. Every part of the saving plan comes from the one will and purpose of God. The central Gnostic error, Irenaeus points out, is their denial of the providence of this one God. They follow Epicurus in proclaiming a superfluous god *deus otiosus* (3.24.2). Plato's god is active in the world (*Laws* 715e), and his goodness (*Tim.* 29e) is consistent with the sovereign grace which Paul teaches. The economy proceeds from God's perfection (2.28.5), nearness (5.16.1) and love (3 pref.).

Human development moves through history and beyond; humans cannot be imprisoned in permanent categories or classes. Development fits, adjusts, accustoms man to God (3.20.2) to ensure man's progress (*proficere, provehi*), growth (*augere*), maturing (*maturescere*) and fruitfulness (*fructificare*).[36] While Adam is in one sense perfect, the possibility of further perfection is set before him.[37] The lord has ordered everything for the perfection of man

---

35 J. Lebreton, *Histoire du dogme de la Trinité*, vol. II (Paris, 1928), 592.
36 The Gnostics used the notion of fruitfulness differently and frequently.
37 See below, chapter 10, and Koch, 'Zur Lehre vom Urstand', 183–214.

(4.37.7). As the new head of mankind, Christ assumes human nature (4.2.4).

Recapitulation provides points of reference which determine what *fits* into man's development.[38] God's revelation (4.11.1) continues to the point where he offers man the gift of adoption. Man was made to grow and the logos uses every means to entice men to glory.[39]

Divine plan and human development are evident in the four covenants: Adam, Noah, Moses and Christ. Like Paul, Irenaeus recognises Abraham as justified before circumcision and the patriarchs as part of the history of salvation. Yet the old testament is commonly identified with Moses and slavery in contrast to new testament liberty (4.9.1).

Yet another development is the universal expansion of Christ in the church. The four winds point to the four Gospels, which with the lifegiving spirit, produce the church (3.11.8). Christ contains in himself those whom he redeems (3.18.7). They are (3.19.1) commingled with the word of the father.[40] There are some things which, Irenaeus insists, do not develop: the apostolic kerygma was already perfect on the day of Pentecost (3.1.1), so the tradition of the apostles is identical with truth (3.3.1). Nevertheless, Irenaeus did make doctrinal progress in a way he could not theoretically allow. His account of the incarnation and human nature, of church and tradition, of history of salvation and of the forces of renewal illuminates the wonder of human development.[41] His sense of human evolution has made Christianity more credible in a scientific age.

4.2.4   ECONOMY AS POLEMIC: HISTORY AS KNOWLEDGE

The highest human knowledge is found in the economy as accustoming, progressive revelation and human evolution. This claim is

---

[38] 'Angemessenheitsgründe', K. Prümm, 'Göttliche Planung und menschliche Entwicklung nach Irenäus' *Adversus haereses*', *Schol* 13 (1938), 344. Once again, the criterion is aesthetic as well as logical.

[39] 'die Menschen seiner Verherrlichung anzulocken', Prümm, ibid., 347.

[40] *commixti Verbo Dei Patris*.

[41] Prümm, 'Göttliche Planung', 355.

central to Irenaeus' attack on Gnosticism.[42] The coordinates of the economy are vertical (descent and ascent of God's son to redeem the earth) and horizontal (the unbroken line of God's saving activity from the beginning to the end of time). These two coordinates leave no place for any other salvation besides that which is given in the Jesus of history and is marked by the ideas of giving/receiving, development and education.[43]

How is a case made for these unambiguous claims? There are two points where Irenaeus interrupts his polemic to state his method. At 1.10.3 and 2.25–8 he points to the one faith of the church, the incarnation of the word, the adaptation of time and the sovereign providence of God.[44] His aim (1.10.3) is 'to explain God's activity and economy which has been directed to mankind'. Knowledge begins from many questions.[45] Why has one and the same God done temporal and eternal, earthly and heavenly things? Why has the invisible God appeared to prophets in different forms? Why do we find more than one covenant given to mankind? How do these covenants differ? Why did God conclude all in unbelief in order to have mercy on all? Why did the word of God become flesh and suffer? Why did the son of God, the beginning, come at the end, in the last days? What does scripture tell us about the coming end? Why has God brought the heathen into the inheritance of the saints (Eph. 3:6)? How will this mortal corruptible flesh put on immortality and incorruption (1 Cor. 15:54)? How can it be claimed (Rom. 9:25) that those who were not a people have become a people, and that those who were not loved have become beloved?

Knowledge of saving history comes from the answers to these questions. The cross, an event within history is taken as normative for all history and decisive for salvation.[46] The vertical coordinates (God to man, man to God) (5.36.3) and the horizontal coordinates ('in the end . . . united to the ancient formation') (5.1.2) point to 'the economy of the cross' which indicates the height, length, breadth and depth, and the two hands which gather the two

---

[42] Bengsch, *Heilsgeschichte und Heilswissen*, 229 30.
[43] Ibid., 230.   [44] Ibid., 4.
[45] Ibid., 53.   [46] Ibid., 54.

scattered peoples under the one head who is God (5.17.4). The work of Christ is 'always' and 'now'.[47]

Irenaeus often describes the economy with an exchange formula (*Tauschformel*): 'the son of God became son of man, so that through him we may obtain adoption, with man bearing, seizing and embracing the son of God' (3.16.3; cf. Gal. 4:4). The person of Christ is central to his work (5.17.1), and hence the exchange formulae are in no way abstract, for Christ really became what we are (3.18.1). This event is the final revelation to which everything else points. Not only is the whole history of salvation directed to Christ, it is all his work.[48]

The continuity of the saving event lies in the person and work of Christ (3.11.8) through all four testaments (3.11.8) and the fourfold gospel. Everything is made by the logos (3.8.2), from whose image man is made (3.23.1), so that the coming of the logos manifests both the formation and the maker (4.33.4). His work fits together logically and aesthetically; it is appropriate to the time and continuous in faithfulness (4.20–7). He is both subject and object of prophecy (4.26.1; 4.10.1); the words of Moses and the prophets are his words (4.2.3) for the prophets received their charisma from him (4.20.4). Moses and the prophets speak of him (4.10.1; 4.9.3). As a fulfilment, Christ cannot be the end of the law unless he be its beginning too (4.12.4). The law taught in advance how man should follow Christ (4.12.5). He is both subject and object of the preaching of the apostles (3.1.1).

Within the economy there can be discontinuity, because God in his freedom chooses certain moments. All things are new because of the newness of the incarnation, so that man might return to God and learn to worship him in a new way (3.10.2). He has made all things new by the gift of himself (4.34.1). The prophets had told of a new covenant (4.33.14) and we know that newness will renew and vivify humanity (4.34.1). This newness is a fulfilment rather than a break with the past, for Christ reigns in the house of Jacob, forever and without a break (3.10.2). There was newness also in earlier seasons (*kairoi*), for there are many precepts and

---

[47] Ibid., 88 108.
[48] 3.12.3; 3.12.8; 3.16.5; 4.8.2; 4.34.2 and 4.

many steps which lead man to God (4.9.3). The prophets spoke of the one and same God 'under many aspects and many titles' (3.10.6).[49]

Because each season has its own character, no one should try to force the saving pace as Mary did at the marriage feast at Cana (3.16.7). Nor could the Jews, not perceiving the word of liberty, hold back what was happening (4.33.1). All must be done at the right time (3.12.11). God does all things with harmony and proportion (*composita et apta*) (3.11.9) and there is 'nothing unseemly, untimely or incongruent in what the father does' (3.16.7).[50] Newness does not imply discontinuity. Even among men newness and identity are found together (4.5.3).

This move from preparation to fulfilment, from promise to reality, reflects an unlikely parallel between the world of prophecy and the world of Plato's forms.[51] There is gradual progress towards the summit of the dialectic which is the first principle of truth, goodness and being. Until the summit is reached the believer or philosopher lives in a world of shadows. Once the finality of Christ is reached, then the shadows all make sense and one is no longer in the shadow but in the light. The horizontal Platonism of Irenaeus from old to new is the movement of Clement of Alexandria's true dialectic, which by joining and dividing moves towards the ultimate truth in Christ, a truth which is also the source of life and being. It is no accident that one of the two passages which Irenaeus cites with approval from Plato concerns the ancient word, which moves through beginning, middle and end.[52]

4.3   TRINITY AND THE HANDS OF GOD

From the beginning to the end of his writings, Irenaeus declares the faith of the church in one father, one son and holy spirit (1.10.1; 5.20.1). In this name Christians are baptised (*dem.* 3). Both son and father are lord and God (*dem.* 47); they are uniquely God (3.6). The word, who made all things, sits above the cherubim, contains

---

[49] *variis autem significationibus et multis appellationibus.*
[50] *nihil ... incomtum atque intempestivum nec incongruens ... apud Patrem.* Cf. also 3.12.11; 5.6.1; 4.37.7.
[51] See below, 8.1.
[52] The second passage declares the goodness of God (3.25.5).

all things, has appeared to men and has given them the gospel (3.11.8). In one place (*dem.* 10), Irenaeus identifies the son and the spirit, the word and wisdom, with the two supreme powers known as cherubim and seraphim. Here there may be echoes from Philo, who had identified cherubim and seraphim as God and Lord. For Philo, God may be seen either under a threefold or single aspect; beneath God, Philo has many intermediaries, which disappear in Christian revelation.[53]

Wisdom is identified not with the word of God (as in Paul and Hebrews), but with the spirit. The spirit shares the fullness of the Godhead (5.12.2). In the rule of faith the spirit comes in third place. As a distinct person, he speaks by the prophets, teaches the patriarchs and guides the righteous (*dem.* 6); he is the sign or seal of the father and the son, imprinted on the believer (3.17.3) and the unction with which the father anoints the son (3.18.3). The spirit is also called paraclete (3.17.3), gift (3.6.4), living water (5.18.1), dew of God (3.17.3) and pledge of incorruption (5.8.1). The pledge within us makes us already spiritual, so that mortal is swallowed up in immortality.

The sovereign grace of God gives autonomy to the action which made all things 'through himself, that is through his word and wisdom' (2.30.9). The divine self-sufficient spontaneity governs all: 'he himself in himself, according to that which is beyond our speech and thought, predestinated and made all things; by his untiring word he made all things that have been made' (2.2.4).

The divine trinity gives nourishment and growth, so that man may gently rise towards the perfection of the uncreated God (4.38). Within the trinity the Intellect/father is the inseparable source of the word/son (2.28.4–6),[54] for the divine Intellect possesses unbroken unity.[55] Father and son exist, as the Fourth Gospel makes clear, in mutual indwelling which gives each a perfect knowledge of the other (2.17.8). The son measures the vastness of the father and as a measure (*mensura*) comprehends him (4.4.2). What is invisible of the son is the father and what is visible of the father is the son: *invisibile*

---

[53] E. Lanne, 'Cherubim et seraphim', *RSR* 43 (1955), 524 35.

[54] Without the separation by which some apologists had distinguished inner from uttered logos.

[55] As we have seen, chapter 2.

filii pater, visibile autem patris filius (4.6.6). The mutual indwelling of father and spirit who is divine wisdom is eternal (2.25.3; 2.30.9; 3.18.1; 4.13.4; 4.20.13). The eternity of the three divine powers is constantly affirmed (*dem.* 11, 30, 43).

Father, son and spirit are united in creation and salvation (5.18.2), and in the progress of the believer who ascends from spirit to son and from son to father (5.36.8). The move through spirit to son and father is traced in different ways (4.20.5, 6; 5.36.2 and *dem.* 7). There is an ascent from spirit to son to father by whom the gift of incorruption is granted (4.20.5; 5.36.2). We move from spirit through son to father, while the father moves to us through son and spirit (*dem.* 7).

A striking way of expressing the divine unity and its embrace is through the description of word and spirit as the hands of God. More recently, George Herbert wrote:

> Wilt thou meet arms with man, that Thou dost stretch,
> A crumb of dust from heav'n to hell?
> Will great God measure with a wretch?
> Shall he Thy stature spell? . . .
> Whether I fly with angels, fall with dust,
> Thy hands made both, and I am there;
> Thy power and love, my love and trust,
> Make one place ev'rywhere.[56]

Irenaeus uses this vivid metaphor of the hands of God in *Against heresies* 4 and 5, and once in the *Demonstration*, to underline the immediacy and continuity of God's activity. Man's mixture of soul and flesh is achieved by God through his hands, the son and the spirit (4.20.1). Continuity is unbroken. Adam never left the hands of God, who made him and finally perfected him in Christ (5.1.3). There was nothing strange in the assumption of Enoch and Elijah into heaven for, from Adam onwards, the hands of God had grown used to ordering, ruling and supporting what they had formed. As God put man in one place and then removed him, so he placed Enoch and Elijah into a place of waiting (5.5.1). God's hand remained on Elijah and Jonah; the three young men were brought out of the furnace by God's hand as a sign

---

[56] George Herbert, 'The temper'.

of his power. No creature can resist the power and will of God (5.5.2).

The healing hands of the incarnate saviour carry on the first formation of man. The word forms us in the womb (cf. Ps. 139:13–16). When the eyes of the blind man were healed, the manner of human creation was declared; the hand which healed the part was the hand which formed the whole (5.15.3).

The hands of God confirm the activity of the creator who made the world *through himself*, that is, through his word and wisdom (2.30.9).[57] He created, modelled, breathed life into and now nourishes us by his creation (3.25.1). The heavens are measured in the palm of his hand (Isa. 40:12). He who fills the heavens and looks on the abyss is with each one of us. God is near and not far off (Jer. 22:23). 'For his hand encloses us in our hidden and secret ways' (4.19.2).

Surrounded with the light of the father (4.20.2), man embraces the spirit of God and enters the glory of the father (4.20.4) who is present through creation, through theophanies, miracles and prophecies.[58] As in the beginning we were shaped in Adam, so in the end we shall be shaped in the word and spirit of God. Adam will become according to God's image and likeness (5.1.3). This likeness points to a desire for intimacy between the creator and his creatures, for God cannot abide separation from what he has made.[59] His purpose is union and communion with men (5.1.3; 5.2.1).[60]

The hand of God is a symbol of the descending love by which God is known. For we do not merely meet God face to face, but are formed by God's hands in ineffable proximity. God does not merely talk and appear: he touches, grasps, shapes and models.[61] His hand is ultimate: we do not look for another substance nor for another hand of God 'besides that which from the beginning even

---

[57] *ipse fabricator, ipse conditor . . . hic conditor . . . qui fecit ea per semetipsum, hoc est per verbum et per sapientiam.* See J. Mambrino, 'Les deux mains de Dieu chez S. Irénée', *NRTh* 79 (1957), 359.

[58] Ibid., 363.

[59] Ibid., 365.

[60] While the action of each of his hands is distinct, Irenaeus affirms nothing of one person which he does not affirm of another.

[61] Mambrino, 'Les deux mains de Dieu', 369.

to the end forms us and prepares us for life, and is present with his handwork and perfects it after the image and likeness of God' (5.16.1).

God did not need angels to make what he had decided should be made. His own hands, his word and wisdom, son and spirit were always with him and through them he made all things freely and spontaneously (4.20.1). At the resurrection, complete, spiritual man will be made like God's son (5.6.1): 'And therefore, throughout all time, man who was in the beginning moulded by the hands of God (i.e. the son and the spirit) is made in the image and likeness of God.'

Continuity and eternity link trinity with economy. God's goodness pours out on his creatures, who must grow towards him as if to the sun, finally receiving eternal life, which is the perfect being of God. Humanity had to be created, to grow strong and to flourish, to recover from sin, be glorified and see God. The vision of God brings immortality in his presence (4.38.3) (Wisd. 6:19).[62] This evolution of mankind is the core of Irenaeus' trinitarian history. It points to the arrangements, harmonies and sequences which make up the divine economy. These form the plan of a loving God who is father, son and spirit.[63]

4.4   RIVER AND MOVEMENT

The economy of the divine architect is packed with artistic detail. It gives order, rationality and sensitivity to the story of God's dealing with mankind, without losing continuity in time or universality in space. The originality of Irenaeus is at once striking and complex. The four themes of accustoming, progressive revelation, human

---

[62] ἔδει δὲ τὸν ἄνθρωπον πρῶτον γενέσθαι, καὶ γενόμενον αὐξῆσαι, καὶ αὐξήσαντα ἀνδρωθῆναι, καὶ ἀνδρωθέντα πληθυνθῆναι, καὶ πληθυνθέντα ἐνισχῦσαι, ἐνισχύσαντα δὲ δοξασθῆναι, καὶ δοξασθέντα ἰδεῖν τὸν ἑαυτοῦ Δεσπότην. Θεὸς γὰρ ὁ μέλλων ὁρᾶσθαι, ὅρασις δὲ θεοῦ περιποιητικὴ ἀφθαρσίας, ἀφθαρσία δὲ ἐγγὺς εἶναι ποιεῖ θεοῦ.

[63] For further discussion of Irenaeus' theory of history, see the following: R. A. Markus, 'Pleroma and fulfilment. The significance of history in St Irenaeus' opposition to Gnosticism', *VigChr* 8 (1954); Marrou, 'La théologie', in *Le origini dello gnosticismo*, ed. Bianchi; J. Daniélou, 'Philosophie ou théologie de l'histoire?', *DViv* 19 (1951); W. Hunger, 'Weltplaneinheit und Adameinheit in der Theologie des heiligen Irenäus', *Schol* 17,2 (1942); J. Daniélou, 'Saint Irénée et les origines de la théologie de l'histoire', *RSR* 34 (1947), 227–31.

development, and history as knowledge are united by the many-coloured disposing and arranging of father, son and spirit. The four elements of God's design are of universal proportion, yet never abstract. They all have a human orientation and the complexity overwhelms.

How did Irenaeus hold these ideas together? He had a sense of movement and a sense of drama. Accustoming pointed to personal action over time. Revelation showed how the great God had, through time, come nearer. Just as individuals grow, so mankind had found spectacular development. Time and change were not to be filtered from the process of knowledge (as Plato wished) for it was within their economies that the mind of God could be learnt. All this was like Heraclitus, one of Justin's 'Christians before Christ', for whom the flux of things was integral to their meaning. In the inexhaustible complexity of the divine economy, there was movement. This sense of movement was linked, I have boldly suggested,[64] with the landscape of Lyons, where two great rivers flowed together. Yet the divine economy went beyond the relentless flow of a great river. Accustoming of man to God his opposite, progressive revelation of divine reality, human evolution towards God, human knowledge of the mind of God – all these were dramatic. They were bound up in human interaction with one God who was father, son and spirit. They were tied to memorable events. God was not found in the vacant spaces but in a powerful, mysterious drama of change. Negation of negation was the impulse of the divine nature. Progress to God was the law of human life.

We began with hopes for a clear plan of history drawn by the divine architect. We end overwhelmed by intricacy and grandeur, with a sense that Irenaeus has told us more than we can receive. That may be so. Only as the accustoming, revelation, development and knowledge reach their goal in Christ will the plan make sense. As surely as the two great rivers – Rhône and Saône – come together, so the divine economy is joined in Christ and nowhere else.

[64] In my *The beginning of Christian philosophy* (Cambridge, 1981), 168: 'How far theologians, like poets, may be affected by their landscape, is a matter of precarious probability; but he would be a dull reader who found nothing of Africa in Tertullian and nothing of Egypt in Clement.' See Gilbert Highet, *Poets in landscape* (Pelican Books, 1959), for the relation between Roman writers and their landscape.

PART III

Recapitulation

Christ is the last syllable which, 'being part of the whole metrical fabric, perfects the form and metrical beauty of the whole'.

Augustine, *On true religion*, 22,42

> And all shall be well and
> All manner of thing shall be well
> When the tongues of flame are infolded
> Into the crowned knot of fire
> And the fire and the rose are one.   T. S. Eliot, *Little Gidding*

> We think that Paradise and Calvarie,
> Christs Crosse, and Adams tree, stood in one place;
> Looke Lord and finde both Adams met in me;
> As the first Adams sweat surrounds my face,
> May the last Adams blood my soule embrace.
>
> John Donne, 'Hymn to God my God, in my Sicknesse'

But indeed our lord is the one true master. He, the son of God is truly good; he, the word of God became son of man, and endured suffering for us. For he has fought and conquered: on one hand, as man he fought for the fathers and redeemed their disobedience by his obedience, on the other hand, he has bound the strong man, set free the weak and poured out salvation on the work of his hands, destroying sin. For the lord is patient and merciful and loves the human race.   (3.18.6)

CHAPTER 5

Recapitulation: correction and perfection

Recapitulation, summing up, does four things. It corrects and perfects mankind; it inaugurates and consummates a new humanity. This chapter looks at correction and perfection as the work of Christ and at the consequence for the person of Christ. The work of Christ corrects and perfects being, truth and goodness. The person of Christ as corrector and perfecter is described as new Adam, divine word, only mediator, son of the father and bearer of the name above all other names.

5.1 RECAPITULATION, A COMPLEX CONCEPT

The idea of recapitulation dominates the theology of the second century. Adumbrated by Justin, it is expounded endlessly by Irenaeus[1] and given decisive place in Tertullian. Clement of Alexandria later takes the important step of uniting it to the Platonic Intellect so that Christian theology becomes biblical and Platonic without a break (*str.* 4.25.156–7): a move which begins from the cosmic theology of Irenaeus in Book 2 of *Adversus haereses* is modified by recapitulation so that the son is divine Intellect and the father is the ineffable One.

The complexity of the concept is formidable. At least eleven ideas – unification, repetition, redemption, perfection, inauguration and consummation, totality, the triumph of Christus

---

[1] The works of C. Hackenschmidt, *S. Irenai de opere et beneficiis domini nostri Jesu Christi sententia* (Strasbourg, 1869) and G. Molwitz, *De ΑΝΑΚΕΦΑΛΑΙΩΣΕΩΣ in Irenaei theologia potestate* (Dresden, 1874), are excellent expositions. Recapitulation is defined as 'iteratio Adami (per idem ac contrarium) a Christo eo consilio perfecta, ut omnia sibi subiceret', Molwitz, 11.

Victor,[2] ontology, epistemology and ethics (or being, truth and goodness) – are combined in different permutations.[3] Are all these ideas necessary to the concept? Even together they are an understatement, because everything that God does is part of his economy and every part of his economy is defined in relation to its recapitulation. So Irenaeus speaks of plurality: 'And the other *economies of his recapitulation*, some they saw through visions, others they announced by word, while others they indicated typically by action' (4.20.8). Redemption (or correction), perfection and inauguration are inseparable from being (or life), truth and goodness. We may distinguish redemption and perfection and see Irenaeus as trying to bridge two different concepts; but it is certain that Irenaeus does not keep them apart.[4] Consummation is tied to inauguration.

The other two ideas are of different orders: 'totality' is applicable to the other variables because God contains all things and is not himself contained. The last idea, 'Christus Victor', is a persistent image which is used to tie the logic of recapitulation together;[5] it continues to dominate the Christian imagination. To find the sense of recapitulation we need all the eleven variables and their relationships. We must elucidate the connection of the parts of recapitulation, tracing the idea to scripture, especially to Paul (Rom. 5

---

[2] W. P. Loewe, 'Irenaeus' soteriology: Christus Victor revisited', *AThR* 17,1 (1985), 14, points out 'Christus Victor remains but a single theme among others, and it draws its meaning from the larger context of that pattern.' Aulen's insight and achievement remain.

[3] My earlier accounts may be found in *The beginning of Christian philosophy* (Cambridge, 1981), 163–205; 'The logic of recapitulation', in *Pléroma*, FS for Antonio Orbe, ed. E. Romero-Pose (Santiago de Compostela, 1990), 321–35; and in *The emergence of Christian theology* (Cambridge, 1993), 142–72. Each time I tackled the problem, it seemed necessary to add another variable. Recently, the primary notion of unification has been brought to my attention by J. Fantino. He rightly makes this idea explicit. See J. Fantino, *La théologie*, 240–58, especially 240 (condenser, parfaire, restaurer).

[4] At some points he does not even differentiate between redemption and perfection or fulfilment; for example, see N. Brox, *Offenbarung, Gnosis und gnostischer Mythos bei Irenäus von Lyon* (Salzburg and Munich, 1966), 186–9. If we separate the different elements of the complex and retain the idea of recapitulation for one of them, the complexity remains under different names.

[5] Another image is the tree, of paradise and of the cross. These images are used, like Plato's myths, to tie the argument together.

and 1 Cor. 15) and John (12 and 17), and through the apostles to Christ, the first and the last, the living one.[6]

Christ came so that fallen man might be corrected to his first integrity and so that imperfect man might be brought to perfection.[7] The saviour includes all men in himself compendiously (*summatim*) and repeats the life of the first man, correcting that life at each point.[8] Christ is in every event of the salvation which is fulfilled in him (3.16.6). He is the treasure hidden in the field (4.26.1). As creator, he comes to his own (5.18.2) and recapitulates his own creation in himself (4.6.2); while true man and true God, he is the end rather than the beginning (4.6.7; 1.10.3). Man who has grown old through sin is made new in the image of God (5.12.4). Recapitulation makes Christ 'head' so that men of all time are brought together under him (3.16.6). Only the incarnate word of God can do this, through his divine and human being (3.18.1; 4.33.4) and through his act of redemption which is obedience to death on the cross (5.16.3).

Christ, the new Adam, unites all by his death on the cross (3.16.9 *et passim*). This union is both physical and moral. The 'physical redemption' doctrine lived on in Athanasius and Gregory of Nyssa, while others followed the moral content of his argument. The moral elements in the recapitulation of Christ were his love, magnanimity or long suffering (3.20.1), his reason (5.18.3; 4.4.3), and his justice, which was indefectible, as he gave his life for our life and his flesh for our flesh.[9]

Recapitulation extends to all human bodies in the world and the resurrection of their flesh follows the flesh of Christ. Flesh is united under Christ as head and finds incorruptibility in Christ (3.18.7). Christ is himself the resurrection (4.5.2). He renews and perfects the world (5.32.1) whose final perfection will come when he returns to reclaim the earth (5.35.2). Millenarianism is for many a foreign body in the thought of Irenaeus,[10] and only at the end of the fifth

---

[6] E. Scharl, *Recapitulatio mundi. Der Rekapitulationsbegriff des heiligen Irenäus und seine Anwendung auf die Körperwelt* (Freiburg, 1941).

[7] Hackenschmidt, *S. Irenaei*, 14.

[8] Ibid., 17.

[9] See A. D'Alès, 'La doctrine de la récapitulation en S. Irénée', *RSR* 60 (1916),185–211.

[10] According to Scharl, *Recapitulatio mundi*, 93.

book does this teaching emerge; but it is needed to fulfil the hope which springs from the recapitulation of all things.

5.2 CORRECTION

The first meaning which Irenaeus links with the concept of recapitulation is that of correction, or rectification of what has gone wrong from the beginning of human history. It is a common theme of tragedy that a decline in human life or fortune begins at a certain point ('where did it begin to go wrong?'); to this may be joined the hope that if the first error could be corrected, subsequent disaster could be averted. With this concept of correction are linked the ideas of the redemption of captive sinners, the justification of the ungodly, repetition, restoration and reconciliation.

Disobedience, slavery, corruption and alienation are corrected by obedience, liberation, incorruption and reconciliation. The change is reflexive, inclusive and repetitive, for God himself corrects, redeems, justifies and rectifies by including the human objects of his action within himself and performing the essential action of correction himself. God is in Christ reconciling the world to himself and the world (sinful humanity) is summed up, united, and included in Christ just as it had been included in Adam. His action is repetitive in that it returns to the point of error and replaces the wrong deed with the right deed, thereby rectifying the ancient fault. Later piety will depict both Christ and Mary in the Garden of Eden.

Obedience

All are sons of God by nature and creation but not all are God's sons by obedience and doctrine (4.41.2). This Johannine theme echoes the dominant Pauline claim that Jesus' obedience to death rectified the disobedience of Adam; one tree was set right on another tree, the cross. This only worked because the obedience of Jesus was directed to the same father as was the disobedience of Adam. In the second Adam we are reconciled to God because *in him* we are made obedient to death (5.16.3).

The disobedience of Adam and Eve was corrected by the obedience of Jesus and Mary. The obedience and faith of Mary are contrasted with the disobedience of Eve (3.22.4). The disobedience of Adam and Eve was 'amended by correction' in Christ (5.19.1).

Liberation from slavery

God offered his own son for our redemption, as Abraham had once offered his son in sacrifice (4.5.4). Man is redeemable because he is free (4.37.1). Freedom and faith are necessary to each other (4.37.5).

Christus Victor[11] included us in his victory and crushed the enemy who had led us captive in Adam (5.21.1). Was there really a contest for the second Adam? Did he not have a certainty of victory? To make a valid contest, he fasted forty days; this gave the enemy a chance and made the recapitulation real (5.21.2). So he overthrew man's enemy, the devil, putting him under the power of man (5.24.4). The victory is perpetuated when we refuse to bend the knee on Sunday and stand upright because it is the day of our liberation from sin and death (frag. 7, Harvey). The enemy who unjustly led man into slavery is himself justly led as a captive and thereby the balance of justice is rectified (5.21.3). Liberation comes through Mary to replace the bondage brought by Eve (3.22.4).

Salvation from corruption

For Irenaeus the incarnation was physically necessary to save humanity from death and corruption. Sin had to be killed, death had to be deprived of power and replaced by life. The corruptible had to be united to the incorruptible so that mortality might be swallowed up in immortality (3.19.1). Man was not by nature incorrupt and needed to be joined to the incorruptible God (3.19.1). God makes himself flesh and blood so that, at the end, he saves in his own person that which at the beginning had perished in Adam (5.14.1). When the creator finds his handwork impaired by wickedness, he heals and restores it until it is sound and whole. When flesh is healed

[11] This image is especially appropriate to themes of correction and liberation.

by God, it can receive life and incorruption (5.12.6). Death, as Paul
had said, is swallowed up in victory (3.23.7), proving the power of
him who raises the flesh from the dead (5.3.2). When the whole
human race is recapitulated, united in Christ, human mortality is
included. Jesus dies on the same sixth day as Adam died through
disobedience, and the second creation begins on the same day as
Adam was created (5.23.2).

Salvation and incorruptibility are free gifts from God (5.21.3). In
the constant interplay of opposites, the fasting of Jesus does away
with the surfeit of Adam (5.21.2). God is the doctor who is proved
by his patients (3.20.2). His healing work does not reject the flesh
because of its condemnation but enables its gradual assimilation to
his own likeness (3.20.2).

Reconciliation through the cross

The new covenant is a law of liberty and peace where plough and
pruning hook replace weapons of war. Both join iron to wood as did
Elisha, in anticipation of the cross which reclaims the savage earth
and gathers with its hook the righteous race of men (4.34.4). Just
as Elisha recovered the lost iron of his axe by throwing the wood
into the river so we who have lost the sure word of God recover
and receive it afresh by the tree of the cross. The height, length
and breadth of that tree reach out to all. Its hands extend from the
one head who is in the middle to join his body into one (5.17.4).
Proliferating metaphors like these mark the poetic achievement of
Irenaeus, the *doctor constructivus* who piles image on image.

While the tree of the cross amends the disobedience of the tree
of paradise (5.19.1), and cancels the written record of our debt,
fastening it to a tree (5.17.3), there is more than a balancing of the
scales of justice or the cancellation of a debt. In a wonderful new
beginning, man who has gone away from God is won back to him;
everything is new because God has come in a new way and should
be worshipped in a new way. This is proclaimed in the blessing of
Zacharias who, filled with a new spirit, announced all these new
good things (3.10.2).

Man had been at odds with his own rationality and at odds with
the righteousness of God. The word who first made man, overcame

that alienation by reforming the human race and destroying its enemy, giving victory to the work of his hands (4.24.1). What happened to man's hostile disobedience to God? It was turned against the serpent who was enemy of God and of man, so that the lord as man should tread on the serpent's head. (4.40.3).

Reconciliation is inclusive and reciprocal. God became what we are so that we might be what he is. He redeemed by his own blood those who were alienated not by nature but by their own apostasy. Giving his soul for our souls, his flesh for our flesh, God joined man to himself by his incarnation (5.1.1). He is our redeemer who with true flesh and blood summed up in himself the ancient formation of Adam (5.1.2). From his perfect work (as in John 17) comes our redemption; even Paul, for whom redemption comes first, also puts it this way. God's strength is made perfect in our weakness (5.3.1).

In recapitulating the original work of the father he reconciles the flesh which had been alienated from God. As Paul shows (Col. 1:22), righteous flesh has reconciled the flesh that was being kept under bondage to sin (5.14.2). The blind man is healed by the hand which created him. That hand of God which formed us in the beginning, which formed us in the womb, has in the last times sought us out in our lost condition. God wins back his own, takes the lost sheep on his shoulders and restores it with joy to the fold of life (5.15.2). In and after Adam, man has fallen into transgression and needs to be washed by baptism, just as the blind man was sent to the pool of Siloam to wash (5.15.3).

Recapitulation means 'to bring together again, to join again into a whole, to bring into unity, to gather up'.[12] The notion of repetition is expressed by the verbs 'reiterate, repeat, renew' (*iterare, repetere, renovare*). The divine initiative which searched for Adam (Adam, where art thou?) is repeated in the same word of God who in the evening of our history comes to call man, reminding him of what he had done in a life hidden from the lord (5.15.4). The word in the garden, the voice of the Lord God, is the same word which remits our sins: 'thy sins be forgiven thee'. Only he against whom

---

[12] 'iterum colligere, iterum comprehendere in summam, in unitatem redigere, recolligere', Molwitz, *De ΑΝΑΚΕΦΑΛΑΙΩΣΕΩΣ*, 3.

a sin has been committed can remit that sin (5.17.1). The one God justifies by faith the circumcised and the uncircumcised alike (5.22.1).

Totality is stressed in a refutation of Tatian (3.23.8), who denied the salvation of lost Adam whom Christ had replaced. Adam, insists Irenaeus, was not abandoned. Alienation was totally overcome. The lost sheep was saved. God needed to save all humankind for his own sake; had man not been saved God would have been defeated. Man must be freed from death and condemnation. God's victory must be entire. The enemy who had captured man was justly captured in his turn by God (3.23.1). It was fitting that the original man be saved because the enemy should not retain any spoils of earlier battles and the fathers should be liberated along with the children (3.23.2).

Totality does not deny opposites and alienation. God indeed subjected the just Abel to the unjust Cain so that the just might be proved by what he suffered and the unjust by the wrong he perpetrated (3.23.4). Adam was smitten with guilt and terror; in his sudden loss of childhood innocence he was contrite and wrapped his loins in rough fig-leaves. These were replaced by a loving God with the softness of animal skins. While God curses the serpent, he leads man on gradually to better things (3.23.5).

5.3.1 PERFECTION OF BEING

Perfection is the second meaning of recapitulation; it derives from John and the Synoptics rather than from Paul, who develops the theme of correction or redemption. The perfection which is described is *both* exclusive, in that it is God's unsurpassable perfection or the word's unsurpassable priority, *and* inclusive, in that it brings together all things within the word of God, requiring the believer to put on the perfection of the head which is Christ. As the transcendent divine Intellect contains all things, as infinite love does not remove itself but encloses mankind in immediacy, so the exclusive perfection of Christ includes all in its unity. This is the answer to the Gnostic separated God: divine perfection is both exclusive and inclusive.

The perfect being of Christ is exclusive

There is one lord, one God (3.6.2), who is in need of nothing (4.17.1 and 5). He is ruler over all his creation (3.6.1). Gnostics try to direct their fantasies above this God (4.19.1); but this is impossible, for God is above principalities, powers and every name (4.19.2). They look for types of types and go on and on in infinite regress (4.19.1, 2).

God's perfection overflows in goodness to what he has made. God does not merely correct what goes wrong. His perfection removes all limits on his being and on his grace which he shows in salvation. Because he is creator he must achieve the goal of his creative work and make perfect what he has begun through his word who is author and finisher. His rich and ungrudging love confers more than man can ask (3 pref.).

This divine perfection belongs to the son as to the father. The purpose of God is declared in the prologue to the Fourth Gospel and is the work of the divine word who begins and finishes the divine plan. Priority and universality are his unique distinctions. His priority is exclusive and his universality is inclusive. His perfection is prior to all things, beyond all men, for he is God, lord, king eternal, incarnate word (3.19.2). Perfect from the beginning (4.13.4), the word of God is beyond comparison (3.8.2). The word/son was with the father before creation (4.20.1-4). The Johannine prologue tells of his originality and his glorious generation. In the beginning was the word. 'For this reason too is that Gospel full of confidence for such is his person' (3.11.8).

The perfect being of Christ is inclusive

From his exclusive priority springs his universal inclusiveness and his work of completion or fulfilment. Because he is first he can perfect all things. He would be powerless over anything prior to and uncaused by himself. The one Christ Jesus sums up and gathers *all things in himself*. With him there is nothing incomplete or out of due season (3.16.7). He is Plato's ancient word which runs from beginning to end and through the middle of things (3.25.5). His universal fourfold gospel points to the four winds (3.11.8).

He is joined to the father as the universal Intellect who sees and thinks all things. Our universal lord accomplished all things in their order and season, at the hour which was foreknown and fitting. He was one and the same, rich and great, not to be divided up as the heretics vainly do. Their fantasy destroys rather than enlarges the wonder of the divine (3.16.7, 8).

He imparts perfection by joining the end to the beginning, linking man to God (4.20.4). All is known to him, for knowledge of salvation did not come from another God but from the son of the one God (3.10.3). At the same time, he was man that he might be tempted, and word that he might be glorified (3.19.3). He was the one man whose obedience, righteousness and life bear fruit in those who were dead from the disobedience of that other one man, Adam, who brought sin and death. Like Adam he was made man by God, so as to be analogous to Adam in respect to origin. Why then was he not made of dust? Because he had to be continuous with Adam, and not of a different race; born of Mary, he was able to sum up man's first formation (3.21.10). He went back seventy-two generations to Adam (3.22.3). This inclusive return to the beginning embraced the fulfilment of all prophecies, no matter when they had been made.

As king and God, the infant Christ received myrrh because of his coming death. The star of Jacob shone upon him (3.9.2). He did not annul but fulfilled the law, as high priest 'propitiating God for men, cleansing lepers, healing the sick, and himself suffering death, that exiled man might go forth from condemnation and might return without fear to his own inheritance' (4.8.2). His passion fulfils the mystery of the Passover in each detail of day, place and hour (Deut. 16:5–6) and the curious inquirer will find every element of the rich imagery of the blessing of Jacob (Gen. 49:10–12) (4.10.2).

At the same time he makes a new beginning, for the last of the four covenants is a covenant of renewal. In himself he sums up all things by means of the gospel which raises man on its wings to the heavenly kingdom (3.11.8). This means that his treasure is new and old, for in his new song and new covenant, he surpasses Solomon, Jonah and the temple (4.9.2). New and old are joined together for he brought all novelty by bringing himself who had been announced (4.34.1).

How does perfect being achieve mankind's salvation?

There are four ways in which Christ's perfection achieves man's salvation.[13]

(i) *Union of God and man, of creator with creature.* Recapitulation means incarnation, where the word, who was in the beginning and always present with mankind has, in the last days and at the appointed time, united himself to his workmanship, that is, to passible man. He recapitulated in himself the long line of human beings (i.e. he united them in himself as head), so that in himself what was lost in Adam might be recovered (3.18.1). When the word/spirit united with the ancient substance of Adam's formation, man was made living and perfect and able to receive the perfection of the father (5.1.3).

For all the magnificent condescension of the incarnation, the creator word of God did not venture into foreign territory, but came to his own, to the world which he governs, and in his flesh hung on the tree to recapitulate all things (5.2.1; 5.18.3). The blood and water which flowed from the crucified proves that he is flesh, which in turn proves the salvation of his own handwork (3.22.2). Indeed the whole dispensation is directed to the salvation of God's work, i.e. flesh (4. pref. 4). Thus he has fulfilled what the creator foretold, alike through all the prophets, and in the service of his father's will brought to completion his own dispensations for the human race (5.26.2).

(ii) *Union of mortal and immortal.* The only way to mankind's incorruption was through union with the incorruption of the word of God (3.19.1). The strangeness of this union was overcome by the word of God who dwelt in man, and became son of man, so that he might accustom man to receive God and that he might accustom God to receive man, all to the good pleasure of the father (3.20.2). Proof that flesh can receive God's gift of life eternal is confirmed by the eucharist, where we are nourished by body and blood of the incarnate lord (5.2.3), and by the way in which God's strength is made perfect in our weakness, as our flesh participates in his wisdom and power (5.3.3).

(iii) *God's own work and presence; soteriology as the exchange of opposites.* The word of God became what we are that he might bring us to be

[13] The term 'physical redemption' does not cover the whole intricacy of Irenaeus' thought.

what he is. Against Ebionites, who deny the divinity of the incarnate lord, Irenaeus argues for the reciprocity of salvation. How can man pass into God unless God has first passed into man (4.33.4)? Time and again we are told that only God himself can save: the lord himself will save them, he will set them free (3.20.4). The sign of the virgin showed that the lord himself saved us (Isa. 63:9) (3.21.1) and the sign of Emmanuel, God with us, declares the same truth of one who, before he knows or chooses evil, will exchange it for what is good (Isa. 7:10–16) (3.21.4).

The unity and universality of salvation derive from the unity of one God, one word, one son and one spirit (4.6.7) who joins himself to humanity.

(iv) *Process to perfection.* Salvation is a process to perfection as the son of God, according to David, perfects praise from babes (4.11.3). Man could not be made perfect from the beginning because what is created must be inferior to and later than the creator (4.38.1). Because of human immaturity, the perfect son of God passed through infancy in order that man might be able to receive him. As a recent creature man could not have received perfection at the beginning (4.38.2), yet he grows to perfection in an ordered universe (4.38.3). He is destined to partake of the glory of God (4.39.2) and to become the perfect work of God (4.39.2).

5.3.2   JOY IN TRUTH; PERFECTION OF TRUTH

The truth of the gospel is always a cause for joy. Abraham knew the father through the word and confessed him to be God. When he learnt of the incarnation, he rejoiced. Simeon perfected the rejoicing of the patriarch and the angels brought tidings of great joy. Mary rejoiced reciprocally in God. So Abraham's joy descended to his children who believed and the childrens' joy rebounded to Abraham (4.7.1).[14]

Jesus points out that all knowledge of God from the beginning has been by revelation of the son himself; he is able to raise children from stones. He gives the faith of Abraham, drawing us away from the religion of stones and hard and fruitless cogitations (4.7.2). He

---

[14] *reciproca autem rursus et regrediente exsultatione a filiis in Abraham.*

reveals the father as word, truth and life: no man comes to the father but by him, and he who has known him will know the father (4.7.3).

Truth is exclusive

Against heretics, who falsely claim pure truth, Irenaeus affirms that the apostles had perfect knowledge (3.1.1). This saving truth is now written on the hearts of the faithful (3.4.2). They know, through love, the God whose greatness would make him unknowable. Only the lamb can open the book and his resplendent flesh displays the immortality of paternal light, for the word was with the father before creation (4.20.1–3). To look on the face of God once brought certain death but in the last days man shall see God (4.20.9–11).

Truth is inclusive

Christ spoke his own truth and showed no respect of persons (3.5.2, 3). Truth springs from the earth in the risen Christ (3.5.1). In him the disciples had seen the father and the father is truth (3.13.2). While the heretics have three Christs, John knew one only (3.16.1, 2), and Paul (3.16.3) and Simeon (3.16.4) affirmed the single identity of the divine word.

Yet the one word is rich in treasure which is new and old, and the new song and new covenant prove him greater than Solomon, or Jonah or the temple (4.9.1, 2). For the love command renews rather than supplants the law; it enlarges and fulfils the law bringing perfection to men (4.12.2). When Jesus read Isaiah in the synagogue he could say 'This day is this scripture fulfilled in your ears' (4.23.1). Scripture is full of proofs of his wonders for the word shows the splendour of the father (4.20.11).

5.3.3 PERFECTION OF GOODNESS

Goodness is central, for as the disobedience of one man Adam brought sin and death, so the obedience and righteousness of the man Jesus Christ brought life in those who were formerly dead (3.21.10). Two features stand out.

(i) *The perfect goodness of Jesus is exclusive.* Free from all ambiguity, Jesus Christ presents an ethical archetype of perfect love. When he had suffered to reconcile sinners, he rose to sit at the right hand of God, perfect in all things. He did not strike back at those who struck him, he prayed for the forgiveness of those who crucified him and, as word of God, only begotten of the father, Jesus Christ our lord, truly brought our salvation (3.16.9).

If the heretics were right in claiming the existence of two Christs, then the one who suffered and prayed 'Father forgive them' was better than the one who flew away (3.18.5). As Emmanuel he exchanges evil for good without reflection or conscious choice (3.21.4).

(ii) *The perfect goodness of Jesus is inclusive.* The Sermon on the Mount extends and fulfils the law; Jesus taught the rich young ruler to keep the commands and then to follow him towards perfection. He included the law because he did not announce another father, son, mother or pleroma (4.12.5). As the end (*finis*) of the law Christ is also the beginning (*initium*) of it. For he who has brought in (*intulit*) the end has himself also wrought (*operatus est*) the beginning (4.12.4).

In completing the law he brings more grace, more love, more glory to the friends of God (4.13.1–3). Under the new covenant of liberty the limits of natural law are widened so that it was given to all men to become sons rather than slaves of God and to know and love the father (4.16.5).

5.4.1 CHRISTOLOGY: TWO ADAMS[15]

Irenaeus has described the work of Christ with unrivalled intricacy.[15] What does this mean for the person of Christ? The christology of Irenaeus is marked by a twofold reference, pointing back to the sin of Adam, which must be reversed, and forward to the perfection which Christ will bring.[16] He begins from the two Adams as expounded by Paul, one whose fall destroys and one whose justice restores all mankind. Recapitulation brings together these two elements under one head (3.16.6).[17] *God and man are united in Christ where the sin of Adam is reversed and the perfection of*

---

[15] L. Duncker, *Des heiligen Irenäus Christologie im Zusammenhange mit dessen theologischer und anthropologischer Grundlehre* (Göttingen, 1843).

[16] Ibid., 158.

[17] Ibid., 162–6.

Christ is fulfilled. As one who perfects the human race, Christ must be a member of that race, and as first of all creatures and first-born from the dead he can bring humanity to perfection (5.1.3; 3.18.7). On the other hand, only God can redeem the human race, for the redeemer must surpass the human being which fell. The joining of God and man comes from God's side, springs from his love and takes place in his birth as a human being, for the humanity of Christ is entire in body, soul and spirit.[18] The notion of exchange – that Christ should become what we are in order that we might become what he is – further ensures his full humanity and the perfection of mankind.[19] Indeed Christ comes to reveal the fullness of humanity and to teach the truth. Yet one cannot learn about God without God; therefore his word is necessary to teach us.[20]

5.4.2 WORD OF GOD

Irenaeus, we have seen,[21] does not divide the thought of the word within the intellect of God from the thought that thinks in God or from God as a thinking being or from the reason of God. Irenaeus moves from the vagueness of the apologists towards a clearer account and makes the person of Christ, the divine word, the centre of his cosmology. Creation and redemption show the word of God to be God. He is 'the visible of the invisible father' (4.6.6).[22] The son of God has been made a son of man (3.19.1) and father, spirit, creation, man, the apostate spirits, demons, the devil and death itself all bear witness to his true divinity and true humanity (4.6.7). Only by a divine incarnation could incorruption and immortality come to men; the corruptible had to be absorbed by incorruption and the mortal by immortality (3.19.1). The word of God is the creator who exists at all times in the world, contains all things that have been made, and hung from a tree in his own creation (5.18.1; 3.18.1). He was a man in order that he might face temptation

---

[18] In spite of his opposition to Docetism, Irenaeus comes close to such a position when he sees the divine logos taking the place of the rational soul in the person of the incarnate Christ; Duncker, ibid., 206.

[19] Ibid., 225.

[20] Ibid., 256.

[21] See above, 2.3.

[22] F. R. M. Hitchcock, *Irenaeus of Lugdunum. A study of his teaching* (Cambridge, 1914), 129.

and he was word of God so that he might be glorified. The word remains quiescent in his trial, humiliation and death, but is evident in his conquest, endurance, beneficence, resurrection and assumption into heaven (3.19.3).

The incarnate word took his flesh, indeed his humanity, from the virgin Mary, for if he did not take the substance of flesh from a human being then neither did he become man, nor the son of man (3.22.1). The virgin birth serves as a sign of our salvation and regeneration by faith (3.16.2; 3.21.5).

5.4.3   ONE MEDIATOR

Against Gnostic and Marcionite claims that Jesus brought a message from a strange unknown God, Irenaeus insists that the son makes the father visible. In Jesus Christ there is no new God but a new manifestation of the only God.[23] In contrast to Justin, for whom it was important to show that there was plurality in God before the coming of Jesus, Irenaeus treats the theophanies of the bible as symbolic representations of a future reality. The world of types points to a word who is as yet invisible and whose manifestation only takes place in the new testament. The life of Christ is indeed a *parousia*, nothing less than an immediate manifestation of God.[24]

The Valentinians divide the son of God, separating Christ from Jesus, the saviour from the word, and the word from the only-begotten. Against such division Irenaeus sets the confession of 'one Christ only, Jesus the son of God incarnate for our salvation' (1.10.1). Because he is only-begotten (*monogenes*) there can be no separation between the only-begotten mind and the word, and because he is anointed Christ by the spirit, there can be no division between the spirit and Christ (*dem.* 53). Nor can there be a separation between the Christ and the man who suffers on the cross, for he reveals the long suffering, mercy and goodness of God (3.18.5). The beauty and strength of the one who dies on the cross breaks down any incompatibility between humiliation and glory (3.19.2). Those

---

[23] Houssiau, *La christologie de saint Irénée*, 127.
[24] Irenaeus does not draw on Greek ideas of a kingly visit but on the new testament to point to the physical nature of the coming of Christ. Similarly, the future coming of Christ is not in antithesis to the human existence of the word in the church but points to the same presence of the word.

who separate the Christ who suffered from an impassible Christ fail to realize the unity of substance in him who was first-born from the dead (4.2.4).

Through his incarnation the mediator, who has primacy over things invisible, extends his primacy over all things visible. How are we to receive, to grasp or to contain this mediator? It is impossible to lay hold of God, yet possible to lay hold of his incarnate word. He who is beyond our grasp, incomprehensible and invisible gives himself to be seen, comprehended and grasped by men (4.20.5). The son of God becomes son of man so that we might receive adoption as his sons; man will carry and receive and embrace the son of God (3.16.3). The son of God, the first-born word descends on the creature, that is, on the work that he himself has fashioned, and is grasped by the creature (5.36.3).

Christ mediates to enable man to participate in God. This unity is described by such words as 'unite, unite together, fuse, union' (ἐνοῦν, συνενοῦν, κολλᾶν, ἕνωσις). Man is joined to God as to another person, and faith is the way to participation (κοινωνία) (4.13.1). The word and spirit are joined to the ancient substance of Adam, to the humanity of Christ and the humanity of all Christians (5.1.3). The son is again joined to his bride, the church, just as the prophet Hosea was rejoined to his wife (4.20.12).

Christ Jesus was born of the virgin in order to unite through himself man and God (3.4.2).[25] Our humanity participates in incorruption because of the union of man to God (3.18.7). Christ is the agent: the union of man with God does not produce the person of Christ; rather, it is the mediation of Christ, which brings together God and man.[26] Opposition to Gnostic dualism leads Irenaeus to stress the unity of the divine word with the creation, in his ability to be seen and to suffer.[27]

5.4.4 FATHER AND SON

The transcendent father is revealed by the son and the invisible is seen by those who believe and receive life (4.20.5). The invisibility

---

[25] There is no trace of two persons in Christ, as was suggested by Loofs.
[26] Houssiau, *La christologie de saint Irénée*, 210–15.
[27] This will lead later to the explicit doctrine of the two natures of Christ; ibid., 256.

of the father ensures that the father is not despised. Through the law and the prophets the word proclaimed himself and the father and then showed the father in visible and tangible form; but not all believed. Yet all saw the father in the son for 'the father is the invisible of the son and the son is the visible of the father'. All, even the demons, called him God, when he was on earth (4.6.6). The son fulfils the law and prophets, as Jerusalem ends in the new covenant. The son is the measure of the father and contains him. God makes all things by measure and order so that nothing is unmeasured and nothing unnumbered.[28] Yet the immensity of the father is contained within the incarnate son (4.4.2).[29] The son is the measure of the father because he comprehends (*capit*) him and is his adaptation. Quintilian speaks of taking an audience as one's measure and adapting to their capacity.[30]

5.4.5 THE NAME

Irenaeus proclaims the power of the name of Jesus Christ,[31] a name which can only be given in the spirit (1 Cor. 12:3). His theology of the name of Jesus is based on Philippians 2:6–11. The good name of Jesus possesses sweetness and beauty which the heretics have replaced with bitter poison (1.27.4).[32] The beauty of Christ (3.19.2; 4.33.11) derives from Isaiah 9:6 and especially Psalm 44:3–5. The power of the name is evident in exorcism and again reflects Philippians 2. The church does not invoke angels or use incantations but turns to the lord who made all things and invokes the name of the lord Jesus Christ (2.32.5). The name of Christ is now glorified among the churches in all nations, thereby fulfilling the prophecy of Malachi (4.17.5, 6).[33] From the royal stamp on coins, name and image are linked by association. To sum up, the invocation of the name, which begins from Philippians 2:6–11, is a source of power for the church, is glorified universally, in the eucharist and in the

---

[28] Wisdom 11:20 tells us that he created all things in measure, number and weight.

[29] *ipsum immensum Patrem in filio mensuratum.*

[30] *submittere se ad mensuram discentis* (*Inst.* 2.3.7).

[31] E. Lanne, 'Le nom de Jésus-Christ et son invocation chez saint Irénée de Lyon', *Irén* 48 (1975), 447 67.

[32] The sweetness of the name may indicate a play upon *Christos* and *chrestos*.

[33] E. Lanne, 'Le nom de Jésus-Christ, 2,' *Irén* 49 (1976), 34 53.

church universal, as the name of the son of God. In all these ways the name is unique and the culmination of worship, vision and glory.

5.5 THE TOTALITY OF RECAPITULATION

The mass of detail which Irenaeus brings to describe recapitulation reflects the theme of inclusive totality.[34] Christ is not merely head or chief but the one who unites a vast plurality. He is not merely the summit but the unity of all things. Romans 5:12–21 and 1 Corinthians 15:45–8, must be added to Ephesians 1:10 for an appreciation of Irenaeus' cosmic view. Irenaeus' first use of the term (1.10.1) is followed by an outline of his theology which plainly flows from this concept.[35] All the questions of human destiny and salvation find their answer in the work of Christ.

The event of recapitulation defines three seasons of the economy.[36] The first season in order of earthly time is creation. There was already a saviour, so there had to be someone whom he could save, lest the existence of the saviour be pointless (3.22.3). The creature was made in the image of God, namely his word (5.16.2). From creation onwards, the saving totality spread wider and wider. The fourth and final covenant, which came in Christ, renewed, summed up and raised humanity to the heavens (3.11.8). This was the climax of a long process of habituation in which man had been accustomed to participate in God and God had become accustomed to dwell in man (3.20.2).

The second of these seasons (logically the first) is the incarnation, death and resurrection of Christ, where totality is evident as he who already has primacy in the invisible realm assumes primacy over the visible realm (3.16.6). The cosmic cross implanted (*infixus*) in creation becomes visible (5.18.3; *dem.* 34). The birth of Christ recapitulates the birth of Adam, to gather up humanity in physical form (3.21.10; *dem.* 32). All the generations between Christ and Adam are also assumed (3.22.4) to show that he is not derived from them but that they, through the gospel, derive their life from him.

---

34 A recent work presents multitudinous detail with sparkling lucidity: Sesboüé, *Tout récapituler dans le Christ* (Paris, 2000).
35 Ibid., 129.
36 Ibid., 131–56. Here and elsewhere Sesboüé draws on Scharl, *Recapitulatio mundi*.

Solidarity with the whole of human life is taken up, as he passes through all ages (2.22.4). He pities the disobedience of Adam and replaces it with his own obedience (4.40.3). In his temptations he overcomes man's defeat by the devil and destroys the adversary (5.21.2). His final trial on the cross extends his unlimited reign in the visible realm and his obedience reshapes humanity. In his incarnation and death Christ has gathered up (*in compendio*) the whole history of salvation and restored the image and likeness of God in man.

Thirdly, the end will come with the return of Christ in glory to sum up all things (1.10.1).[37] Here he who is the beginning becomes the end. The totality of Christ's work is reflected in the eucharist. The new wine at Cana compressed the time of natural ripening, just as he compressed all things within himself (3.11.5; 3.16.7).

What then is recapitulation?[38] Who is the agent? It is the work of the incarnate Christ. What is summed up? The totality of humanity and the universe is recapitulated in Christ. What happens in recapitulation? First, the whole history of salvation is resumed, so that beginning, middle and end are brought together (3.24.1). Secondly, the sovereignty of Christ over all things is assumed; just as he reigns over the unseen world, so he is lord of the visible world, which he supports by the axis of his cross. Thirdly, all things are recreated, restored, renewed and set free.[39] Lastly, all things achieve the purpose for which they were made; they are not merely repaired but are brought to perfection in Christ.

---

37 Sesboüé, *Tout récapituler*, 154.
38 Ibid., 159.
39 Ibid., 162: 'C'est la dimension rédemptrice de la récapitulation.'

CHAPTER 6

Recapitulation: inauguration and consummation

This chapter examines the way recapitulation runs from the inauguration of new life in the church to the consummation of all things. Irenaeus had learnt from Paul of correction and from John of perfection. Ephesians told him of a new order of being in Christ, of the body, which grew from and into the head, displaying the eschatological miracle of the cross which brought restoration and perfection. This salvation radiates through the church, in which life, truth and goodness descend from Christ through the apostles and spread throughout the world. Life or being is the note of the church for those who have been raised with Christ to be united with him in heavenly places. The church is guided by the economy of apostolic truth and its members display a new pattern of life. Ordered by ministry and mission, the church lives by baptism and eucharist until the final consummation when God alone will reign. Christ will come again and the dead will be raised. Recapitulation continues to the end, uniting the faithful and rejecting apostates, defeating Antichrist and restoring humanity to God.

6.1.1 INAUGURATION OF NEW LIFE

Those who were dead in trespasses and sins, ruled by the prince of the power of the air, have, together with Christ, been made alive, raised and seated in heavenly places (Eph. 2:5, 6: συνεζωοποίησεν, συνήγειρεν, συνεκάθισεν). Newness is shown in a new spirit, a new order, a new worship of one God (3.10.2). New life came from God, for the power of the most high God overshadowed Mary to bring a new kind of generation which inherits not death but life, a life imparted through the eucharist. What does Irenaeus mean when he speaks of Mary as the source of our regeneration (4.33.4 and 11)? He claims that, in becoming the mother of the new Adam, the source of new life, Mary has conveyed life to all, who recover life in and with him.[1] This linear view of the divine economy is typical of Irenaeus. Nothing is automatic, for there are many who do not receive union with God and who remain in the old Adam who was conquered and expelled from paradise (5.1.3). As in the natural Adam all were dead, so in the spiritual Adam all may be brought to life (5.1.3).

The new life is marked by immortality, for the father will receive the righteous into incorruption and everlasting enjoyment (4.6.5), as his order of salvation moves forward to set free his servant, adopt him as son, bestow an incorruptible inheritance, and so bring man to perfection (4.11.1).

Truth comes with grace, for the revelation of the father, which comes through the word, gives life to those who see God (4.20.7). Here alone they find glory, for those who are in the light do not produce the light which enlightens them; they contribute nothing to it (4.14.1). The glory of man is to continue and abide in the service of God, and so to participate in the glory of the lord (4.14.1). As those who see light are within light and share its brilliance, so those who see God are in God and share his splendour (4.20.5). Only by serving God can his glory be acquired (4.16.4).

6.1.2 LIFE THROUGH THE CROSS

At the cross, conflict between Irenaeus and the Gnostic dualism is explicit.[2] For Gnostics, suffering and death cannot be related to God. Only those who are removed from the sphere of the physical world can be saved by the spiritual element within them. Irenaeus, following both Paul and John, joins the humiliation of incarnation and cross with the exaltation of resurrection. The cross is itself the sign of victory and the power of salvation. For both Paul and John (and for Irenaeus), the glory of Christ is seen in his cross.

---

[1] P. Galtier, 'La vierge qui nous régénère', *RSR* 5 (1914), 143. Massuet takes this as a reference to the church.
[2] T. Scherrer, *La gloire de Dieu dans l'oeuvre de Saint Irénée* (Rome, 1997), 181–206.

The exaltation of Christ's resurrection is declared by Irenaeus through several prophetic passages. Psalm 110:1–7 speaks of humiliation and exaltation in glory (*dem.* 48). Isaiah 11:10 speaks of the exaltation[3] of the risen Christ who will rule all things from his glory (*dem.* 61). The lord is exalted above all flesh (Isa. 2:17) (4.33.13) and ascends Mount Zion (Ps. 68:18) as the gates are opened for the king of glory to enter (Ps. 24:7, 9) (*dem.* 83, 84).

Humiliation and exaltation are joined in the saviour who is both a man without beauty (*homo indecorus*) and beautiful in form (*decorus specie*). He is man so that he might be tested and word of God that he might be glorified. When he is dishonoured and crucified, his humanity is absorbed in the victory, which he wins through suffering and the demonstration of his goodness. The unity of the word of the father and son of man is declared in this saving act (3.19.2, 3). In robust imagery, Irenaeus tells how the prophets foretold the humility of Christ in the weak and inglorious man who enters Jerusalem on an ass and presents his back and his cheeks to be struck. A lamb to the slaughter, he drinks vinegar, is abandoned by friends and holds out his hands all day long. The object of derision and insult, his clothes are divided and he descends to the dust of death. All these things are foretold by scripture, and his humiliation is a condition of his exaltation in glory. This glory is both hidden and revealed in his suffering (*dem.* 71).

So there can be no separation between the humiliation of Christ's flesh and his exaltation in glory. The mystery of the cross, for Irenaeus, demands both these things. Only a man could have overcome the enemy which had conquered man (3.18.7). Irenaeus has an intricate argument to show how the humiliation of the passion is a thing of glory because it points to the reality of salvation. For the Gnostics, the passion of the twelfth aeon produced ignorance, death, corruption and error. In contrast, 'by his passion the lord has destroyed death, nullified error, destroyed corruption, overcome ignorance; he has manifested life, displayed the truth and given incorruption' (2.20.3). The disruption of death, error and corruption are linked causally with the manifestation of life, truth, and the gift of incorruption. The cross is a sign which points to life

---

[3] Reading 'ἀνάστασις' for 'ἀνάπαυσις'.

and truth, and a reality which communicates incorruption. Herein lies the glory of the cross, and in this glory all may share. As eagles flock to devour a carcass, so all gather to participate in the glory of the lord (4.14.1).

The cross points to the kingship of Christ and his power as judge. The government is on his shoulders, for the cross declares his kingship (*dem.* 56). The necessary unity of him who has suffered on the cross with the king who reigns in majesty joins the *consecutive* account (as in Phil. 2:5–11) with the *unitive* account (as in 1 Cor. 1; Gal. 6:14; John, *passim*). 'He who has suffered under Pontius Pilate, he is the lord of all men and their king, their God, their judge, for he has received power from him, who is God over all, because he became obedient unto death, even the death of the cross' (3.12.9).

The cross is the source of life, as he who is lifted up draws all to himself and gives life to the dead (4.2.7). The apostles preached that the son of God in his passion destroyed death and brought life to the flesh so that he might destroy the enmity against God, bringing us peace with God by doing that which is agreeable to him (*dem.* 86). All of which is profoundly Pauline; for Paul, the cross goes on in life-giving power. The cross is never an episode in the story of the resurrection; the resurrection is an episode in the story of the cross.[4]

The final glory of the cross is the love, which is demonstrated for the father and for us. The submissive love of the word of God on the cross is the means of our salvation (3.16.9). The prayer of pardon, 'Father, forgive them', declares the long-suffering patience, mercy and goodness of Christ, who puts into practice his command that we should love enemies (3.18.5). Truth and goodness spring from the cross where the word of God and son of man fought and conquered. By his obedience he redeemed us from disobedience and bound the strong man (3.18.6). All this pointed to his love and mercy, to the cross as the proof of the goodness of Christ[5] which displays the love of Christ for the whole human race (3.18.6; cf. Titus 3:4).

---

[4] E. Käsemann, *Perspectives on Paul* (London, 1971), 59; *Paulinische Perspektiven* (Tübingen, 1969), 106–7.

[5] *ostensio bonitatis Christi.*

The cross is an epiphany of cosmic significance for Irenaeus, when (following Justin) he points to the sign of the cross in the universe. The word of God is co-extensive with creation, which it sustains in length, breadth, height and depth. The word of God, who rules the universe, was also crucified in four dimensions, the son of God giving himself the form of the cross in the universe (*dem.* 34). Epiphany and soteriology are joined as Irenaeus combines the theology of Paul, Ephesians and John. So far from being a distraction, Gnostic pessimism concerning the passion has impelled Irenaeus to blend the several ways in which Paul and John combine a theology of the cross with a theology of glory.

6.2.1 CHRIST AS HEAD AND CORNERSTONE

In his recapitulation, the lord, king and judge receives power from the God of all because he has been obedient to the death of the cross (3.12.9). Consequently, the people which believes in God through him is no longer under the power of angels but under his rule as lord (3.12.9). He, the head, rose from the dead, and is followed by his many members who are joined together in one body (Eph. 4:16) (3.19.3). He became what we are that he might bring us to be what he is himself (5 pref.). He gave his flesh for our flesh, his soul for our souls, and poured out the spirit of the father 'for the union and communion of God and man' (5.1.1).

He went through the process of human birth so that he could acknowledge himself as son of man (4.33.2). Those who are redeemed by the flesh of the lord are re-established in his blood, 'holding the head from which the whole body of the church, having been fitted together, draws its growth' (5.14.4; cf. Col. 2:19). Son and father work together to give life and salvation (4.20.6), so that what is partial is perfected through more and more gifts towards an end where the same Christ is still supreme (4.20.7).

Those who are united under Christ look back to Abraham as the father of all God's pilgrim people, the believers of both covenants. God builds them into one building with Christ as the chief cornerstone (4.25.1). He who is the chief cornerstone gathers together those who are far off and those who are near (3.5.3) into one body which proclaims throughout the world the one way of salvation.[6] The light and wisdom of God which saves all men is declared openly on the streets, pronounced faithfully in public squares, proclaimed on the tops of walls, and spoken with confidence at the gates of the city (Prov. 1:20, 21) (5.20.1).

The epiphany of the church is described with the metaphors of light, proclamation, tower, vineyard, water, garden, four pillars, treasure, glory and stars. Within the church, the apostles deposited all the riches of truth and life (3.4.1). By its preaching the church brings light and truth (1.10.2). It is the beautiful, elect tower of the vineyard and the epiphany of God's grace because it shines everywhere as its wine-press is dug, 'for those who receive the spirit are everywhere' (4.36.2). The beauty of the church derives from the presence of God's gift of the spirit in all the church, 'for where the church is, there is also the spirit of God, and where the spirit of God is, there is the church and every grace. And the spirit is truth' (3.24.1).

In contrast, those who do not receive from the pure fountain of Christ dig broken cisterns (Jer. 2:13) and from holes in the earth drink dirty water. They shun the faith of the church because they fear being convicted, and reject the spirit so that they may not be instructed (3.24.1). The spring which gushes from the body of Christ is splendid in its purity.[7] The nourishment of the church comes from the scripture, which is the milk of the church for her children. Exuberance rules. The church is also a garden in the world from which all the fruits should be eaten: 'eat of every scripture of the Lord; but do not eat with a proud mind and keep away from heretical strife' (5.20.2). The unity of church, scripture and spirit spreads through the world, and just as the church is universal, so the fourfold gospel breathes in every direction incorruption (3.11.8).

The church is the channel of God's love, displaying his glory. Charity is more precious than knowledge and more glorious than prophecy. The presence of this gift in the church is seen everywhere and, especially, in the martyrs who go on ahead to the father (4.33.8, 9). As the love of God displays his glory in the church, so

---

[6] Scherrer, *La gloire de Dieu*, 207–38.
[7] *nitidissimus.*

does the liberty which expresses the faith and love of the believer. The free obedience of the church is more glorious than the submission of servitude (4.13.2). We are not freed in order to separate ourselves from our Lord, but rather that we might receive his grace, love him more and partake of a greater glory when we stand in the presence of the father (4.13.3).

So, within the church, friendship, service and glory are joined together. The love of God brings glory to man who loves, supplying his need with the friendship of God. For God does not need the love of man, but man needs the glory which flows from the love which he returns to God (4.16.4). To serve God is to be illuminated by God and to share in his splendour, 'for this is the glory of man, to persevere and to remain in the service of God'. Chosen by the lord, those who follow him are glorified as they receive the vision of glory which he asked for them (Jn 17:24). It was his will to share glory with his disciples, who come from the East and the West to participate in the glory of their lord (4.14.1). This glory is the spiritual sacrifice foretold by the prophets and reflected in the eucharist which is offered throughout the world. The name of Christ is glorified in the church as he glorifies the father and gives glory to man (4.17.6). The martyrs are glorious in the perfect love of God which was shown in Stephen who asked that the sin of his persecutors be not laid to their charge (3.12.13). On the testimony preserved in Eusebius, the martyrs of Lyons hurried on with joy to the glory of Christ (*H.E.* 5.1.6; 5.1.35; 5.1.48; 5.1.23).

6.2.2 THE UNITY OF THE CHURCH

Unity dominates the theology of Irenaeus – his accounts of God, redemption, christology and, inevitably, his account of the church.[8] The church is universal but manifested locally. The structure of the church displays 'the same shape of church order' (5.20.1) and the 'ancient structure of the church throughout the whole world' (4.33.8).[9] In a clear reflection of the cosmic Intellect, the church believes the elements of faith 'as if she had but one soul, one and the same heart, and she proclaims and teaches them and hands them down with perfect harmony, as if she possessed one mouth' (1.10.2). United in teaching, the church is united in worship as she offers universally a pure sacrifice (4.17.6; 4.18.1 and 4). As mother, the church alone can nourish the faithful from her breasts (3.24.1).

The unity of the church with the trinity is apparent from the affinity of the church with the father who is intellect, with Christ in whom all is brought together, and with the holy spirit who acts in every local church. The spirit constantly vivifies the church in which he dwells, transforming the believer 'so that the flesh forgets itself and takes on the quality of the spirit' (5.9.3). The spirit communicates Christ (3.24.1) so that the whole church is shaped according to the image of the son (4.37.7) and follows its head through passion, death and resurrection (3.19.3).

While the church is never so assimilated to Christ that their identities are merged (the relation is compared with that of husband and wife) (4.20.12), yet restored humanity rises to the father (5.36.1).[10] The unity of the divine Intellect spreads its trace through the whole universe by the action of the divine trinity. The son is always with his creation to reveal the father. 'Therefore, then in all things, and through all things, there is one God the father, and one word, and one son, and one spirit, and one salvation to all who believe in him' (4.6.7). Schism is usually trivial in origin, and can never be justified by any compensating reform (4.33.7).[11] Irenaeus stood against Victor for unity and peace (*H.E.* 5.24.10–11) and pointed to the example of Polycarp and Anicetus (*H.E.* 5.24.16–17). In his action and theology, Irenaeus pioneered the first comprehensive ecclesiology.[12] He did this because the church took a central place in his account of the recapitulation of all things.

Irenaeus is often and dubiously associated with early catholicism (*Frühkatholizismus*), a pattern of thought whereby the locus of salvation began to move from Christ to the church as institution. This

---

[10] *novus homo . . . semper nove confabulans deo.*

[11] E. Lanne ('L'église de Rome', *Irén* 49 (1976), 309–11) links this claim to the action of Victor in excommunicating the churches of Asia. See Kereszty, 'The unity of the church', 215.

[12] Kereszty, 'The unity of the church', 217.

may be seen in Ephesians, where (in contrast to 1 Cor. 12) Christ is the head of the body rather than the whole body, and the concept finds its consummation in Cyprian. In the twentieth century early catholicism gained attention through the advocates and critics of the ecclesiology of the ecumenical movement. Controversy lapsed when protagonists like Käsemann and Küng recognised that they were saying the same things, and above all when Käsemann showed the roots of early catholicism in Paul himself, who directly and indirectly, consciously and unwittingly, prepared its way. Paul speaks of the church as the body of Christ and first links ecclesiology and christology. Of course in Paul the body of Christ is still a metaphor used to exhort Christians to fulfil their obedience, while in Ephesians it is a metaphysical entity which grows as the extension of Christ. Again, for Paul, the sacraments are not the medicine of immortality, because what is given is never separated from the giver and the act of its gift. Christology and ecclesiology are not interchangeable.[13]

The imprecision of *Frühkatholizismus* as a concept is striking. Harnack linked the process with the influence of Greek ways of thinking which he believed to be various modes of idealism. Sohm pointed to the growth of institutions and ordinances. Bultmann put this succinctly by saying that law became constitutive rather than regulative for the church.[14] Werner, like Käsemann, took the fading of future eschatology as the significant trend, a decline which is certainly not found in Irenaeus.[15] Yet the fading of eschatological

---

[13] Yet the tendencies of Ephesians can claim precedents in Paul. 'He did in fact make the sacramental incorporation into the worldwide body of Christ the criterion of being a Christian, and thus rejected a mere historical or ethical connection with Jesus of Nazareth as this criterion. For him also the lordship of Christ on earth rests on the fact that the exalted Lord, present in the Church, binds his own to himself and to one another. By endowing them with the Spirit, he makes them capable of permeating the old world as the inbreaking of the new, following his own precedent, and thus of demonstrating his omnipotence in every place and time', E. Käsemann, *Exegetische Versuche und Besinnungen*, vol. II (Göttingen, 1965), 246; ET, *New Testament questions of today* (London, 1969), 243. The whole essay 'Paul and early catholicism' should be consulted for an account of the issue.

[14] R. Bultmann, *Theology of the New Testament*, vol. II, (London, 1955), 97-8.

[15] In Irenaeus there is a heightened future eschatology. See J. D. G. Dunn, *Unity and Diversity in the New Testament* (London, 1977), 341-66 for a useful summary of the discussion and a valuable summing up; note also C. K. Barrett's criticism of Käsemann (*Luke the historian in recent study* (London, 1961), 70) and the discussion in H. Conzelmann, *An outline of the theology of the New Testament* (London, 1969), 289-94.

hope is not a feature of catholicism, which first emerges unambiguously in Cyprian with a heightened, urgent eschatology.[16] The church, governed by its magisterial bishops, is a new kingdom under *Christus imperator*.[17] Its structure is necessary because the end is near when the lord takes over the sovereignty of the earth.[18]

With 'early catholicism' we have a term which, like 'deification' in the early church fathers, points to a genuine truth but lacks precision. In the case of deification, common sense suggests an avoidance of the term. With 'early catholicism', blurred edges remain and the term may fall into well-deserved neglect by interpreters of Irenaeus.

6.3 THE ECONOMY OF APOSTOLIC TRUTH

The epiphany of the church is no chance irruption but part of *God's universal plan*, which he made known as *universal truth* in scripture and the world. We have seen how Irenaeus turned to nature for confirmation of the four Gospels, which the four cherubim declared (3.11.8). Indeed all living creatures were tetramorphous, and this applied to the gospel, and to the covenants of the lord, the fourth of which renews mankind (3.11.8).

Since God made all things in due proportion, the outward aspect of gospel is well arranged and harmonised (3.11.9). The gospel begins from one God, who made the world and spoke through Moses and the prophets to declare his unicity (3.11.7). The truth goes on, as the presbyters of the church preserve this faith in one creator God, and increase that love for the son of God who accomplished such wonderful dispensations for our sake (4.26.5). This variety in unity is marvellous in its finality: we should never look for another father, nor another substance, nor another hand of God besides that which, from beginning to end, forms and prepares us for life; always present with his handwork, God perfects it in his own image and likeness (5.15.4).

Truth is not known to all, for if the Jews had known of the future existence of Christians they would have burned their scriptures, which declare that other nations partake of life while they

[16] *De unitate* 27; *Epistles* 58.10.
[17] See W. Telfer, *The office of a bishop* (London, 1962), 124ff.
[18] See E. Osborn, 'Cyprian's Imagery', *Antichthon* 7 (1973), 68.

are disinherited from the grace of God (3.21.1). Yet the origins of truth point to its perfection. In Jerusalem the *universal* truth was declared by the voices of a church from which others originated, the voices of the great city of citizens of the new covenant, the apostles, the disciples who are truly perfect, perfected by the spirit after the assumption of the lord (3.12.5). From the same apostles the church has spread in every place and perseveres in one and the same opinion (3.12.7). Its prayers, offered in every place, rise as incense to God (4.17.5). Inscribed on the hearts of countless nations is the tradition, rule of faith and salvation, which makes them wise, righteous, chaste and pleasing to God (3.4.2).

What is the mark of truth? It comes from God through the visible line of the apostles. Irenaeus makes five points: the uniqueness of God, the uniqueness of truth, the apostolic succession, catholicity, the opposite effects of martyrdom and heresy.

(i) *The uniqueness of God.* 'For the lord of all gave to his apostles the power of the gospel, through whom also we have known the truth, that is, the doctrine of the son of God, to whom also did the lord declare: "he who hears you hears me; he that despises you despises me and him that sent me"' (3 pref.) (Lk. 10:16).

There can be no other God for prophets, apostles and disciples, nor for us who follow them (3.5.1). Analogously to the twelve tribes of Israel, Christ generates the twelve-pillared foundation of the church in a foreign country (4.21.3).

After considering the four Gospels, Irenaeus turns to the other apostles (3.11.9). The book of the Acts proves the unity of apostolic doctrine. First, Peter (3.12.2–4) declares that there exists no other God and repeats the same truth before the council and Cornelius (3.12.5–7). Then Paul on the Areopagus (3.12.9) and Stephen the martyr (3.12.10) show the agreement of all apostles on faith in one God (3.12.11). The claim that Paul had his own private revelation and doctrine is absurd when Luke was so close to him and remembered so many details (3.14). There can be no division between the apostles, for Peter and Paul were apostles of the same God, and God is not so limited as to have but one apostle who understood the dispensation of his son (3.13.1). Nor did apostles hold back any secret truth: Paul taught with simplicity what he knew, the entire counsel of God (3.14.2).

(ii) *The uniqueness of truth.* The result of this faithful transmission is clear. There is one identical, life-giving faith, handed down in truth and preserved in the church from the apostles until now (3.3.3). The apostles deposited the truth in the church as a bank for safe keeping and ease of access. We should not seek truth from others when it is easily obtainable from the church (3.4.1).

Maligned by vain sophists as hypocrites, the apostles followed the revealed truth (3.5.1). We have Luke's testimony that the apostles were true, open and steadfast, and that they held nothing in reserve (3.15.1). As preachers of truth and apostles of liberty they proclaimed father and son as the only God (3.15.3), while those who are alienated from truth ever wallow in error (3.24.2). If we want true knowledge we shall find it in the doctrine of the apostles and the ancient constitution of the church which is spread throughout the world (4.33.8).

(iii) *The succession.* Our link with God and truth is through the succession which joins us to Christ and the apostles. We have learned the plan of our salvation from those through whom the gospel has come down to us; first they proclaimed it publicly and then, by God's good will, handed it down to us in scripture, so that the same gospel might be the ground and pillar of our faith (3.1.1). People were as important as books: Clement of Rome could still hear the echo of the preaching of the apostles and see their traditions before his eyes (3.3.3).

For Irenaeus the personal link with the apostles and eye-witnesses of the lord was Polycarp, whom he ever pictured in his memory:[19] 'For I have a vivid recollection, revolving these things accurately in my mind' (Eusebius, *H.E.* 5.20). Polycarp was instructed by apostles, had talked with many who had seen Christ, and was appointed by apostles as bishop in Smyrna. This gave him authority and made him a more steadfast witness than others. Little wonder that he denounced Marcion as the first-born of Satan, just as John had denounced Cerinthus (3.3.4). Apart from Polycarp, there is a lot more evidence of the apostles, especially of Peter in the book of their Acts, to which Irenaeus gives great importance (3.12.1). The twelve apostles are our guarantee of authenticity in the foreign country

---

[19] See above, 1.1.

where the twelve tribes were born; any who depart from continuity
with Christian beginnings are rightly to be suspected (4.26.2).

To prove the integrity of all the churches we have but to list
the succession whence they are sprung. To do this for all churches
would be tedious; it is enough to list the succession of the 'very
great, very ancient and universally known church founded and
organized at Rome by the two most glorious apostles, Peter and
Paul' (3.3.2). From the apostles there have come down to us in this
place the order, succession, tradition, preaching of truth, and the
one life-giving faith (3.3.3). The doctrinal succession is definitive,
not Rome, which is only important because it possesses the doctrine
which serves as a standard for others 'But the meaning of Irenaeus
is *not*: on condition that the churches keep the apostolic tradition
they are under moral obligation to agree with Rome, but rather:
there are *in fact* other apostolic churches, and by reason of this they
cannot have any other kind of relationship with the apostolic church
of Rome than agreement with it.'[20] Irenaeus gives no ground for
attributing priority to Rome.

(iv) *Catholic.* A further guarantee of the authentic truth is its
universal extent. In every place we find the same tradition of the
apostles, the same faith in the same God the father, the same dispensation of the incarnation, the same gift of spirit, the same commandments, the same church order, the same expectation of the same
advent and the same salvation of both soul and body. The one true
way of salvation is displayed so that the epiphany of Christ shines in
every place as his truth is preached. The church is planted as a paradise in the world, Eden restored. Here on earth the heavenly recapitulation of all things in Christ takes on human form. Here he joins
man to the spirit, making the spirit head of man as Christ is head of
the spirit. Only through the spirit can we hear and speak (5.20.1, 2).

It has been needlessly claimed that Irenaeus sees the universal
church from a regional perspective and gives priority to Rome because of its relation to Lyons. Tertullian has a similar perspective,
looking to Corinth, Philippi, Ephesus and Rome. Irenaeus looks
to each of these main churches as well as to Rome, having special

---

[20] L. A. Abramowski, 'Irenaeus, Adv. Haer. III 3,2: Ecclesia Romana and omnis ecclesia
and Ibid., 3,3: Anacletus of Rome', *JThS* 28 (1977), 103.

regard for Ephesus and Polycarp. The subjection of all churches to Rome would be unthinkable for Irenaeus.[21] With still less justification, it has been claimed that Rome had a priority in matters of faith, but not in matters of discipline;[22] for we have seen that Irenaeus saw Rome rather as emblematic and not prior to other churches.

(v) *Helped by martyrs and harmed by heretics.* No one does more for new life in the church than do the martyrs. The apostles and their disciples were perfected, born aloft to what is perfect, as was Stephen for whom the heavens opened (3.12.13). They were sheep for the slaughter; but, in their consecration to God, they minister to our faith, through selfless neglect of earthly treasures (4.16.1). Through their suffering and loss the church grows in numbers (4.33.9).

At the opposite end of the scale, heretics fail in all the characteristics of the apostolic church (3.17.4) and deny either the divinity or humanity of Jesus, the very things by which he is able to save us (4.33.4). So also schismatics are condemned, because they have no love of God and consider their own interests rather than the unity of the church (4.33.7). The devil, the first apostate, is the cause of all later apostasy (4.41.3); but the devil does not daunt Irenaeus, who believes that by his writing he may bring heretics back to the truth (3.2.3).

6.4 NEW WAY OF LIFE

The church displays a new way of life which is marked by purity, exuberance, spiritual flesh and peaceful citizenship.

Our offerings to God have moral conditions, for it is the pure conscience of the offerer that sanctifies the offering (4.18.4). We are sons of God only through obedience and doctrine (4.41.2); those who disobey their parents do not inherit (4.41.3). The earnest of the spirit dwells in us to make us spiritual even now while the mortal is swallowed up in immortality. By the spirit we are no more slaves of fleshly lusts, but ruled by the spirit. Following the light of reason, we become spiritual men (5.8.1, 2).

[21] N. Brox, 'Rom und "jede Kirche" im 2. Jahrhundert. Zu Irenäus, adv. haer. III 3,2', in *Festgabe Hubert Jedin zum 75. Geburtstag*, ed. W. Brandmüller and R. Bäumer (Paderborn, 1969), 77–8.

[22] H. J. Vogt, 'Teilkirchen-Perspektive bei Irenäus?', *ThQ* 164,1 (1984), 58.

The kingdom of heaven belongs to the violent, who strenuously and swiftly snatch it up when the opportunity is presented (4.37.7). The more vigorous our effort, the more highly esteemed is our goal (4.37.7).[23] There is an exuberance about Christian giving, for the Christian gives as a freeman not as a slave; his gift is not paid as a tithe but offered joyfully and freely as a widow's mite (4.18.2).

Paul contrasts works of the flesh unfavourably with the works of spirit (5.11.1). However, when he says that flesh and blood cannot inherit the kingdom of God, he is speaking of carnal lusts; the flesh which is so prone to sin can be joined to the body of Christ. Just as a branch of a good olive may be grafted into a wild olive which may accept or reject the graft, so the flesh may bear fruit in a king's paradise and regain pristine manhood in the image and likeness of God (5.10.1).[24] It is in our physical members that we are brought to life by doing the works of the spirit (5.11.2).[25] The righteous flesh of the son of God has reconciled the flesh which was being kept under bondage to sin, and brought it into friendship with God (5.14.2).[26]

For Irenaeus, the ideal man is the glorified Christ, who is endowed with spiritual flesh. The concept of flesh brings together many aspects of his theology. The trinity is indicated when the father offers the substance of earth, when the word models man in the future form of Jesus, and when wisdom or holy spirit deifies man to the fullness of the glorified Christ. Eschatology announces the raising of all in body and soul to the physical condition of Christ where they behold God. In the economy, man reconciles in his body the two extremes of flesh and spirit which God brings together through his plan of salvation.[27]

---

[23] Erasmus delighted in the *priscum vigorem* of the gospel which he found in Irenaeus.

[24] The wild olive is Paul's metaphor (Rom. 11:17; see E. Käsemann, *Commentary on Romans* (ET; Grand Rapids, 1980), 308; *An die Römer* (Tübingen, 1973), 295) which misinterprets the practice of grafting. Irenaeus corrects Paul's error. The wild olive receives a graft of the cultivated olive and becomes a cultivated olive while remaining, in its root stock, a wild olive. See D. Minns, *Irenaeus* (London, 1994), 77–8. Also see D. Minns' review of A. Orbe, *Teología de san Ireneo. Comentario al Libro V del' 'Adversus Haereses'*, vol. 1, in *JThS* 38 (1987), 194.

[25] Here Irenaeus is aggressively Pauline. See E. Käsemann, *Essays on NT themes* (London, 1964), 135; *Exegetische Versuche und Besinnungen*, vol. 1 (Göttingen, 1960), 34; *Perspectives on Paul*, 114–15 and *Paulinische Perspektiven*, 197–8.

[26] On reconciliation of the flesh, see also below, 10.4.

[27] A. Orbe, 'El hombre ideal en la teología de s. Ireneo', *Greg* 43 (1962), 491.

Deification moves from the image and likeness, by means of the trinitarian economy, to the vision of God which gives incorruptibility. The work of the spirit bears fruit in the salvation of the flesh, which it makes capable of incorruption (*capax incorruptelae*) (5.12.4). Participation in incorruption comes from union with the flesh of Christ, communion with the spirit, incarnation, eucharist and final resurrection. Flesh and spirit are joined in present sacraments and final glory. For Irenaeus as for Tertullian, the flesh of Christ is central. The church is the place of new birth by water and the spirit (3.24.1). Incorruption is marked by the glory and love of God. The cross is the centre of the economy (5.17.4). The word, impressed in the form of a cross on all creation, became flesh, hung from the tree and recapitulated all things in himself (5.18.3). Here the sign of life hangs from the tree, whence flows the spirit who is the living water (5.18.2, 3). 'Man fully alive is he who has received incorruptibility and eternal glory. It is he who is the glory of God; and the glory of man is the vision of the father who envelops him in his "paternal light" and grants him "paternally" incorruptibility.'[28]

How do Christians regard the world when they make their triumphant exodus from the land of captivity? As the Israelites despoiled the Egyptians so we may keep the property which we once acquired from the mammon of unrighteousness (4.30.1). There is a difference: the Hebrews owed the Egyptians nothing, but we do owe the Romans the benefits of peace (4.30.3). Indeed the earthly rule under which we live has been appointed by God and not by the devil. Earthly governors arouse fear which restrains the savage strife of man with man; without such fear, men would devour one another like voracious fishes (5.24.2).

6.5 BAPTISM, EUCHARIST AND MINISTRY

Irenaeus' account of ministry depends on his soteriology and anthropology. Few have achieved such a rich and remarkable synthesis.[29] Ministry begins at baptism, when the spirit begins to work and renew within (3.17.1). The same spirit brings the

---

[28] Y. de Andía, *Homo vivens: incorruptibilité et divinisation selon Irénée de Lyon* (Paris, 1986), 344.
[29] See M. A. Donovan, 'Insights on ministry: Irenaeus', *Toronto Journal of Theology* 2,1 (1986), 89.

first-fruits of all nations to unity in Christ (3.17.2) and gives every grace and truth to the church (3.24.1). This truth or reality is guaranteed by the rule of faith, which has been handed down, and by the prophetic gifts of presbyters, bishops and others, who teach, baptise, celebrate the eucharist, see visions, prophesy, and perform exorcisms and healing. Even the raising of the dead is possible to those who have received and who give freely (2.32.4).

With its threefold reference to remission of sins, seal of life eternal and regeneration, baptism glimpses the range of Irenaeus' theology. It declares the unity of father, word and spirit, one God who creates and renews the whole man in his entirety. Flesh, soul and spirit share in the life of God. The saving work of father, son and spirit is effective for all who believe. Irenaeus' theology is brought into focus by baptism, so that one could say of baptism as Irenaeus said of eucharist (4.18.5), that his thought agrees with baptism and baptism confirms his thought.[30]

The baptism of Jesus was needed for his work of salvation, first, because the anointing of the spirit (3.9.3) was essential for a messiah and, second, because the descent of the spirit was necessary that the spirit might be accustomed to live in mankind, so as to work the will of the father by removing sinful habits (3.17.1).[31] But what effect could baptism have on one who was from the moment of his spotless generation the incarnate word of God (3.19.1)? Can it be more than a sign of God's purpose that humans should participate in the spirit manifest in Jesus?[32] Irenaeus does indeed distinguish the incarnation, where the word is made flesh in Mary, from the anointing of the spirit at the Jordan. The baptism 'affected the flesh (that is the human nature) of Jesus: until then he was united substantially to the Son of God, but not *fisicamente* – physically (that is qualitatively) – equipped for his saving mission'.[33] Can the baptism be the most important filial moment for Jesus, when it is not mentioned in the crucial text of 3.19.1?[34]

[30] A. Houssiau, 'Le baptême selon Irénée de Lyon', *EThL* 60,1 (1984), 59.

[31] D. A. Smith, 'Irenaeus and the baptism of Jesus', *TS* 58 (1997), 618–42.

[32] E. Fabbri, 'El bautismo de Jesús', 19, cited in Smith, ibid., 631.

[33] A. Orbe, *Introducción a la teología de los siglos II y III* (Rome, 1987), vol. II, 666.

[34] Scholars have provided much illumination on this point. See Fantino, *La théologie*, 375 and de Andía, *Homo vivens*, 185–201. See also Smith, 'Irenaeus and the baptism of Jesus', 640.

We eat of the bread, which is Christ's body, through the presence of the holy spirit in the eucharist. Here Christ nourishes us with himself. The spirit acts as mediator between Christ and us so that we share in Christ through him (3.24.1). The density of the claims of Irenaeus concerning the eucharist can only be understood within the total scheme of his theology and the presence of Christ and the spirit. Because we communicate with Christ in his flesh, so our flesh which has been nourished by this eucharist will be raised again to the glory of God the father. For the word of God will grant immortality to what is mortal and incorruption to what is corruptible, because his power works in weakness (5.2.2, 3).

The words of Irenaeus concerning the two elements in the eucharist have been interpreted in different ways. Luther, Pusey, Calvin, Grabe, Baur and Steitz identify the earthly element as the bread while Massuet and Batiffol take it to be the body of Christ. The heavenly element is variously identified as the body of Christ, the power of the holy spirit, the divine word, and the words of consecration. The doctrine must preserve Irenaeus' concern to rehabilitate matter. The eucharist is part of the total activity of God through creation and redemption which ends in the gift of incorruptibility to the flesh. While there is no precise formula of substantiation, a constant attention to material reality is present in the account of the eucharist.[35]

6.6.1 CONSUMMATION: ONE GOD ALONE WILL REIGN

For all the finality of the correction and perfection achieved in Christ, there remains a further fulfilment. The new humanity begun in Christ lives by hope in a future kingdom.

The one and same God the father has prepared good things for his subjects who desire his fellowship and has prepared eternal fire for the apostate devil and fellow rebels. One God, father and son, will send some into eternal bliss and others into a furnace of fire (4.40.1). There is a third group, of those who, like Enoch and Elijah, are translated directly into paradise, where they will remain until the consummation, enjoying a foretaste of immortality (5.5.1).

---

[35] A. D'Alès, 'La doctrine eucharistique de S. Irénée', *RSR* 3 (1923), 24 46.

There is no difficulty in believing that flesh could last for ever, since Jonah emerged unscathed from the whale's belly and the three young men in the furnace did not even smell of the fire through which they had passed. This was God's doing, for he alone could send, to join the three, a fourth like the son of God. 'Neither the nature of any created thing, therefore, nor the weakness of the flesh can prevail against the will of God' (5.5.2). Why did Jonah and the three young men emerge from their trial? Because God declared his power through them (5.5.2). This same God shall be glorified in humanity, the work of his hands, shaping it to resemble his son (5.6.1). Then shall men see God face to face (5.7.2).

We now receive a certain portion of his spirit, pointing to perfection, preparing us for incorruption, the earnest of our inheritance (3.24.1; 5.8.1), and we already cry 'Abba, father'. It will be much more when, face to face with that same God, 'all the members shall burst into a continuous hymn of triumph, glorifying him who raised them from the dead, and gave the gift of eternal life' (5.8.1).

6.6.2   WHEN CHRIST SHALL COME AGAIN

In his second advent, Christ will come on the clouds to bring the day which burns as a furnace, smiting the earth with the word of his mouth, slaying the impious with the breath of his lips, having a fan in his hands, cleansing his floor, gathering wheat into his barn but burning chaff with unquenchable fire (4.33.1). Some saw him with the father in glory, some saw him coming on the clouds, while some saw his wounded side and others saw a burning furnace (4.33.11). Both John and Daniel predicted the dissolution and desolation of the Roman empire, followed by the end of the world and the eternal kingdom of Christ (5.26.1, 2). The final truth about man and God will emerge at Christ's judgement, when he separates believers from unbelievers, obedient from disobedient. Here he will show himself to be just and good, following the will of the father who made men alike and with power of free choice, without ceasing his universal providence which makes his sun rise upon the evil and on the good and sends rain on just and unjust (5.27.1).

The Christ who lived and died will return, in the same flesh in which he had suffered, to reveal to us the glory of the father

(3.16.8).[36] This will be the display of our salvation (*ostensio salutis*). The return of Christ in glory will be both a proof and a revelation of our salvation (3.16.6). His flesh will show the truth of his gospel as it reveals the glory of his salvation. All evil will be destroyed at the coming of the Lord who lays waste Babylon and the beast (5.26.1). The face, glory and power of the lord will bring judgement when he comes to be glorified in his saints (4.27.4). The final separation of light from darkness will be an act of both God and of man (5.27.2–28.1). Those who have rejected the light and have not believed have chosen darkness and judgment for themselves. The mythology of the triumphant return is given existential point by the choice between light and darkness.

While all have freedom of choice, moral freedom can only come through the grace of God, which brings a new heart and mind.[37] To follow the one who gives salvation means to participate in salvation, just as to follow the light means to receive light. Those who serve and follow God share in life eternal (4.14.1). The free service of God raises man to perfection (4.37, 38). Some affinity with Stoicism may be noted in Irenaeus' account of man's divinity (Seneca, *Epistles* 41). The God within was real for both Stoic and Christian. Man possessed a fragment of the divine (Marcus Aurelius, *Meditations* 5.11). However, for Irenaeus, natural man did not possess the spirit which was a gift of God.[38]

True perfection belongs to the unbegotten God alone (4.38). Participation in the gift of divine life comes through the holy spirit, the lord and life-giver (5.12). The members of the human body 'are inherited by the spirit when they have been translated into the kingdom of heaven' (5.9.4).

6.6.3 RESURRECTION[39]

The resurrection of the flesh is sure (5.13.3) and our bodies, although decomposed, shall rise restored (5.2.3), for a saved man is

---

[36] Scherrer, *La gloire de Dieu*, 241 9.

[37] E. Klebba, *Die Anthropologie des hl. Irenäus. Eine dogmengeschichtliche Studie* (Münster, 1894), 157. See below, 11.1.

[38] See Klebba, ibid., 181. See below, 10.3.

[39] See also below, 10.4.

a complete man as well as a spiritual man (5.6.1). Like a grain of wheat the body must die in order to live (5.7.2). That flesh which is now under the dominion of death shall put on incorruption and immortality (5.13.3). Death shall be defeated and the flesh which it has held in subjection shall emerge from its dominion. The corruptible must put on incorruption, and the mortal must be clothed in immortality (1 Cor. 15:53) (5.13.5).

The sign of Jonah points to the resurrection of the body by reference to Christ's resurrection, which was anticipated in the earlier economy. The flesh must rise to the glory of God, for we are prepared by the word our saviour to participate in the eternal hymn of praise to the holy God.[40]

Irenaeus, joining Revelation 20:1–21:4 and 1 Corinthians 15:24–8, speaks of two resurrections, the first being the resurrection of the just in the kingdom of the son (5.36.3) and the second being the general resurrection which follows the delivering of the kingdom by the son to the father. In the kingdom of the son man will continue to grow and progress towards perfection in Christ (4.11.1; 5.35.1), and the creation will be restored (5.33.3).

Eternal life will be already enjoyed in this kingdom, which is the link between the present period of the church and eternity, of which man cannot speak.

For as long as the eschatological event is delayed there will continue to be conflict in some form or another, but when man has reached his destination and grown to the *imago* and *similitudo*, the power of Satan will then have been completely expelled, and God's universal dominion, unimpeded by hostile opposition from any quarter, will be the ultimate reality which 'no eye has seen'.[41]

6.6.4 COMMUNION AND SEPARATION

Those who continue in love to God, receive from him that communion which is life and light, while those who deliberately depart from God earn separation. Deprived of all good, apostates endure

---

[40] See G. Jouassard, 'Le "signe de Jonas" dans le livre IIIe de *l'adversus haereses* de saint Irénée', in *L'homme devant Dieu. Mélanges offerts au Père Henri de Lubac* (Paris, 1963), vol. I, 235–46.
[41] Wingren, *Man and the incarnation*, 187.

every kind of punishment. Since God's good things are without end, their loss is eternal, just as those who are wilfully blinded are forever excluded from light (Jn 3:18–21) (5.27.2).

Those on the left of the great judge are sent into eternal fire, for they have deprived themselves of all good (2 Thess. 2:10–12) (5.28.1, 2). Those on the right have been joined by communion with the son of God and are restored to the divine likeness and presence. There is one son who perfected his father's will, confirmed and incorporated his handiwork, by descending to contain the creature which his hands had moulded. While the son descends, 'on the other hand, the creature should contain the word and ascend to him, passing beyond the angels to be made after the image and likeness of God' (5.36.3).

Man's story runs from beginning to end without a break, but the end is not smooth. In communion with God, man does not slip imperceptibly into divinity. He was moulded at the beginning by the hands of God, by the son and the spirit in accordance with the image and likeness of God. On the basis of his choice and obedience, he is, at the judgement, thrown away as chaff or gathered in as wheat. The wheat must be broken up, ground fine, moistened by the patience of the word of God and exposed to fire so that it may be fit for a king's banquet. Tribulation is necessary for those who are saved. One of our men (the martyr Ignatius), says Irenaeus, longed to be ground into fine flour that he might become the pure bread of God (Ignatius, *Epistula ad Romanos* 4) (5.28.4).

6.6.5 ANTICHRIST AND CHILIASM[42]

Another key player in the drama of salvation has yet to appear. Antichrist recapitulates in his own person all mixed wickedness due to the antediluvian apostasy of angels (5.29.2). His name is symbolised by the number 666; but his identity remains uncertain until he comes, for many names (for example, *ΕΥΑΝΘΑΣ*, *ΛΑΤΕΙΝΟΣ*, *ΤΕΙΤΑΝ*) would qualify numerically (5.30.3). After laying all things waste he will reign from the temple of Jerusalem

---

[42] See the useful article: C. R. Smith, 'Chiliasm and recapitulation in the theology of Irenaeus', *VigChr* 48 (1994), 313–31.

for three and a half years; then the lord will come from heaven. The Antichrist and his followers will be sent into the lake of fire while the righteous enter their promised rest and inherit that kingdom where many shall come from the East and the West to sit down with Abraham, Isaac and Jacob (5.30.4).

What is the point of chiliasm, of the earthly kingdom after resurrection? There are at least two reasons, one which looks forward and the other which looks back. Prospectively, the resurrection of the just into an earthly kingdom marks a transition into incorruption where those who shall be worthy will be gradually accustomed to partake of the divine nature. Retrospectively, they receive a reward for passing the trials of their former lives. It is right that in that very creation in which they were tested by labours and manifold suffering, they should receive the reward of their afflictions. 'For God is rich in all things and all things are his' (5.32.1). His bounty is evident in the exuberance of natural things in this kingdom. John told the elders that the vines would have ten thousand branches, the branches would have ten thousand twigs, the twigs would have ten thousand shoots and the shoots would have ten thousand clusters and the clusters would have ten thousand grapes and every grape would yield at least twenty-five amphorae of wine. All crops would perform similarly. Animals would have so much to eat that they would not prey on one another and would submit to man in perfect obedience, eating the food which God intended for them. There shall be no strife between wolves and lambs or lions and oxen in the perfect peace of the lord's holy mountain. 'For if that animal, the lion, then feeds upon straw, of what quality must the wheat itself be whose straw shall serve as suitable food for lions?' (5.33.4). The whole creation shall grow and increase through an abundance of water (5.34.2). The righteous shall reign in the bountiful earth, growing ever stronger by the sight of the lord (5.35.1).

Resurrection prepares for incorruption, and discipline leads through the times of the kingdom to the glory of the father in the city of God. As John foretold (Rev. 21:5–6), this is the truth of the matter (5.35.2).

Irenaeus' eschatology is not an embarrassing postscript but a necessary consequence of a creator God who so surrounds all things (*concludens omnia*) and loves his creature that he becomes incarnate to restore its failings. That restoration completed, Christ inaugurates for ever the renewal of all creation. The restoration of human lives, which is the present concern of the church, will be complete in a restored universe. The inauguration of a new humanity is fed by the hope of final glory.

Splendid as inauguration sounds, it presents the most difficult problem among all Irenaeus' concepts. The epiphany of the church is presented without spot. Yet strife with evil is not over and battles in this field are still fought and lost. Gnosticism offered a way out of this dilemma through the illusion of instant perfection. Paul found the same perfectionism at Corinth among those who reigned with Christ. Irenaeus offers the same solution as did Paul, who began with the cross and ended with the final resurrection. The cross is never left behind but remains the grace by which weakness is made strong. Hope for a final victory when Christ hands over the kingdom to the father springs from the presence and victory of the cross. So the church lives between cross and parousia and gains life from these sources. Its splendour shines through the world where in every place it offers a pure sacrifice of thanksgiving. The medium of truth as well as grace, it guards the deposit of the gospel through its succession from the apostles. For it is a pilgrim people on its way from cross to parousia.

Many interpreters of Irenaeus have been embarrassed by his millenarianism. Surely evil has been overthrown in Christ, they say, and such fantasy is inappropriate. Yet Irenaeus and his readers today are part of a world where evil is alive and well. They need an apocalypse of the consummation, when God shall dwell with his people, when death, sorrow and evil shall be no more. The recapitulation of all things in Christ is the pledge of their hope.

Recapitulation and consummation are thus tied together, and the whole of recapitulation is oriented to the end when creation and redemption fulfil their purpose. 'By His becoming man the bond between God and man has been made unbreakable, and man has free access to the source from which his life flows.'[43]

---

[43] Wingren, *Man and the incarnation*, 213. Cf. 4.34.6.

PART IV

Participation

Participation in God runs through truth (logic), glory (aesthetics), life (anthropology) and goodness (ethics).

We share in his truth by faith, reason (ch. 7) and the world of prophetic images (ch. 8). We achieve beauty in the light of his glory (ch. 9). We share in his life by the breath and enlivening spirit which he gives (ch. 10). We participate in his goodness by loving those who wrong us (ch. 11).

> The word of God, our Lord Jesus Christ, through his immeasurable love, became what we are, that he might bring us to be even what he is himself.   (5 pref.)

> Into this paradise of life, the lord has introduced those who obey his preaching, 'summing up in himself all things in heaven and earth'; but the things in heaven are spiritual, while those on earth are of the human order. Therefore these things he summed up in himself, by uniting man to the spirit and causing the spirit to dwell in man, by himself becoming the head the spirit and giving the spirit to be head of man. For it is by this spirit we see, hear and speak.   (5.20.2)

> In a flash, at a trumpet crash,
> I am all at once what Christ is, since he is what I am, and
> This Jack, joke, poor potsherd, patch, matchwood, immortal
>   diamond,
> Is immortal diamond.
>   Gerard Manley Hopkins, 'That nature is a Heraclitean fire and of the comfort of the Resurrection'

CHAPTER 7

Logic and the rule of truth: participation in truth

Participation is the fourth of Irenaeus' key concepts. Because it is the human response to the divine Intellect, economy and recapitulation, it takes many forms. However complex the first three concepts are, they are unitive and point to one God, one saving economy, one Christ. Participation is distributive, God's sharing out of his truth, beauty, life and goodness to humans in many ways. We begin with participation in truth as it comes through the rule of truth and logic.

The canon and criterion of truth was central to Hellenistic philosophy. Christians designated the central elements of their faith, gospel or kerygma with the same term.[1] The rule had been handed down from God through the apostles. Human conversion marked a turning to divine truth from inadequate or false conceptions. Heresy issued a challenge for it claimed a source which was above argument; yet heretics showed all the weaknesses of sophists. Against them Irenaeus used the weapons of parody and pastiche, not for personal ridicule but to show that their opinions were inappropriate. His final test of truth was *consonantia*, a harmony which was both logical and aesthetic.

7.1 CANON AND CRITERION

The authority of the rule or canon in Irenaeus reflects a philosophical use. *Kanon* and *kriterion* dominated Hellenistic philosophy,

---

[1] A more extended discussion is found in my article, 'Reason and the rule of faith in the second century AD', in *The making of orthodoxy*, FS for H. Chadwick, ed. Rowan Williams (Cambridge, 1989), 40–61. See also my *The emergence of Christian theology*, 243–7.

as the tests for Stoics and Epicureans of objective truth. Epicurus devoted a work to the theory of criteria,[2] and in a fragment *On Nature*[3] insisted that no valid inquiry is possible without a canon which tests opinions.

A *kanon* is a rod to be used for testing straightness or measuring length. It must be straight.[4] Lucretius wrote of how a bad rule produced catastrophic results.[5] Three terms (rule, square, plummet line)[6] explain the importance of the canon for good foundations.[7] Without a canon there is no security.[8]

Since a canon is a means of judging, legal terms enter philosophical use.[9] The verdict goes to the sensations whose testimony is sure.[10] The *Canonice* of Epicurus is for Seneca concerned with judgement and rule.[11] The credibility of a rule which could decide all questions was ridiculed by Cicero.[12]

Stoicism with its grasping impressions[13] offered a straightforward test of truth.[14] Epictetus talks about preconceptions, common notions, canon.[15] The rule distinguishes truth and reason from appearance. In Epicurus and the Stoics there are several ways of understanding canon and criteria.[16] The persistence of the theme is evident in Alcinous, who begins his account of Platonic dialectic with a discussion of the criterion which he finds in the forms (*Didask.* 4).

---

[2] Περὶ κριτηρίου ἤ κανών. Listed tenth among the books of Epicurus, D. L. (Diogenes Laertius) 10.27.

[3] Arrighetti fr. (34) 31, 11–27.

[4] Aristotle, *De Anima* 1.411a5.

[5] *De rerum natura* 4.513–21.

[6] *regula, norma, libella*.

[7] Cf. H. Oppel, 'KANON', *Ph*, supplementary vol. 30 (1937), 80–1.

[8] *De rerum natura* 4.505–6.

[9] Sextus Empiricus, *adv. Math.* 7.211–16.

[10] D.L. 10.32.

[11] *Epistulae morales* 89.11.

[12] *De finibus* 1.63.

[13] Sextus Empiricus, *adv. Math.* 7.248, 426.

[14] Striker, 'Κριτήριον τῆς ἀληθείας', NAWG.PH 1 (1974), 90.

[15] *Dissertationes* 1.28.28–30; 2.11.13–25; 2.20.21; 3.3.14–15; 4.12.12; *Enchiridion* 1.5. *prolepseis, koinai ennoiai, kanon*.

[16] Striker, 'Κριτήριον', 102.

7.2 COMPENDIUM OF TRUTH

Irenaeus was the first Christian theologian to speak precisely of the rule of truth or rule of faith.[17] The rule is the original true and firm knowledge of God which the church preserves. With the truth itself and God's open testimony, there is no excuse for scattering into strange opinions and questions and rejecting firm and true knowledge (2.28.1). Strictly, the compact body (*somation/corpusculum*) of truth (1.9.4), in contrast to the fabrication (*plasma/figmentum*) of the heretics, refers not to a written source but to absolute truth. There is only one message of salvation and one reconciliation wrought in Christ incarnate.[18]

The rule joins bible and tradition. Irenaeus can refer to individual texts or books of the bible as a 'rule of truth'. His *Demonstration of the apostolic preaching* proved the truth of the kerygma from prophetic oracles, which disclosed the divine Intellect. 'The content of scripture and the rule of truth really coincide.'[19] This is what the apostles handed down (3.4.1). The 'content of the tradition' (1.10.2) is universal.

The rule joins faith and life. Dogmatic truth evolved from a way of life, an experience of God, which belonged to the distinctive tradition of the Wisdom literature. Irenaeus' divine Intellect was the God of the Wisdom literature.[20] This God, as intellect and love, surrounds all things and penetrates by his wisdom into hidden places (Wisd. 7:2–27). In response to such a universal wisdom, kerygma and faith are maintained by the universal church believing 'as if she had but one soul, and one and the same heart', proclaiming and teaching as if she had one mouth. In different languages, the

---

[17] A. Faivre, 'Irénée, premier théologien "systématique"?', *RevSR* 65 (1991), 11–32. Generally the latter term was preferred for internal use within the church and the former term was preferred when argument was directed to heretics.

[18] This follows B. Hägglund, 'Die Bedeutung der "regula fidei" als Grundlage theologischer Aussagen', *StTh* 12 (1958), 1–44. Hägglund acknowledges his debt to J. Kunze, *Glaubensregel, Heilige Schrift und Taufbekenntnis* (Leipzig, 1899).

[19] Hägglund, 'Die Bedeutung der "regula fidei" ', 12. The rule of truth is the saving revelation of father, son and holy spirit in creation and redemption; to this truth, baptismal confession, scripture and preaching bear witness.

[20] 'De la sorte, la foi implique aussi un rapport au monde comme possibilité de vie pour l'homme, malgré les expériences qui peuvent témoigner du contraire. Il en découle des façons spécifiques d'user du monde', D. Lührmann, 'Confesser sa foi à l'époque apostolique', *RThPh* 117 (1985), 110.

tradition is the same. Just as the sun, God's creature, is the same throughout the world, so the light of the 'preaching of the truth gives light to all who will to know the truth' (1.10.2). Without written sources, barbarians believe, 'and because of faith are very wise indeed' (3.4.2). From baptism onwards, the believer retains 'the rule of truth unchangeable in his heart' (1.9.4). The universal truth is summed up in a rule. Brevity is a distinctive quality of Christian truth. In contrast to the long-windedness of the law, God gave in Christ a short word[21] which summed up all that was needed. He was salvation in summary.[22]

7.3 CHARISMA AND TRUTH

Bishops have a certain gift of truth. The charisma of the spirit works in all true believers to give understanding of doctrine (4.33; 5.20.2). Bishops have no unique gift of truth but an assured, reliable commission to teach.[23] 'Not only their ethical disposition and the succession, but also the spirit who already "perfected" the apostles and since then is active in the church, equips them to hand on the truth intact.'[24] The charismatic activity of the spirit embraces the church (3.24.1) and any office is a means through which he works. However, an office which hands on the word displays this gift decisively, and must be exalted in face of Gnostic detractors, for only in the church are the true 'pneumatics' to be found (4.33.1–7).

To complete his argument, Irenaeus moves from the question of truth to apostolic tradition (3 pref.).[25] After Book 2 of *Against heresies* he deepens his argument, turning to rule (Book 3) and charisma (Book 4). Apostolicity is supported by episcopal succession of bishops and charisma of truth. Certainty is linked with the truth of

---

[21] *Dem.* 87 supports brevity in the 'short word' of Isaiah 10:22–3 with Matthew 6:7; 27:37–8; Romans 9:28; 13:10.

[22] 3.18.1. For the seven formulae of the rule in this work, see Benoit, *Saint Irénée, introduction*, 209–16, and the conclusion 'L'unité demeure sa note fondamentale; elle est comme Dieu, le Christ, l'Evangile, la Tradition et la foi, une et toujours la même.'

[23] N. Brox, 'Charisma veritatis certum (zu Irenäus adv. haer. IV 26, 2)', *ZKG* 75 (1964), 331.

[24] Ibid.

[25] Faivre, 'Irénée, premier théologien "systematique"?'

the tradition 'the *veritas* is the *charisma*',[26] and not with presbyteral infallibility.[27]

The divine origin of the rule gave it authority. Irenaeus had no doubt that the rule had come from God, through the economy of law, prophets, Christ, apostles and church.[28] The prophetic truth of one God came to the heathen through the creation, for the world reveals its maker. To Christians it came as apostolic tradition (2.9.1), where those who heard the apostles would hear the lord and those who reject the apostles would reject him (3 pref.). Rule, tradition and gospel coincide. Receiving perfect knowledge from the spirit, the apostles 'departed to the end of the earth, preaching the glad tidings of the good things from God to us, and proclaiming the peace of heaven to men, who indeed do all equally and individually possess the gospel of God' (3.1.1). After preaching, the apostles handed down their message in written form.

Bishops succeeded the apostles in the scattered churches, to hand down the truth which apostles had passed on. No secrets were withheld from their successors (3.3.1). It would be tedious to list all the successions, so Irenaeus selects the church of Rome. From Peter and Paul the succession came to Linus, Anacletus[29] and Clement, who declared in a letter the tradition of one creator God who spoke to Abraham, Moses and the prophets, and is the father of the lord Jesus Christ. This letter proves the identity of the tradition, which is now held by Eleutherus as the twelfth in succession:

By this order and by this same succession the tradition of the church from the apostles and the preaching of the truth have come down to us. This is the most complete proof that there is one and the same life-giving faith

---

[26] 'This is the only interpretation which makes sense of the passage' — H. von Campenhausen, *Ecclesiastical authority and spiritual power* ET (London, 1969), 172. Yves Congar began from the same view ('the objective deposit of truth') but later allowed the possibility that the phrase could include a charism for action or function. The vast literature includes contributions from E. Molland, K. Müller, N. Brox, L. Ligier, A. Ehrhardt, R. M. Grant, J. N. D. Kelly and H. von Campenhausen.

[27] See J. D. Quinn, '"Charisma veritatis certum": Irenaeus, *Adversus haereses* 4.26.2,' *TS* 39 (1978), 520–25. The phrase drew the attention of First and Second Vatican Councils in their accounts of episcopal and papal magisterium.

[28] Irenaeus lists witnesses to revelation nineteen times. H. Holstein, 'Les témoins de la révélation d'après saint Irénée', *RSR* 41 (1953), 410–20.

[29] Abramowski points out that Anencletus (Anacletus) is the ἀνέγκλητος of Titus 1:7; 'Irenaeus, Adv.haer. III 3,2', *JThS* 28 (1977), 104.

which has been conserved in the church from the apostles and handed on in truth. (3.3.3)

Tradition, apostles and church all depend on Christ who is the truth and who, as David says, has sprung triumphantly from the earth. There can be no falsehood or deceit in him (3.5.1). He never aimed to please his hearers but spoke the truth as he alone knew it. He is the one 'I am' to whom Moses and Elijah looked.

The canon of truth is the fullness of right belief found in scripture and tradition.[30] As for Clement of Alexandria, so for Irenaeus, it is the true gnosis (4.33.8).[31] Irenaeus presents the rationality of the divine economy as credible, acceptable and consistent, in contrast to the irrationality of the Gnostic accounts which are incredible, fatuous, impossible and inconsistent.[32] Irenaeus attacks the Gnostics because they do not have an order and rule. They are Cynics in their indifference yet boast of Jesus as teacher, while ignoring his hostility to evil in any form.[33]

An influential study designates the church as the fundamental reality for truth,[34] the body of which the different doctrines are members (1.8.1), the formula for the interpretation of scripture, and the source of doctrine.[35] The rule is relevant to baptism, because a narrative or exposition (*narratio* or *exegesis*) which declares God's love for man from creation to resurrection is part of the baptismal liturgy.[36]

The *Demonstration* points to four tests of authenticity. The rule is a simple expression of baptismal faith in the church's proclamation. Apostolicity defines the tradition which governs the church and its scriptures. Progressive revelation joins the old testament with the new testament in a continuity which displays the saving plan of God. Finally the autonomy and free choice of every human must be affirmed.[37]

---

[30] Brox, *Offenbarung, Gnosis und gnostischer Mythos*, 105 6.

[31] Ibid., 166.

[32] Ibid., 202.

[33] *qui non solum a malis operibus avertit suos discipulos, sed etiam a sermonibus et cogitationibus* (2.32.2). Brox, ibid., 456.

[34] D. van den Eynde, *Les normes de l'enseignement chrétien, dans la littérature patristique des trois premiers siècles* (Gembloux and Paris, 1933).

[35] Ibid., 291.

[36] See V. Grossi, 'Regula veritatis e narratio battesimale in sant'Ireneo', *Aug* 12 (1972), 437 63.

[37] E. Peretto, 'Criteri di orthodossia e di eresia nella Epideixis di Ireneo', *Aug* 25 (1985), 666.

7.4 WHAT DOES THE RULE SAY?

The content of the rule of faith is entirely theological, without the ethical and ecclesiastical content, which it held in Paul and to which it returned in Augustine. The rule may be found in binary or ternary form. Binary examples are 'faith in one God the father almighty and in one Lord Jesus Christ the son of God' (1.3.6), and 'one God maker of heaven and earth, announced by the law and the prophets, and one Christ son of God' (3.1.2). The best example of ternary form comes at the beginning of Irenaeus' exposition in 1.10.1 and is worth quoting in full:

For the church, although scattered through the whole world to the ends of the earth, has received from the apostles and their disciples that faith which is in one God, the father almighty, 'who has made the heavens, earth, sea and all that is in them' and in one Jesus Christ, the son of God who was incarnate for our salvation, and in the holy spirit who has proclaimed by the prophets the economies of God and the advent, the birth from a virgin, the passion, the resurrection from the dead and the bodily ascent into heaven of our beloved lord Jesus Christ, and his coming from heaven in the father's glory to 'sum up all things' and to raise up all the flesh of the whole human race, so that to Christ Jesus our lord, God, saviour and king, according to the will of the unseen father 'every knee should bow, of things in heaven, in earth and under the earth, and every tongue should confess' him, and that he should judge all justly, sending into eternal fire the spirits of evil, the angels who have transgressed and turned apostate, and the wicked, unjust, lawless and blasphemous among men, but granting the grace of life incorruptible and conferring the gift of eternal glory on the righteous, holy, who have kept his commands and persevered in his love, some from the beginning and some since conversion.

Certain points emerge. There is no distinction between the kerygma, the faith and the tradition of the church. The rule is much longer than the canons of philosophers and needs a demonstration from the prophets who saw the mind of God. The canon of truth lay for Platonists in the world of forms and that world was replaced by Justin and Irenaeus with the divine economies as seen by the prophets.[38]

---

[38] This will be the starting point for chapter 8.

7.5   CONVERSION, RECOVERY OF REASON,
FAITH AND SIGHT

Conversion[39] is a move into a new way of thought, indeed a recovery of reason in the rational soul. God, we have seen, is universal intellect and light (2.28.4), who alone possesses perfect knowledge (2.28.8). By his goodness, we have partial knowledge (4.20.4) which at the last day will become complete (2.28.7).[40] Our wisdom consists in not going beyond what ought to be known (Rom. 12:3), and those who go beyond this knowledge are ejected from the paradise of life (5.20.2). To deny the one creator of the world is an outrage (2.28.2). He has given us a mind which is sound, sure, pious and devoted to the love of truth, and this mind should be exercised to gain knowledge (2.27.1).

Irenaeus, we have seen,[41] begins from a universal human awareness of God which falls short of what scripture gives. To learn about God we need God's help, through his word (4.5.1). The Jews departed from God, because they thought wrongly that God could be known apart from his son and word (4.7.4). While creation and prophets point to the son and to the father (4.6.6), knowledge of God comes only from God and from him who is the way, the truth and the life (4.7.3). Saving knowledge brings perfection (3.12.5), is rational (5.8.2; 4.4.3) and linked with the presence of the holy spirit (5.8.2).

7.6.1   HERESY

The notion of 'heresy' (*haeresis*) has an interesting history.[42] In philosophy and medicine it was used from the second century BC to designate schools of thought.[43] For Philo, the disciples of

---

39   '"L'epistrophé" è anzitutto un mutamento del modo di pensare e di porsi di fronte al Dio dell'Antico e del Nuovo Testamento. È un ritorno ad una tradizione accettata nella sua globalità nel passato e caratteristica del cristianesimo, ma che è stata abbandonata', E. Peretto, 'La conversione in Ireneo di Lione. Ambiti semantici', *Aug* 27 (1987), 163.

40   See above, chapter 3.

41   See above, chapter 2.

42   A comprehensive account is found in Alain Le Boulluec, *La notion d'hérésie dans la littérature grecque IIe–IIIe siècles*, 2 vols. (Paris, 1985). Further, I am indebted to the convenient survey and original contribution of D. T. Runia, 'Philo of Alexandria and the Greek *haeresis*-model', *VigChr* 53 (1999), 117–47.

43   J. Glucker, *Antiochus and the late Academy* (Göttingen, 1978).

the prophet Moses seek knowledge of the God-who-is and follow a life-giving philosophy.[44] Philo saw himself as a mere expositor of Moses, to whom he added 'nothing of his own'.[45] Later biblical writers (Jeremiah, Psalms, Proverbs) are disciples of Moses. Divisions are found in Josephus who designates distinct groups (Pharisees, Sadducees, Essenes) as sects (*haireseis*),[46] compares them with Greek schools, and tells how, when young, he tested them before he became a Pharisee. Philo does not speak of schools within Judaism, for the philosophy of Moses is undivided and those who deny it are apostates to be punished by death.

As the earliest surviving Christian anti-heretical work, Irenaeus' treatise is important. While the detail of heresy overwhelms, Irenaeus offers a clear impression through his metaphors. Heresy is a false imitation of a precious stone (1 pref. 2), a wild beast which can only be destroyed if it is brought into the open (1.31.4), and a deadly mixture of lime and water which masquerades as milk (3.17.4).

Irenaeus uses the word 'heresy' rarely. The adjective 'all' (*omnis*) is applied to half the examples because he wants to present a sum of heresy over against a sum of truth. He also speaks of heretics rather than heresy, prefers the plural to the singular (forty-nine instances to two), and uses the word more in the last three books than in the first two (forty-three to nine). His concern is less with the distant founders than with the present disciples.[47]

While the succession of heresies could be traced back to Simon Magus (1.23.2; 1.27.4; 2 pref.), this did not imply continuity of ideas. Indeed there was constant separation and division (1.22.2). Blindness to truth brought heretics to divide perpetually so that their ideas were scattered in every direction (5.20.1). Heresy emerges as an antitype to the church, marked by multiplicity in contrast to the unity of the true faith.[48] It is only accessible because Valentinianism recapitulates all heresies so that objections against it apply to other forms of error (4 pref. 2). Diversity remains and

[44] *De specialibus legibus* 1.345.
[45] *De opificio mundi* 5: οἴκοθεν μὲν οὐδέν.
[46] See *Bellum Judaicum* 2.119–66, *Antiquitates Judaicae* 13.171–3 and 18.11–22.
[47] A. Benoit, 'Irénée et l'hérésie, les conceptions hérésiologiques de l'évêque de Lyon', *Aug* 20 (1980), 59.
[48] Ibid., 61.

increases through elements borrowed from poets and philosophers, with an endless variety of permutations and combinations.

It is therefore remarkable that four common denials run through the variety of heretical opinion:[49]

(i) while there is an appeal to scripture enlarged by their own Gospels (3.11.7) and an appeal to oral traditions of their own (3.2.1), there is a denial of old testament scripture;

(ii) the saving God is not the creator (1.22.1) and the prophets are not part of the divine economy (4.34.1);

(iii) the word of God did not become flesh (3.11.3). In the eucharist they offer bread and wine to a god other than the creator, who must be outraged by gifts which are foreign to him (4.18.4);

(iv) the flesh cannot be saved into incorruption (5.2.2).

The busy mastermind behind heresy is the devil, who offers pride, falsehood and seduction.[50] Pride, which rebels against the creator God, has an intellectual element, for it is ignorance of man and of God (5.2.3). To this ignorance is joined a claim to total knowledge (*universa agnitio*) (2.28.9), including knowledge of God's ineffable mysteries (2.28.6). Irenaeus ridicules the claim and the content of these portentous mysteries (1 pref. 2).[51] God alone has perfect knowledge and we place ourselves in peril if we search for another God above him (2.28.8). Pride also puts the heretic above the law which God has given, and loses the ability to distinguish between good and evil (1.25.4). Secondly, falsehood is disguised by heretics, to make it appear true (1 pref.). Satan inspires them to mutilate scripture in order to conceal falsehood. (5.21.2). Thirdly, just as Satan seduced Eve (1.30.7), so heretics seduce the simple (1 pref.; 3.15.2). The sophistry of heretics destroys the faithful (1 pref.; 3.17.4) as the devil, a liar and murderer from the beginning, has always done (Jn 8:44) (5.22.2). Finally, heretics claim a secret tradition (following Matt. 11:25–7) of hidden knowledge (1.20.3) and this gives them the right, they believe, to twist everything their own way and to follow no rule. The apostles, they claim, could only speak to the Jews of the Jewish God and no one could learn

---

[49] Ibid., 63–6.

[50] Y. de Andía, 'L'hérésie et sa réfutation selon Irénée de Lyon', *Aug* 25 (1985), 624–30.

[51] *portentuosissima et altissima mysteria*. See also 3.15.2; 2.2.2; 4 pref. 4.

anything new from them. Every heretic has his own rule which means that there is no rule at all (3.12.6).

7.6.2 CONTEMPORARY ASSESSMENT

In the twentieth century some sympathy for Gnosticism grew out of modernism with its flight from authority and rejection of tradition.[52] For modernism, heretics had to be right because tradition was wrong. A recent study of heresy by Alain Le Boulluec aims at a fair assessment. It begins from a perceived contrast between the Nag Hammadi writings and the Gnostic heresies depicted by Irenaeus and Epiphanius,[53] which suggests that Irenaeus and others provided a biased, inaccurate account.[54] It then turns to Michel Foucault, who has investigated the decision of the socially powerful to separate the normal from the abnormal, to define rationality on the basis of this exclusion,[55] asking for a 'cut-off' point and disowning all that is beyond it.[56]

The value of Le Boulluec's treatment is beyond question. There is space merely to indicate four points where Foucault hampers Le Boulluec's investigation. First, powerplay is not important for Irenaeus; the second century had different centres of power for 'orthodox' and heretic alike.[57] Argument was far more important. Secondly, Justin introduced the notion of heresy after his journey through philosophical schools. His rejection of these schools was based on their rational inadequacy, not on their social power, for he finishes up with the least powerful (Christian) school. Thirdly, the conflict of Irenaeus with Gnostics is not a species within an established genus of heretical controversy; it is an historical phenomenon in its own right.[58] Fourthly, according to Altendorf, Bauer

---

[52] Jeffrey Stout, *The flight from authority. Religion, morality, and the quest for autonomy* (Notre Dame, 1981), 2–3.

[53] Le Boulluec, *La notion d'hérésie*, I, 7.

[54] Ibid.: 'apercevant les procédés d'un travestissement polémique'. Others have been struck by the lack of such contrast and the fairness of Irenaeus' presentation. Arbitration between these two verdicts would be lengthy and inconclusive.

[55] Ibid.

[56] Ibid.

[57] See H. D. Altendorf, 'Zum Stichwort: Rechtgläubigkeit und Ketzerei im ältesten Christentum', *ZKG* 80 (1969), 61–74.

[58] Ibid., 74.

introduced an inappropriate schema: unbelief, right belief and false belief; he further spoke of 'orthodoxy' as a successful movement based on Rome, putting forward, says his critic, the fruits of his 'lively and constructive imagination which played on the argument from silence'. [59] Much of what Bauer wrote is useful; but it simplifies complex evidence. As ever, the fourth century, with the accounts of Eusebius and Epiphanius, gives little help in understanding the second century, when Marcionites saw themselves as church reformers and Valentinians as church members who had achieved deeper understanding. Conflict between groups used every weapon to hand and was agonistic like all polemic in the ancient world. [60]

Social theory must give way to history of ideas, for it cannot explain two things: why Irenaeus' arguments against Gnosticism are also put forward by Plotinus, who could not have known or cared less about Christian power struggles; and why Irenaeus is so blatantly eirenic about the East–West power struggle on the Quartodeciman question and so militant against Gnostic ideas. Only a concern for truth rather than power will answer these puzzles. Irenaeus prays that heretics will not remain in the pit they have dug, becuse he loves them more effectively than they think they love themselves (3.25.7).

Social theory obscures the great value of the heretical confrontation, where Gnostic theosophy forced Christian theology into philosophical method and values as a means of defence and exposition. It was not enough for Irenaeus and others to set the rule of faith beside the Gnostic myth and make an unreasoned choice; an effort was needed to show that the renewing of the mind to which Paul had pointed (Rom. 12:2) was able to produce, from scripture and the rule of faith, a synthesis of greater coherence than the alternatives.

7.6.3 SOPHISTRY

Christian thought entered the European tradition in the midst of a long-established conflict between philosophy and sophistry,

---

[59] Ibid., 64: 'die lebhaft mit dem *argumentum ex silentio* spielende konstruktive Phantasie des Verfassers'.
[60] Ibid., 68.

a conflict which had blurred edges but which remained relevant to culture.[61] From Plato onwards philosophers attacked sophists, alleging their danger to lie in their proximity to the matter of philosophy (argument) and their alienation from its aim (pursuit of truth). This truth was foreign to heresy.[62] 'Strangers to the truth, they inevitably wallow in all error, which tosses them to and fro, so that they think differently on the same subjects at different times, never holding a stable opinion, wishing rather to be sophists of words than to be disciples of the truth' (3.24.2). Abandoning the one rock, they build on sand which contains many stones. Their trivialities run from number games to the hypostatisation of the aeons out of mere words. Their hair-splitting distinction between justice and goodness is incompatible with Plato's cosmology and with his metaphysic (3.25.5). As false, deceiving sophists, they call the creator 'father' and 'God' only as a matter of courtesy and, divining falsehoods (*falsa divinantes*), they dispute every point of God's economy with baseless trivia (4.1).

The sophists of words fabricate the aeons and diversify the meanings of 'God' and 'father'. As depraved grammarians they deny any difference between direct and oblique meanings. Their fabrication of names promotes a ridiculous fantasy (1.11.4). Following a lust for disagreement (5.13.2), they invent fables to support their teachings. Irenaeus quotes their myth of Pandora which describes the generation of the Saviour, the common fruit of all the aeons (1.2.6; 1.3.1), and shows it to be inappropriate (4.2.2). As sophists of Pandora, heretics try to be more perfect than the perfect, but end by showing themselves to be mindless (1.11.1). They are melons (1.11.4), or even squashes, which lack salt.[63]

Sophists seek without finding. In their account of the man who was blind from birth, they accuse the divine logos of ignorance and blindness. This is the way in which they plumb the mysteries of the deep things of God (1 Cor. 2:10). Philo had developed similar criticisms. Cain symbolises the sophist who provokes the simple

---

[61] See Brian Vickers, *In defence of rhetoric* (Oxford, 1988), especially 83–147, 'Plato's attack on rhetoric', and 148–213, 'Territorial disputes: philosophy versus rhetoric'.

[62] The following paragraphs are indebted at many points to Le Boulluec, *La notion d'hérésie*. I, 136–54.

[63] Ibid., 139. Here Irenaeus follows the style of Timon of Phlius who ridiculed other philosophers in his 'Silloi'. See below, 7.7, Parody.

Abel (*Quod deterius potiori insidiari solet* 1). The tower of Babel, built by the descendants of Cain, represents the skills of sophists (*De posteritate Caini* 53). The sorcerers cannot stand against Moses because the law declares that all sophistry is overcome by wisdom (*De migratione Abrahami* 85). Philosophy is the royal alternative to the sophistic way (*De posteritate Caini* 101), which deforms the beauty of wisdom (*Quod omnis probus liber sit* 4).

Sophistry was linked with greed for financial gain (1.4.3) or with sexual lust (1.13.3). Plato had criticised the financial rewards required by sophists (*Hippias Major* 281b; *Cratylus* 384b), and Lucian made the same attack in his 'Philosophers for sale'.[64] Heretics could be excluded simply on the grounds of their financial gain, for the lord had said, 'Freely you have received, Freely give!' (Matt. 10:8). Irenaeus contrasts the liberality of the church with the greed of Gnostic teachers (2.31.3; 2.32.4). New testament writers condemn those who are greedy for shameful gain (Titus 1:7) and the *Didache* requires that a prophet who asks for money should not be heard (11.3).

Irenaeus sets the simplicity of Christian faith against the pretensions of the Gnostics (2.26.1). The sacrifice of the church is marked by simple thankfulness to the God of creation (4.18.4), while heretics offer nothing because they have no gratitude to their creator (4.18.4). The simplicity of Christians follows one God and looks to the salvation of the whole man, body and soul (5.20.1). Heretics smash this simplicity into pieces and lose its meaning (5.20.1). The simplicity of the faithful (5.20.2) established the unity of the church where the simplicity of the dove overthrows the wisdom of the serpent, as Mary conquered where Eve failed (5.19.1).

7.7   PARODY: THEOLOGY FOR HORSES

For Xenophanes, the god who is divine Intellect renders anthropomorphic gods ridiculous and worthy of parody. The same move is made by Irenaeus who reflects Xenophanes' (KRS, 167–9) use of

---

[64] For an amusing example of sophistry see Lucian's 'Philosophers for sale', 22 (LS, 37 L; *SVF* 2.287). You know your own father, but if a veiled human is placed in front of you, you must admit you do not know who it is. Since that person happens to be your father, you do not know your own father.

parody to make a perceptive critique of anthropomorphic Gnosticism. In each case the concern is to display logical and aesthetic inadequacy rather than personal comedy.

Xenophanes states his objections:[65]

But mortals consider that the gods are born, and that they have clothes and speech and bodies like their own.

The Ethiopians say that their gods are snub-nosed and black, the Thracians that theirs have light blue eyes and red hair.

But if cattle and horses or lions had hands, or were able to draw with their hands and do the works that men can do, horses would draw the forms of the gods like horses, and cattle like cattle, and they would make their bodies such as they each had themselves.

Irenaeus' chief complaint against the Gnostics was that they used words without logical control. They gave no reasons for their procession of aeons (1.11) and anyone could make up a list of names which had no reality. He uses parody to make this point, and writes of the Valentinian account of creation as follows:

And what comes from all this? It is no trivial tragedy, indeed, which each of these men pompously expounds, each in a different way, from which passion and from which element, each essence derived its origin ... For who would not spend his entire fortune to learn that from the tears of the aeon involved in passion, the seas, springs, rivers and all liquid substances derived their origin, that the light came from her smile, and the corporeal elements of the world came from her perplexity and anguish? However I want to make my contribution to their 'fructification' ... For, since all tears have the same property, it is unlikely that from them come both salt and fresh waters. It is more probable that some are from her tears and some from her perspiration. Furthermore since there exist also in the world waters which are hot and acrid, it is for you to understand what she did to produce them and from what part of her they came. Such are some consequences of their hypothesis. (1.4.4)

Later, he provides a second piece of parody:

With this monad coexists a power of the same essence which I in turn call the one, Hen. These powers then, Monotes, Henotes, Monas and Hen, produced the rest of the aeons ... There exists a certain pro-principle, kingly and beyond all thought, prosubstantial and proprocylindrical, which I call the 'Pumpkin' and along with this gourd exists a power which I call in turn 'Superemptiness'. This Pumpkin and this Superemptiness, being one, have emitted, without emitting, a fruit entirely visible, edible and sweet which is properly termed 'Cucumber'. With this Cucumber coexists a power of the same substance which I further name 'Melon'. These powers, namely, Pumpkin, Superemptiness, Cucumber and Melon, have emitted the remaining conglomeration of the delirious melons of Valentinus. For if one may apply common language to the primary tetrad and if anyone may assign names as he wishes, what is to stop us from using these names since they are more credible, in common use and known to all? (1.11.4)[66]

Irenaeus compares Gnostic exegesis with a pastiche concocted from widely separate lines of Homer (1.9.4). Genuine lines of Homer are used to tell a story Homer never told. Irenaeus quotes:[67]

> Having thus spoken, he sent forth from his house with deep sobs
> The noble Hercules, doer of mighty deeds,
> Eurystheus, son of Sthenelus, descended from Perseus,
> Charging him to bring from Erebus the dog of gloomy Pluto.
> And he went like a mountain lion confident of strength,
> Swiftly through the city, while all his friends followed,
> Both maidens, and youths, and much-enduring old men
> Mourning for him bitterly as if he went to death;
> But Hermes and the blue-eyed Athena conducted him
> For she knew in her heart how her brother laboured with grief. [68]

Pastiche, a common form of parody, has been defined as 'an imitation or forgery which consists of a number of motives taken from genuine works by any one artist recombined in such a way as to give the impression of being an independent original creation by that artist'.[69] The 'double-coding' of a pastiche need not have

---

[66] The Greek names of the vegetables are confirmed by Epiphanius, *Panarion haer.* 32. The cucumber and melon could have come from Numbers 11:5. See A. Rousseau and L. Doutreleau, *Irénée de Lyon. Contre les hérésies*. 1, *SC* 263, (Paris, 1979), 235.

[67] J. Daniélou sees in this cento an allegorical concoction of Valentinus. See *Gospel message*, 82–4. However, see also R. L. Wilken, 'The Homeric cento in Irenaeus' "Against Heresies"', 1.9.4', *VigChr* 21 (1967), 25–33.

[68] *Odyssey* 10.76 and 21.26; *Iliad* 19.123 and 8.368; *Od.* 6.130; *Il.* 24.327; *Od.* 11.38; *Il.* 24.328; *Od.* 11.626; *Il.* 2.409. The concoction is attributed to Irenaeus who either composed or borrowed it, by H. Ziegler, *Irenäus der Bischof von Lyon* (Berlin, 1871), 17.

[69] P. Murray and L. Murray, *A dictionary of art and artists* (Harmondsworth, 1960), 234. Cited in M. Rose, *Parody: ancient, modern and post-modern* (Cambridge, 1993), 72.

a comic effect. A pastiche can refer to any composition which joins different sources or to a picture where different styles are stuck together.[70] Quotation or 'cross-reading' joins disparate texts, 'so that either their concealed identity or lack of identity will be brought into the foreground with some comic effect'.[71]

By the fourth century BC, *parodia* ($\pi\alpha\rho\omega\delta\iota\alpha$) was used to describe comic imitation and transformation of an epic verse work, and was later extended to cover other forms of comic quotation or imitation. Quintilian defined *parodia* as 'a name drawn from songs sung in imitation of others, but employed by an abuse of language to designate imitation in verse or prose' and his definition led others almost to identify parody with imitation. $\Pi\alpha\rho\alpha\tau\rho\alpha\gamma\omega\delta\epsilon\omega$ meant 'to tell in a false tragic style' and was used of comic 'meta-fictional' as well as of satirical writing, practised notably by Aristophanes.

In modern times, the use of parody has shown a positive purpose. Parody as writing which is meta-fictional, critical and comic, is exemplified in *Don Quixote* and *Tristam Shandy*. It has been defined as parasitical, burlesque, double-planed and double voiced. Foucault hailed *Don Quixote* as the first modern work of literature because in it the certainty of similitude is replaced by difference and a laughter that shatters.

7.8 CONSONANTIA

The rule of faith and the scriptures are of little value in the pursuit of truth without the principle of *consonantia* which covers both logical coherence and aesthetic fitness. In its rhetorical use[72] the verb *consono* moves beyond its original Pythagorean sense of harmony to the general principle of coherence. Yet it retains the presumption of opposites from which a harmony is formed.[73] This means that the Heraclitean strain which runs through the rest of Irenaeus' thought is present in his epistemology as in his metaphysics. The heretics

---

[70] Ibid., 73 4.
[71] Ibid., 77.
[72] Quintilian, *Inst.* 9.3.45, 73, 77.
[73] Philolaos had written $\dot{\alpha}\rho\mu\text{ovía}$ $\delta\dot{\epsilon}$ $\pi\dot{\alpha}\nu\tau\omega\nu$ $\dot{\epsilon}\xi$ $\dot{\epsilon}\nu\alpha\nu\tau\dot{\iota}\omega\nu$ $\gamma\dot{\iota}\nu\epsilon\tau\alpha\iota$ $\ddot{\epsilon}\sigma\tau\iota$ $\gamma\dot{\alpha}\rho$ $\dot{\alpha}\rho\mu\text{ovía}$ $\pi\text{o}\lambda\nu\mu\iota\gamma\dot{\epsilon}\omega\nu$ $\ddot{\epsilon}\nu\omega\sigma\iota\varsigma$ $\kappa\alpha\dot{\iota}$ $\delta\dot{\iota}\chi\alpha$ $\phi\rho\text{o}\nu\epsilon\dot{\text{o}}\nu\tau\omega\nu$ $\sigma\nu\mu\phi\rho\dot{\text{o}}\nu\eta\sigma\iota\varsigma$, DK, n. 44, B 10, cited in de Andía, 'L'hérésie et sa refutation', 640 3, who takes coherence as a harmonic, and not a logical principle. In Irenaeus it has to be both.

wrongly look to letters, syllables and numbers to find their way to God. But in his creation God has fitted, arranged and prepared things into forms which have meaning and are never accidental. 'For the rule does not emerge from numbers, but numbers from a rule, and God does not derive his being from created things but created things derive their being from God' (2.25.1). Everything is seen to spring from the one God, when attention is paid to coherence. For the whole displays the judgement, goodness, wisdom and skill of the creator, while the individual parts are contradictory and discordant (2.25.2). Logic and aesthetics go together, as the variety of notes produces the harmony of the whole (2.25.2). Man the creature must humbly learn from the maker of all things, both the dispensations of things and the order of knowledge (2.25.3, 4).

Coherence comes from love, the higher knowledge which gives wholeness to life, leads to the knowledge of Christ crucified, holds the system of truth together and points a way through the mysteries of providence. As with creation and providence, so with the understanding of scripture, harmony (*consonantia*) is decisive. Love of truth and daily study will lead to the body of truth, where members fit together without clashing. There is enough that is clear and unequivocal in scripture to provide a basis for knowledge. In the ambiguity of parables everyone has a different opinion (2.27.1). When the rule of faith is followed, the scriptures fit together, unequivocally and harmoniously; for this is what the plain parts of scripture indicate. There is no hope for those who abandon what is certain, to build on sand instead of rock (2.27.2, 3). When we follow the rule 'all scripture which has been given to us by God will be found harmonious . . . through the polyphony of texts one harmonious melody will resound in us, praising with hymns the God who has made all things'.[74] Knowledge and praise are joined by the rule of faith (2.28.3).

Consonantia of the four Gospels and the four living creatures (3.11.8), of the preaching of Paul and the testimony of Luke (3.13.3), and of the different testaments (3.12.12), confirms the rule of truth. Indeed harmony of salvation (*consonantia salutis*) marks the whole activity of God whose spirit speaks with the sound of many waters

---

[74] *omnis scriptura a Deo nobis data consonans nobis invenietur . . . et per dictionum multas voces consonantem melodiam in nobis sentiet, laudantem hymnis Deum qui fecit omnia.*

(4.14.2) (Rev. 1:15), and the proclamation of the church which has one mouth (1.10.2). Worship is also '*consonans*' with the rule. Faith in incarnation is confirmed by the eucharist. 'For our opinion is consonant with the eucharist and the eucharist on its part confirms our opinion' (4.18.5).

In this chapter we have seen how faith and Pauline 'love which rejoices in truth' mark the beginning of participation in Christ. For the rule of faith indicates how the divine wisdom and the charisma of truth may be shared. The truth is the charisma and conversion recovers reason and grants vision. Socratic love of truth rejects the emptiness of heresy and parody displays the need for the *consonantia* in which love and truth unite.

CHAPTER 8

Scripture as mind and will of God: participation in truth

We have seen that the rule and apostolic preaching look to scripture for reciprocal demonstration. The bible is the highest source of truth because the prophets were inspired of God. Their visions take the place of Platonic forms and depict the mind and will of God. Just as Alcinous found the criterion of truth in the world of forms rather than in a formula of one line, so the Christian rule of faith expands to a brief statement of scriptural claims behind which lies the universe of biblical imagery. Prophecy moves from future reference to present reality as illuminated by a rebirth of biblical images. These images unite the bible as the divine source of truth in which the believer participates.

Irenaeus provides the first clear evidence of a Christian bible, although his 'new testament' is not yet a document (4.9.1). He has a central concern for right use of the scripture (5.20.2) and is commonly contrasted with the Alexandrian fathers because he gave less importance to the place of philosophy and stayed closer to biblical categories. *Against heresies* draws extensively on new testament writings, mainly Gospels and Acts of the Apostles, then the sayings of the lord and the Epistles of Paul.[1]

Much has been written on Irenaeus' interpretation of the bible.[2] He extols the bible as the measure of truth (2.28.1), perfect because from God (2.28.2), ordered and coherent (1.8.1), and never without meaning (4.31.1). What God has so entrusted to men must be

---

[1] It is difficult to count quotations because they fade into allusions. Benoit finds 629 references to the old testament and 1065 to the new testament. A. Benoit, 'Ecriture et tradition chez S. Irénée', *RHPhR* 40 (1960), 33.

[2] The literature is enormous. The fine work of J. Hoh, *Die Lehre des hl. Irenäus über das Neue Testament* (Münster, 1919) is a comprehensive introduction.

handled with integrity, zeal and daily practice (2.27.1). Of course many questions must be left in the hands of God (2.28.6), for our knowledge is partial (2.28.7). We should despise the bible if its truths were universally accessible, for we are lesser and more recent than the word and spirit of God (2.28.2). In face of the tension between plain simplicity and divine mystery, Irenaeus turns always to the rule of faith as a criterion. Above all, the agreement of the Gospels and the prophets points to the supreme event of incarnation from which the life of humanity is renewed (4.34.1).[3]

8.1.1   FROM PROPHETIC SPIRIT TO ETERNAL WORD

Irenaeus finds in the prophets the economies of the divine Intellect. All is recapitulated in Christ and the linear extent in time gives way to synchronisation. Prophecy and fulfilment still affirm the historical dimension, but the recapitulation of all things brings simultaneity to the noetic world. Irenaeus' argument begins with Justin Martyr's linking of prophetic images and Platonic forms.

Prophetic spirit

The authority of scripture depends on a metaphysic of mind[4] which is common to Justin and Irenaeus. The movement of their argument is first set out in Justin's account of word, spirit and mind of God.[5] More than a third of Justin's *Apology* is taken up with prophecies which have been fulfilled or are yet to be fulfilled. These are the unique source of truth. Even Plato learned from the prophets, who are 'our teachers' (*1 apol.* 59). Philosophers and poets are able to talk about the immortality of the soul and other doctrines because they received hints from the prophets which have led them to the truth. The prophetic spirit will be seen to fulfil exactly the same function as the spermatic logos except that the seeds are traced to scripture rather than to human minds (*1 apol.* 44).

---

[3] For a lucid exposition of these problems see N. Brox, 'Die biblische Hermeneutik des Irenäus', *ZAC* 2 (1998), 26–48.

[4] See above, chapter 2.

[5] See my, 'Word, Spirit and Geistmetaphysik', *Prudentia*, Supplement (1985), 64–6.

Word of God

Justin explains the anthropomorphic language of the old testament in terms of the cosmic Intellect whom Irenaeus knows as God. When we read that God shut Noah into the ark or came down to see the tower which the sons of men had built, we must not think that the unbegotten God himself came down or went up anywhere.

> [He] stays in his own place, wherever that is, being quick to see and quick to hear, having neither eyes nor ears but being of indescribable might; he sees all things, and knows all things and none of us escapes his observation; and he is not moved or confined to a spot in the whole world, for he existed before the world was made. (*dial.* 127)

On the contrary, it was Christ, as lord, God, son of God, who appeared in power as man, angel and burning bush. He is not an impersonal force, emanating like light from the father and sinking when the father wills; rather he is numerically distinct like a fire kindled from another fire, distinct but not depriving the original fire in any way (*dial.* 128).

Scripture tells that God begat before he began creating things; his only begotten was a 'certain rational power', whom the holy spirit calls with many names, such as glory of the lord, son, wisdom, angel, God, lord, and logos. God's begetting was like our thinking and speaking,

> for when we produce some logos we beget the logos, not by cutting it off so that there is less logos left in us, when we produce it, just as we see also happening in the case of fire, which is not made less when it has kindled another fire but stays the same, and what has been kindled by it is seen to exist by itself, not taking away from that which kindled it. (*dial.* 61)

This word declares that those who prefer opinion to truth cannot find success, and whatever the word forbids, no sensible man will choose. (*1 apol.* 12). Truth belongs to Jesus Christ because he is God's proper son, his word, first-begotten and power (*1 apol.* 23). The word of God is his son; as angel he tells us what we should know; as apostle he is sent to declare whatever is revealed.

Word of men

Logos, in Socrates, condemned the demons and was in turn condemned (*1 apol.* 5). Long before Christ came there was hostility from those who lived without reason towards those who lived with reason (*1 apol.* 46). The difference between the reality of the logos and the dim perception of human minds is explained by the Platonic theme of participation. The logos himself is the reality in which direct participation is possible. Other ways to the truth are indirect through seeds and imitations (*2 apol.* 13). This idea is plainly of Stoic origin but it has become part of a Platonic metaphysic which allows for degrees of truth and reality.

Words of Jesus

The highest truth is that of the word himself; he spoke with terseness and brevity, unlike the sophists, for 'his word was the power of God' (*1 apol.* 14). Justin's conversion leads him to the prophets and the writings of the friends of Christ. Here he finds the only safe and useful philosophy. The source is the words of the saviour, for these have a terrible power of their own, and bring dread to those who stray from the right path, but rest to those who faithfully practise them (*dial.* 8).

Every argument of Justin's *Dialogue with Trypho* depends on the acceptance of scripture as 'the mind and will of God' (*dial.* 68). His attitude to scripture is one of acceptance of a complex world of divine truth. Historical exegesis would be inadequate within this world of word and spirit (*dial.* 85), and history has to coexist with simultaneity.

Isaiah speaks of all the powers resting on the one who is to come. This means that all the powers came together on Jesus and ceased to be found elsewhere. Just as Jesus is the whole logos so the fullness of the spirit is in him and not elsewhere (*dial.* 88).

8.1.2 MIND AND WILL OF GOD

Justin's argument from prophecy, therefore, does not begin from Jesus as the fulfilment of predictions, but from the prophets who saw the economies of the divine mind which were joined to ordinary events. The logos is active within the events and realities of the world.[6] This link of the particular and the universal is consistent with the omnipresence of God who is Intellect. Prophetic vision is linked with particular events but is not reducible to them.

Justin's account of prophecy in the *Dialogue* presents the key idea. Here he shows that the prophets saw the divine, noetic reality and that their writings are therefore the only sound basis for philosophy. 'Philosophy is the knowledge of being and truth, the recognition, and the well-being which is the reward of this knowledge and wisdom' (*dial.* 3.4).

Plato, Justin continues, says that the eye of the mind sees being when it is pure and clear. The mind is the cause of all intellectual objects (*noeta*) and does not see with physical sight. Being is beyond all substance, unspeakable and inexplicable, alone good. The vision of that which is comes suddenly to souls of a good nature because of their affinity and their desire to see the good (*dial.* 4.1).

The bridge between philosophy and the bible is that intellect sees intellectual objects and the prophets can cross this bridge. Justin insists that the prophets alone had this vision of the God-who-is and of the higher reality which depends upon him. They saw and declared the truth without respect or fear of men. They spoke only what they saw and heard and were able to give knowledge of the beginning and the end of things. This knowledge is the proper knowledge of philosophy. The prophets, because of their direct perception of reality, needed no proofs for what they said. They were witnesses of the truth, above demonstration and worthy of belief.

The truth of prophecy does not depend upon its fulfilment in the coming of Christ, but on its original source in the vision of those who saw directly and accurately what every philosopher needs to see. Justin can speak of the events of the Gospels as the true philosophy because they reflect the prophetic vision of reality. This fusion of Plato and the bible is fundamental to the understanding of the economy of salvation and the nature of scripture in both Justin and Irenaeus.

The words of the prophets are continued in the words of the lord wherein Justin finds a terrible power. Irenaeus similarly affirms an

---

[6] Justin includes Heraclitus in his 'Christians before Christ'.

identity between the prophetic account of the divine mind and the words of him who was himself the divine mind and word. Truth depends on this direct access to the mind of God, as for Plato it depended on access to the forms and the form of the good. The words of the prophets and the words of Christ are joined by the projection back of Christ into the thought of the ancient prophets. Abraham rejoiced to see the day of Christ, for Christ was his contemporary.

8.1.3 PROPHECY: FROM PREDICTION TO PRESENCE

Yet the predictive element of prophecy remained. Irenaeus, like Justin, sees the prophetic vision of the divine economies as a noetic apprehension of the divine mind. As for Philo, Moses looked on the divine forms when alone on the mountain. The law was given to lead the people from the secondary to the primary, from types to reality, from temporal to eternal, carnal to spiritual, and earthly to heavenly things. For forty days, Moses contemplated the divine logoi and paradigms, spiritual images, and types of things to come (4.14.3). At the same time, the future reference of prophecy remained important for two reasons. First, the fulfilment of prophecy in Christ demonstrated the truth of the apostolic preaching. What is for men impossible has been foretold by prophets so that when it happens faith is strengthened and doubt removed (*dem.* 42). The son of God has in his own person confirmed the truth of all prophecies about him, to provide for our faith a foundation which cannot be shaken (*dem.* 98).[7] Secondly, the time between prefiguration and realisation was a time of preparation and education.[8] The divine economy made sense of the time between prophecy and fulfilment 'for through types they learned to fear God and to persevere in his service' (4.14.3). Through patriarchs and prophets Christ trained his inheritance in advance for the economies of God (4.21.3).

These two predictive factors went together. The preparation and education meant that the new testament message was not new; the only novelty was its fulfilment in Christ. The Ethiopian eunuch

---

[7] See Daniélou, *Gospel message*, 226–34.
[8] R. M. Grant, *The letter and the spirit* (London, 1967), 83.

(Acts 8:26–40) had been catechised in advance by the prophets concerning God and salvation. He needed to be told only that the son of God had come.

Prediction, however, gave way to presence. Prophecy, for Irenaeus, defends the oneness of God and the one plan of salvation against Gnostic divisions.[9] All God's economies are united in one economy, which leads to Christ. The central moves are clear in one passage (4.20.1–8). The invisible and incomprehensible God created all things by his word and wisdom. To his incarnate word all things were subjected and by the same word God was known. He gave a *charisma* to the prophets so that they could foretell his incarnation and announce future events, declaring that God would be known according to his love. Prophetic vision participates in the incarnate God and God's love permits us to see him.

Prophetic vision saw and made known the continuous activity of God, father, son and holy spirit, as the word constantly gave knowledge of the father through the changing economies. Through the spirit, God was seen prophetically, through the son he was seen adoptively, and through the father he will be seen paternally in the kingdom of heaven (4.20.5). The vision of God is participation in God, and only within the glory of God can man live (4.20.5).[10] The tension between the immensity (*magnitudo*) and love (*dilectio*) of God requires that the divine economy be gradual.

This leads to the important move from continuity to simultaneity. How this happens is shown in a recent study, which concludes by setting out the chief ideas of Irenaeus on prophecy.[11] In the end we may define prophecy backwards rather than forwards as 'one of God's saving economies by which, through the mediation of the spirit, the same God brings the reality and the results of the incarnation of the word back to the time of the Old Testament'.[12]

This careful and extended study reveals the move from prediction to presence, from economy to recapitulation. Economies

---

[9] This section draws supporting argument from Rodrigo Polanco Fermandois, *El concepto de profecía en la teología de san Ireneo* (Madrid, 1999).

[10] Ibid., 32.

[11] Ibid., 384–97.

[12] Ibid., 393.

remain, but their temporal extent becomes secondary. Irenaeus reaches the noetic world of Justin without Plato's help. Recapitulation brings all the economies together. The temporal dimension is not lost but included among all things in Christ.

The prophets had presented the mind of God to Justin because they saw the *noeta*. After Irenaeus, the insistence that the object of Christian hope was also the ultimate being which philosophers sought – the fusing of the ontological and eschatological – turned scripture into a higher world which gave the believer understanding of the world in which he lived.[13] The world of prophecy takes the place of the world of Plato's forms in a way far more effective than did the aeons of Valentinus.

The synchronisation of gospel, prophets and law was to have enormous consequences. A whole culture found the imagery of the old testament (when joined to the new) a source of inspiration in every aspect of its life. Yet the world of the spirit was never divorced from history, and the particularity of Jesus remained the key to all understanding.

8.1.4 A REBIRTH OF IMAGES

Irenaeus fits prophetic images into Platonic epistemology, only after they are transformed in the life and teaching of Jesus. Christianity is 'a visible rebirth of images'.[14] Jesus took and transformed a treasury of images and handed them on to his followers who were further led by the spirit into all truth. To understand the movement requires intellectual effort but mere calculative reason is not enough. 'The images must live again in the mind, with the life of the image of Christ: that is inspiration.'[15]

Nowhere is this renaissance more evident than in the Apocalypse, where John sees the slaughtered lamb and gives himself over to the images which flow from it. This is the open heaven. This is the answer to the ineffability of what God has done in overturning time to make the future present and eternity close at hand. It is

[13] For an extended treatment of this development, see G. Apostolopoulou, *Die Dialektik bei Klemens von Alexandria* (Frankfurt, 1977).
[14] A. Farrer, *A rebirth of images* (London, 1949), 14.
[15] Ibid., 17.

communicated, in John as in Irenaeus, 'by playing simultaneously on several registers'.[16]

Irenaeus follows Justin in identifying these images with the mind of God or the world of forms.[17] They are joined by logic and aesthetic, but imagery is more powerful than logic. It has an amazing multiplicity of reference. It presents reality with all the interconnections. 'There is a current and exceedingly stupid doctrine that symbol evokes emotion, and exact prose states reality. Nothing could be further from the truth: exact prose abstracts from reality, symbol presents it. And for that very reason, symbols have some of the many-sidedness of wild nature.'[18]

Prophetic imagery draws another world by using pictures of this world: the lamb, the candle sticks, light, lost sheep and shepherd, virgin mother, child and suffering man. Truth and beauty appear in physical shape. We are on the way to incarnation.

We cannot find our way by discursive reason alone. Only the mind of God understands our world. So we must share the mind of Christ, live in the bible and look to the open heaven and the solid earth, from which our bodies were made. Just as Plato's dialectic disappears into the form of the good, so Irenaeus' images submit to the glory of the cross. 'Jesus Christ clothed himself in all the images of messianic promise, and in living them out, crucified them: but the crucified reality is better than the figures of prophecy. This is very God and life eternal, whereby the children of God are delivered from idols.'[19]

8.2.1 THE UNITY AND TRUTH OF SCRIPTURE

The truth is derived from scripture and handed down in the church. 'This, beloved, is the preaching of the truth and this is the manner

---

[16] 'en jouant simultanément sur plusieurs registres et en disant par exemple que Dieu bouleverse le temps: le futur peut être présent et l'éternité à portée de la main', P. Prigent, *L'Apocalypse de saint Jean* (Paris, 1981), 379.

[17] Justin compares his proofs from prophecy to mathematics; they are like saying that two plus two equals four.

[18] Farrer, *A rebirth*, 20.

[19] A. Farrer, 'An English appreciation', in *Kerygma and myth*, ed. H. W. Bartsch (London, 1953), 223.

of our redemption, and this is the way of life which the prophets proclaimed and Christ established, the apostles delivered and the church in all the world hands on to her children' (*dem.* 98). The *Demonstration* is a proof from scripture. The apostolic preaching is shown to be true because it declares what scripture has foretold. Irenaeus knows of no other proof which can stand beside the testimony of the scriptures. The source of truth is the holy spirit who spoke through the prophets the word of truth. Scripture is validated by the rule of faith which is threefold, declaring father, son and holy spirit (*dem.* 6).

Scripture can be misused. The heretics have taken the parables, the prophets and the words of the apostle, and dismembered them to destroy their coherence and truth. 'They disregard the order and the connection of the scriptures' (1.8.1). They gain their views from other sources than the scriptures and then twist logic to justify them. The heretics perversely select the parables and every other obscure section of scripture. They produce, according to their own inclination, a false interpretation of a parable, and they set up their opposed systems on the basis of such interpretation. The proper subject of parbles is the one God who is father of all, and to desert him removes any possibility of understanding what parables are about (2.27).

Knowledge has limits. There will be parts of scripture which we cannot understand. When we cannot find an explanation we should not look for another God besides the one true God (2.28.2). Because we trust in the one true God and love him forever, we may hope to receive always more and more from God. Scripture, which God has given us, will finally be to us completely consistent and the parables will fit together with those passages which are perfectly plain (2.28.3).

Christ, the treasure hidden in the field, is the content of scripture. If anyone reads the scriptures carefully he will find an account of Christ and his new calling (4.26.1). The prophets prefigured all things of Christ, being joined as members of Christ, each one setting out some part of the truth. He is the whole body whose many members are prefigured by the prophets (4.33.10).

8.2.2 SCRIPTURE AND TRADITION

There is nothing unsure about the writings of the apostles and their testimony. There are those who saw John face to face and who can confirm the number (666) which is found in the 'most approved and ancient copies' of the Apocalypse (5.30.1). Written and oral testimony stand side by side. Polycarp spoke with John and others who were eye-witnesses of the word of life and all the words which he heard were in harmony with the scriptures (*H.E.* 5.20).

The relation between scripture and tradition[20] in Irenaeus has been commonly misunderstood: tradition has been seen as a saving supplement which rescues the inadequacy of scripture. However, while Irenaeus speaks of scripture five times in the *Demonstration*, and 160 times in *Against heresies* he refers to tradition in the technical sense only twenty-one times (noun) and forty-one times (verb). His citations of old testament (629) and of new testament (1065) dominate *Against heresies*. Looking at the *Demonstration*, R. Seeberg identified Irenaeus as the first great representative of biblicism.[21] Nothing could be further from the truth, because Irenaeus analyses the theology of scripture more rigorously than most theologians. His own theology blends Paul and John in a way which is beyond proof-texts and based on a profound understanding.

Gnostics reject scripture, which they claim to be corrupt, and prefer the living voice of tradition. Irenaeus defends the truth of scripture but also sets out true tradition in contrast to that of the Gnostics. His account of tradition is therefore a second line of defence which points back to the truth of scripture. The scriptures provide the basis, and tradition is appealed to as confirmation of the scripture. We should 'take refuge in the church, be reared in her bosom and be nourished by the scriptures of the lord' (5.20.2).[22]

8.2.3 PRINCIPLES OF INTERPRETATION

Irenaeus works with eight principles of scriptural interpretation.

---

[20] Benoit, 'Ecriture et tradition chez Saint Irénée', 32–43.

[21] *Dogmengeschichte* (Leipzig, 1922), 1, 365.

[22] *Confugere autem ad ecclesiam et in eius sinu educari et dominicis scripturis enutriri.*

(i) *Rule of truth.* The rule of truth is the starting point. Behind it stands the one canon and content of the faith written on the heart by the holy spirit.[23]

(ii) *Logical coherence and aesthetic fitness.* 'It is fitting, it is possible, therefore it is' is a constant refrain for Irenaeus.[24] Logical coherence is also a constant test. The rejection of the logically incoherent and the aesthetically inappropriate go together: the heretics have taken a mosaic and jumbled the pieces around to produce a fox instead of a king; they have made a new poem by juggling remote lines into a new order (1.8).[25] Scripture is an unbroken unity, he argues, for the word of God is found in all parts of scripture (4.35.2).[26] Coherence is the final text because coherence is the way God works. The exuberance of Irenaeus' exegesis goes beyond logical analysis. The poetic associations which spring from the lost axe of Elisha point to connections which only lively imagination can achieve. This comes for Irenaeus from 'chewing the cud' of scripture. Daily rumination for Christians as for Jews is part of exegesis (5.8.3).

(iii) *Fulfilment of prophecy and recapitulation.* Scripture shows the fulfilment in Christ of what the spirit foretold through the prophets. Christ sums up the purposes of God, and crowns the long dispensation of saving history. Recapitulation, we have seen, unites a wide range of concepts.

(iv) *Eschatology.* Irenaeus sees the victory of Christ continued in the kingdom of the son, who will reign for a thousand years on earth. All the wonders of chiliastic plenty will cover the earth.

---

[23] 1.9.4; 1.22.1; 2.27.1; 3.2.1; 3.11.1; 3.12.6; 3.15.1; 4.35.4; *dem.* 3.

[24] Hoh, *Die Lehre des hl. Irenäus*, 112.

[25] See above, 7.7, on parody.

[26] The Gnostics put forward a collection of narratives for which the principle of logical coherence was not seen to be relevant. Irenaeus, however, brought against them the principle of no contradiction, and he based this on the central thought of Platonic origin that God is the highest and all-embracing reality. There can be no other God beside God (2.1.2). Beyond God there can be no other reality, no strange God and no higher necessity. Everything depends upon the principle that God is all-embracing and all-powerful. There is nothing over which he does not rule and transcend. With this idea goes inevitably the principle of rationality, for without such a first principle there is no limit to thought. Unending worlds and gods will follow (2.1.4). Thinking must have clear limits and a clear orientation and these are lost when one goes in search of a god higher than God; Schwager, 'Der Gott des Alten Testaments', 294.

(v) *From the certain to the obscure.* How stupid it is to put on blinkers and begin from obscurities in order to find one's own private God (2.27.2)! When the bridegroom comes, the unprepared trafficker in obscurity, with his dim lamp and untrimmed wick, is excluded from the brightness of the wedding chamber. Since parables are obscure, no lover of truth will begin from them rather than from what is clear and certain. It is dangerous to abandon what is certain, indubitable and true (2.27.3).

(vi) *Moral integrity of interpreter.* Those who claim knowledge of the unspeakable mysteries, which not even God's son knew, are disqualified as irrationally puffed up (2.28.6).[27] Pride leads to falsehood (5.22.2). Those who desert the church drink from broken cisterns and filthy puddles (3.24.1). Alienated from truth, they think differently[28] at different times, and blaspheme their creator. Because they dishonour God, his light does not shine to them (3.24.2).

(vii) *History.* Irenaeus has a sense of historical context. For example, he writes of the tension between Jews and Gentiles (3.12.15; 4.24.1; 3.5.3), and of the identity of Paul's preaching to the Gentiles with the preaching of Peter to the Jews (3.13.1). Paul's message of freedom to the Gentiles (Gal. 2) is not neglected (3.13.3) and the solidarity of Luke and Paul is indicated by the 'we' passages (3.14.1). He notes the continuity between Jesus and Paul in their concern for the poor and lowly.

(viii) *Grammar.* Irenaeus readily argues points of grammar, claiming, for example, that 2 Corinthians 4:4 does not point to more than one God (3.7.1, 2).

Gnostics fail on every principle of exegesis. They do not hold to the rule of faith; they select arbitrarily (*eligentes*, 2 pref. 1), use other sources outside scripture (1.8.1), ignore context (1.8.2, 3), turn to what is obscure rather than what is certain and true (2.27.3) and explain the obscure by what is more obscure (2.10.1). They ignore important names when they can find no numerical relevance (2.24.1, 2; 1.14.4) and they personify key terms such as Sophia (1.8.4),

---

[27] See above, chapter 2.
[28] *aliter atque aliter.*

Aion (1.3.1), Stauros (1.3.5) and the members of the Ogdoad such as Pater, and Charis (1.1.1; 1.9.2).[29]

Their moral fibre is displayed as deficient, because of their pride (3.12.12) and intellectual arrogance (1.10.2, 3) which monstrously sets itself above God (2.26.1). Paul insists that our knowledge now is partial (1 Cor. 13:9) while Gnostics claim complete knowledge (2.28.9), when some questions should be left to God (2.28.3). Further, their sexual behaviour is spectacularly bad (4.26.3).

8.4 IMAGES OF THE ECONOMY: THE FOUR GOSPELS

Following his criterion of fitness and proportion, Irenaeus finds it impossible that the written Gospels should be more or fewer in number than they are (3.11.8).The world has four zones and the church is scattered throughout all the world. There are four winds which blow, so the church is made alive by the gospel and the spirit which exhales in four directions. The argument shows how literally Irenaeus took the unity of creation and redemption and of the noetic and physical worlds. The same word who made everything and who contains all things has given the gospel under four aspects. The world, which the word sustains by his creative power, displays on every side the fourfold sign of the cross which marks his triumph and his recapitulation.[30]

To annul the shape of the gospel (3.11.9: $\dot{\alpha}\theta\epsilon\tau o\hat{\upsilon}\nu\tau\epsilon\varsigma \ \tau\dot{\eta}\nu \ \dot{\iota}\delta\dot{\epsilon}\alpha\nu \ \tau o\hat{\upsilon} \ \epsilon\dot{\upsilon}\alpha\gamma\gamma\epsilon\lambda\dot{\iota}o\upsilon$) is to be vain, ignorant and audacious. It is wrong to represent the gospel as being in its aspects either more or fewer than four. The heretics, however, do not see this. Montanists look to John's Gospel, Marcion boasts that he has the one Gospel, although he has cut himself off from the gospel. But the worst people of all are the followers of Valentinus because they have put forward their own compositions as Gospels, and claim to have not fewer but more Gospels than there are. They even call a recent writing by the title 'The Gospel of Truth'. This writing does not agree with the Gospels and, if it is true, then what the apostles have handed down is not the gospel of truth. 'But', says Irenaeus,

---

[29] Irenaeus' point is that the meaning of these terms 'wisdom, aeon, cross, father, grace' has no relevance to Gnostic use.

[30] P. Ferlay, 'Irénée de Lyon exégète du quatrième évangile', *NRTh* 106 (1984), 227.

'I have proved through many arguments of great force that only those Gospels of the apostles are true and worthy of acceptance and that their number cannot be either increased or diminished. God always works things in proportion and proper arrangement and therefore the external or outward aspect of the gospel is ordered, arranged, harmonized' (3.11.9).

Irenaeus' reverence for scripture is joined to the metaphysic of mind which governs his account of God and the world. 'The creative word ($\tau\epsilon\chi\nu\iota\tau\eta s$ $\lambda\acute{o}\gamma os$) who sits upon the cherubim, holding ($\sigma\upsilon\nu\acute{e}\chi\omega\nu$) all things together, when he had appeared to men gave to us the tetramorphous gospel, which is held together ($\sigma\upsilon\nu\epsilon\chi\acute{o}\mu\epsilon\nu o\nu$) by the one Spirit' (3.11.8). The fourfold cherubim (not four-faced as Irenaeus claims)[31] had been joined by an earlier source to the living creatures of the Apocalypse (whom Irenaeus does not mention). Christ is enthroned between the lion, ox, man and eagle, which represent John, Luke, Matthew and Mark as '*images of the economy of the son of God*'.

John (lion) tells of the pre-eminent, effective and glorious genera-tion of him who was in the beginning God, who made all things, and who displays audacity. Luke (ox) is a priestly work, beginning with Zachariah offering sacrifice and telling of the fatted calf sacrificed for the returning prodigal. Matthew (man) displays the humanity and humility of one born as a man from the line of David and Abraham. Mark (eagle) points to the gift of the spirit as it com-mences with a reference to Isaiah and embodies the brevity and scope of prophetic utterance.

There remains one gospel message of Christ possessed of cosmic scope. This came to us through the apostles who first preached it and then wrote it down so that it would become the foundation of our faith (3.1.1). Fixed in writing, it guards against the heresies which the spirit had foreseen. Only the four Gospels are 'true and firm', for they are the one gospel which has come from the apostles (3.11.9; 3.5.1). The Gospel of Truth is rejected because it is recent and quite inconsistent with the Gospels of the apostles (3.11.9).

Well before the end of the second century codices containing the four Gospels were in use.[32] Irenaeus uses the Gospels together. In

---

[31] See discussion of T. C. Skeat, 'Irenaeus and the four-gospel canon', *NT* 34,2(1992), 198.
[32] G. N. Stanton, 'The fourfold Gospel', *NTS* 43 (1997), 329.

3.10.3, when discussing Luke, he uses John without indicating that he has switched; he weaves texts together, cites inexactly, adds oral traditions without distinguishing sources.[33] Unlike Justin, who also knows at least four 'memoirs' of the apostles, Irenaeus is interested in the different approaches of the four Gospels. There are four reasons why there should be four Gospels. The four Gospels provide 'solidity' in contrast to Gnostic ropes of sand. They also provide 'harmonious proportion';[34] the aesthetic unity of the Gospels (*bene compositam et bene compaginatam*) reflects the unity of the creation (*composita et apta*) (3.11.9). Further, in Irenaeus metaphors fructify and there is always need for plurality in language about God; the voice of the word is like the sound of many waters.[35] Finally, biblicism (one verse–one vote) was not yet a possibility, given the formative state of the canon; Irenaeus followed Paul (Rom. 10:5–13) in turning to the spirit rather than to the letter, and defining all thought about God christologically (3.18.2).[36]

The unity of revelation in scripture is further guaranteed by the identity (*unus et idem*) of the spirit who in the prophets announced and explained the coming of the lord and who in the apostles declared the fullness of the time of adoption (3.21.4). Irenaeus summarises his account of the universal word and spirit as manifest in scripture (4.33.15):

(a) the prophetic utterances cover a long series of scriptures;
(b) they are understood by the reader who is truly spiritual;[37]
(c) they display the entire work of the son of God;
(d) the unity of this work derives from one God, father, son and holy spirit, through knowledge always of the same God acknowledging always the same word of God (although he is only now manifest), acknowledging also always the same spirit of God (although he has been recently poured out in a new way);
(e) the spirit descends on the human race from creation of the world to its end;

---

[33] Ibid., 321.
[34] Like the Tetrapylon at Aphrodisias; ibid., 320.
[35] See above, 7.8, *Consonantia*.
[36] Käsemann, *Paulinische Perspektiven*, 237–85, ET *Perspectives on Paul*, 138–66. Käsemann gives unaware a similar exegesis to Irenaeus.
[37] For Origen, this means that inspiration must be twofold – of both writer and reader.

(f) from the spirit flows salvation for those who believe in God and follow his word.

Scripture belongs to the lord (*dominica*) (2.30.6; 2.35.4; 4.33.15; 5.20.2). He is the source of charisma to the prophets (4.20.4). Indeed the prophets were themselves members of Christ and prophesied as his members (4.33.10). Hence their words were spoken by both word and spirit of God (2.28.2). As far as the apostles were concerned, their link with Christ is obvious, since they were 'observers and ministers of the word of truth' (4 pref. 3; cf. Lk. 1:2). Yet the prophets also wrote the words of Christ. Commenting on John 5:46–7 – where Jesus declares. 'If you had believed Moses, you would have believed me' – Irenaeus claims that Christ could not have indicated more clearly that he had spoken words which Moses wrote. Further, if this is the case, there is no doubt that the words of the other prophets are his, a claim which Irenaeus has already made (4.2.3; 4.10.1).[38]

8.5.1   FORMATION OF THE CHRISTIAN BIBLE

God, the giver of all charismata (2.32.4), is the origin of all scripture, old and new, all of which, because it comes from him, may be called 'divine' (2.35.4). Irenaeus' account of the formation of the scriptures derives from the same theology as is evident in his account of God, the trinity and history. God's unity is unbroken and universal in scripture as in creation. 'How therefore did the scriptures testify of him unless they were from one and the same father?' (4.10.1). This holds of the present as of the past. Scriptures do not end with the prophets but include the apostolic writings, which take precedence over the works of the prophets: 'first the apostles, second the prophets, but all from the one and same God' (3.11.4).

We turn now to historical questions. Irenaeus tells us more than anyone about the beginning of the Christian bible. The new

---

[38] While J. Ochagavía (*Visible Patris Filius. A study of Irenaeus' teaching on revelation and tradition*, OrChrAn 171 (Rome, 1964)) believes Irenaeus goes beyond the Gospel text here, D. Farkasfalvy ('Theology of scripture in St Irenaeus', *RevBen* 78 (1968), 326) argues that Irenaeus 'uses a variant of Jn 5:47 that preserves the perfect parallelism between the act of faith with respect to Moses' writings and the words of Christ'. Farkasfalvy's article provides a useful background to the topic of the present chapter.

testament emerged against a background of theological disagreement over the difference between Jew and Christian. Marcion rejected both Mosaic law and creation and in this he was joined by
most Gnostics. They agreed that the God of the Jewish scriptures
could not be the father of Jesus Christ. The only way to hold on to
both Jewish and Christian scriptures was to believe 'that there was
a difference between the eras in which one and the same God had
acted, and to see in the old testament a stage (or various stages)
of that providential guidance of salvation-history which attained
its goal in Christ'.[39] In the face of the two tendencies, dominical
sayings were defined by the preface 'it is written' (Justin), or by
reference to those who had known the apostles (4.27.1), or to what
may be read in the Gospel (4.29.1).

The possibilities were to select a single Gospel (as Marcion did),
to produce a new Gospel from authentic elements, or to choose a
few Gospels and make them a unity. Irenaeus belongs to a church
which chose the final option and accepted a Four Gospel canon.
This acceptance was gradual and cannot be tied to a specific
time and place.[40] The contrast between Justin, who generally cites
old testament as scripture, and Irenaeus, who cites new testament
alongside and above old testament, is clear. The move of Irenaeus
is not the result of an ecclesiastical decision but of his own rational
acceptance of the rule of faith which embodies the new testament
message. For 'Irenaeus is not, like a later canonist, concerned with
formal safeguards for their own sake, but with the one substantial
truth of the Christian message, through which mankind receives
salvation.'[41]

Irenaeus has no ecclesiastical guarantee for the standing which
he gives to the new testament, nor does he argue from the general
category of scripture, transferring to the new testament the status
accorded to the old testament. He begins with the claim that gospel,
truth and the teaching of the son of God are to be found in what
the apostles preached and handed down in writings (3 pref.; 3.1.1).
The apostles have full knowledge of the truth and their writings
do not need to be cut back or supplemented. He offers historical

[39] H. von Campenhausen, *The formation of the Christian bible* (London, 1972), 166.
[40] C. F. D. Moule, *The birth of the New Testament* (London, 1972), 188.
[41] Von Campenhausen, *Christian bible*, 182.

argument for their authority and arranges them in order: first the teaching of the apostles (four Gospels, Acts), sayings of the lord, and the apostolic letters of Paul. Irenaeus grants Paul equal authority to that of the other apostles.

If Marcion first propounded a Christian canon of scripture, then Irenaeus' canon could be seen as a catholic response. Yet it was not a canon either in the exclusive sense of Marcion or in the later sense of a formal list. Irenaeus does not try to iron out inconsistencies as does Tertullian. His interest is not historical but theological, governed by 'a feeling for the essential and unitary: the one God, the one Christ, and the one salvation'.[42] Before Irenaeus, Justin had already won the victory for the old testament against the Gnostics through the concepts of one God and one economy of many epochs. After Irenaeus the church always looked to a bible with two testaments, the second of which controlled the first.

8.5.2 CANON OF SCRIPTURE

Irenaeus does not supply a list which anticipates fourth-century definitions of the canon, but his defence of the four Gospels, and his intensive use of John and Paul, represent an important stage of its development. Beyond the theological considerations already considered, what other factors produced the change from Justin's Memoirs to Irenaeus' four Gospels?[43] The rapidity of the change was due to the power of Gnostic exuberance rather than the threat of Marcionite restriction. Christians had indeed received 'an explosive revelation which required . . . the constitution of a canonical corpus . . . a group of writings with a fixed outline and a fully recognised normative function'.[44]

Can the canonical uncertainties of Irenaeus' time illuminate Christian existence as it lives by the tension between an historical figure of the past and the immediacy of a risen lord?[45] Four questions may be asked:

[42] Ibid., 206 7.
[43] Y-M. Blanchard, *Aux sources du canon, le témoignage d'Irénée* (Paris, 1993), 283: 'la rapidité de l'évolution' may need qualification, but there was 'une influence extérieure massive'.
[44] Ibid., 283. Irenaeus' canon was a response to the Gnostic lack of a canon, rather than to Marcion's limited canon.
[45] Ibid., 311.

(i) How did Gnostics regard the scriptures? Some disregarded scripture in their esoteric excursions. Neither their works nor those of their opponents can be restricted to exposition of identifiable texts.[46]

(ii) What part was played by harmonisations such as Tatian's *Diatessaron*? They were not concoctions based on the four Gospels but attempts to produce a Gospel at a later date. In response to heresy, Justin and Irenaeus harmonised the words of Jesus from the apostolic accounts; however, Tatian went further and produced his own account of the historic ministry of Jesus. His work was rejected by Irenaeus lest new Gospels proliferate, and the shape of the gospel was defined as four-fold. The theory that a Roman school produced harmonies of texts[47] fails because it presupposes that only a text could link the words of Jesus to second-century writers. On the contrary, the *Diatessaron* depends on a double reference to Christ through the living tradition of his words and the written records of scripture.

(iii) How are we to account for the different, indeed inverse, order of the Gospels (to which infancy narratives are a late addition) and the account of Justin (where infancy narratives take precedence)? Mark, the earliest Gospel, gains the least recognition in the second century. In Justin he is, like Paul, 'le grand absent'.[48] There seems no clear answer to this question.

(iv) What part did lectionaries and liturgy play? Liturgy and living recollection played a part during the period when two sources (Gospels and a collection of sayings) governed the life of the early church. The free oral tradition preceded the text and, as Irenaeus shows, continued alongside it.[49] Christianity never became purely the religion of a book.[50] For Irenaeus, Christ remains the subject who speaks a word rather than the object of a writing. The historical writing gives bodily stature to the voice, but does not replace it.

---

[46] Blanchard points out that Pagels wrongly assumes the contrary; ibid., 313.
[47] A. J. Bellinzoni, *The sayings of Jesus in the writings of Justin Martyr* (Leiden, 1967), 141.
[48] Blanchard, *Sources*, 319.
[49] Ibid., 323.
[50] An opinion which some have wrongly attributed to Irenaeus.

'On the one hand, the gradual acceptance of a canon of scripture indicates a radical difference between the historical Christian faith and the mythical language of the Gnostics. On the other hand, the creative spontaneity at work in the operation of the sayings of Jesus points to a living relation with the Risen One.'[51] The second century makes a permanent theological point: scripture must never be a dead letter but always a spoken language, which is ever new and fresh.[52]

There is a long transition between the second-century appearance of the new testament writings and their fourth-century reception in a formal canon.[53] The great achievement of Irenaeus is twofold: he organised the structure of scripture and he set out the apostolic tradition using both the sayings of the lord and the writings which were to be canonised.

8.6.1   TYPOLOGY AND TRUTH

'The exegesis of Irenaeus is of the greatest precision and density, worthy of scrupulous analysis.'[54] One principle of exegesis (according to the Presbyter) is that what appears scandalous in scripture should not be rejected, because God put it there and he has higher standards than we have. It should be seen as part of the total economy, and discerned as a type. This point was taken up by Origen, who claimed that God placed offensive material in the text of scripture so that readers would look beyond the literal to the spiritual sense.

A good example is the account of the incest of Lot and the entire salination of his wife (4.31). Irenaeus reverses their order

---

[51] 'D'une part, la mise en place progressive d'un Canon scripturaire marque la différence radicale entre la foi chrétienne historique et le discours mythique des systèmes gnostiques; d'autre part, la spontanéité créatrice à l'oeuvre dans l'effectuation des logia atteste une relation vivante au Ressuscité', Blanchard, *Sources*, 330.

[52] Ibid., 331: 'une langue, laquelle ne sera vivante que portée à la parole, dans la nouveauté et la liberté qui caractérisent tout acte d'énonciation'.

[53] The history of their reception is as important as the history of their redaction. Its complexity is great but cannot be overlooked; the early fathers are essential to the understanding of the new testament.

[54] A. Orbe, 'Los hechos de Lot, mujer e hijas vistos por San Ireneo', *Greg* 75 (1994) 63. Cf. 'Whatever may be his other gifts, he shows no special wisdom in the application of hermeneutical methods', F. W. Farrar, *History of Interpretation* (New York, 1886), 174 5.

because the meaning within the economy (i.e. under the rule of faith) gives priority to the incest and it is the more difficult and more illuminating episode. He does this despite the literal truth that the incest would not have taken place if Lot's wife were still alive. The inebriated innocence of Lot and the simple altruism of the daughters are stressed. The story relates the two churches (two daughters) to the one divine father (Lot) who can procreate children. Lot stands for the word who created the human race and then poured out on all the life-giving seed which is the spirit who remits sins and gives life.[55] When the seed or spirit of God was joined to flesh which God himself has made, the two churches produced from their own fathers living sons (Jew and Christian) to the living God.

Lot's wife also represented the church, the salt of the earth, with a plurality of meaning which only typology could contain. Corruptible flesh is replaced by a salt rock which endures for ages and provides a firm foundation for faith. Like Lot's wife, the church is left behind on earth (after her lord has ascended), and sends forth children of the one father, losing members but standing firm.

Typology[56] shows the logic of revelation, which moves from pattern to reality. Moses, for example, is told to make all things according to the type or pattern which he saw on the mountain; in this way he will move from temporal to eternal, from carnal to spiritual and from things earthly to heavenly (4.14.3). The movement is complex, proceeding vertically, upwards to heaven (*typum caelestium*), downwards to the church (*imagines eorum quae sunt in ecclesia*), and horizontally to the future (*prophetiam futurorum continens*) (4.32.2).

Horizontally, this means a move from prediction by patriarchs and prophets to description of the reality of Christ (4.25.3), but all takes place in one God. Since the subject of typology is the recapitulation of all things in Christ, there is no limit to the scope of its content. Inevitably, with such width, there is ambiguity and enigma. Christ is the treasure hidden in a field of types and parables, a complex of riddle and uncertainty (4.26.1). Yet, like the different

---

[55] See below, 10.3.
[56] The discussion of the remainder of this section is indebted to M. Simonetti, 'Per typica ad vera', *VetChr* 18 (1981), 357–82.

members of one body, prophecy is a unity, where 'all the prophets prefigured one thing. . . the work of Christ' (4.33.10). This gives to the world of types a global unity which Gnostics try to shatter.

The modern tendency to divide types from allegory does not find support in Irenaeus and Justin.[57] Indeed types have a vertical reference linking earthly and heavenly realities rather than the horizontal/temporal application which has often been given to them (4.19.1 and 4.32.2). In Irenaeus, typology becomes a generic term for all symbolic representation. It gives global relevance to the presence of Christ in scripture.[58] Sometimes it points beyond the incarnation to the eschaton, when the just will rise from the dead to reign in the earth (5.33.3). Whereas the Gnostic interpretation is unnatural and diverges from the rule of truth (1.9.4) and the tradition of the elders (4.26.2), the final achievement of Irenaeus is that he was the first church theologian to join systematically old testament and new testament through the world of typology.[59]

8.6.2   TYPOLOGY AND ECONOMY

The whole argument of Irenaeus in Book 4 of *Against heresies* rests on the words of the lord and the prophets, which are incompatible with Gnostic interpretations. The unity of Book 4 has been proved by a careful analysis of the literary structure.[60] The words of the lord are used to refute the Gnostic divisions between the old and new covenants.[61] Irenaeus begins with a proof from the clear words of the lord that there is one creator God who is the author of the two covenants. In the second part he proves that the old testament is a prophecy of the new and has prepared the faith of the church. The

---

[57] Nor can it be justified from patristic literature. 'Et le mot qui reste le plus fréquent, le plus constant, au moins dans la tradition latine, est *allegoria*', H. de Lubac, ' "Typologie" et "allégorisme" ', *RSR* 34 (1947), 187. See also the valuable account, F. M. Young, *Biblical exegesis and the formation of Christian culture* (Cambridge, 1997), part III, 119–212.

[58] Simonetti 'Per typica ad vera', 367.

[59] Ibid., 380.

[60] P. Bacq, *De l'ancienne à la nouvelle alliance selon S. Irénée. Unité du livre IV de l'Adversus haereses* (Paris, 1978).

[61] Book 4 has three parts:
   (i)   unity of testaments proved from the clear words of the lord;
   (ii) the old testament as prophecy of the new;
   (iii) the unity of the two testaments proved by the parables of Christ.

unity of this Book 4 must be seen less in linear argument than in the sequence of the words of the lord, which are the purest expression of the divine mind.[62] The writings of Moses are owned by Christ (Jn 5:46–7), and the unity between the writings of Moses and the spoken words of Christ is clear (4.2.3).

Within the motif of the words of the lord, Irenaeus plays on several registers. His central theme remains the unity of the divine economy, including the many partial economies in a continuity which depends upon the words of the lord spoken in the prophets and spoken by Christ. The two claims of recapitulation, as growth and evolution on the one hand and as a return to the beginning on the other, are held together by scriptural citation.[63] In his use of scripture and his account of the economy, Irenaeus puts forward a christology which is more and more ontological; that is, Christ speaks because of what he is.

Christology is Irenaeus' answer to the problem of contradiction between old and new testaments. Is the economy coherent? Harnack was emphatic that the contradictions were too strong and Braun claimed that the possibility of linking new testament with old testament texts is today excluded.[64] Biblicist approaches face the difficulty of linking an old testament text with a new testament text when old testament texts are constantly being reinterpreted.[65] Here the new testament has no alternative but to adopt an eclectic approach to old testament traditions. An example of the difficulty of resolution may be seen in Psalm 109, which has been taken either as Christ cursing the Jews or as David cursing the Christians. Is it possible to find a total view within which the various types can find their place?[66] Choosing spirit not letter, Irenaeus has followed Paul in making Christ the centre of all exegesis and has achieved his aim through the concepts of recapitulation and economy.

---

[62] There are other themes as well. Irenaeus always writes harmony or counterpoint, never a simple melody.

[63] The claim that Irenaeus used a distinct document on prophecy is difficult to maintain, for the alleged document is in total harmony with the rest of *Against heresies*; Bacq, *De l'ancienne à la nouvelle alliance*, 340. However, Irenaus tries to harmonise all his sources.

[64] Schwager, 'Der Gott des Alten Testaments', 309.

[65] G. von Rad, *Theologie des alten Testaments*, 5th edn (Munich, 1968), vol. II, 409; cited in Schwager, ibid., 310.

[66] Schwager, Der Gott des Alten Testaments', 310 11.

8.7 JOHN

The Fourth Gospel has a dominant role in the theology of Irenaeus, not because it is cited more frequently than others, but because it contains the understanding of one God, incarnation, creation, glory, life, and knowledge which forms his thought. His account of God, word, incarnation and creation is taken explicitly from the prologue and provides his starting-point. Glory is the most striking Irenaean idea for many readers[67] and its link with incorruption points back to John. Recapitulation is governed by the Johannine themes of unification and perfection; it is implicit in the prologue of John and in chapter 17 which brings John's teaching together and balances the prologue.[68]

The prologue relates the 'sovereign, effective and glorious generation of the word from the father' and 'is filled with *an unqualified boldness*, which defines its character' (3.11.8). The incarnation tells how the word became flesh. God becomes the son of man in order that man might become the son of God, and that the human nature which had departed from God might be won back (3.10.2). His taking of flesh accustoms him to the new-born sons of God, born of faith in his name. In the unity of the father and son, the son does all according to the will of the father (Jn 5:19–23). The word came to his own to recapitulate, to return all things under his lordship to the father. The incarnate word received power over all things and by becoming flesh he assumed sovereignty on earth. The word 'received power over all things when he became flesh. Just as he held first place in heaven as the word of God, so he has, as the righteous man, taken first place on earth' (4.20.2).

The word assumed the power which was his as creator and extended his lordship to those who had died before he came. John does not oppose the centrality which Paul gives to Christ crucified but joins it with the incarnation. To the mysteries of Christ's birth and death, John adds the time between them; it is important that Christ lived through all the ages from infancy to maturity in order

[67] R. Tremblay, *La manifestation et la vision de Dieu selon Saint Irénée de Lyon* (Aschendorff Münster, 1978); Scherrer, *La gloire de Dieu*.

[68] G. Siegwalt, 'Introduction à une théologie chrétienne de la récapitulation', *RThPh* 113 (1981), 259–78. E. Käsemann, *Jesu letzter Wille nach Johannes 17* (Tübingen, 1966); ET, *The testament of Jesus* (London, 1968).

to restore all to fellowship with God (3.18.7). The unity of father and son is evident in the knowledge of Nathanael through the instruction of the father (3.11.6), since only through the father may the son be known and vice versa. Again, the knowledge which Christ has of humans (Jn 2:25) is marked by mercy (*dem.* 60) and the relation into which he calls them is that of a friend of God: 'by declaring his disciples friends of God he shows plainly that he is the word' (4.13.4).[69]

The creative word is ever present to the father (*dem.* 43) and the human race (3.18.1). This intimate presence which Irenaeus underlines by the Xenophanes allusion[70] springs open in the incarnation;[71] for the incarnate word is the creator word who comes to what is his own, to the world which is his own territory created by him according to the will of the father (5.18.2). At the marriage feast at Cana the incarnate word drank first the wine made by God on the vine (3.11.5).

When he became man he was already in the world, imprinted on all creation in the form of the cross (5.18.3).[72] This, we found earlier, is the point at which the cosmic word is joined to the historical Jesus. The indefatigable immediacy of the creator to the creature is further underlined by the metaphors of the finger of God (3.21.8) and the hand of God (3.21.10).[73] Irenaeus joins the creation of man (Genesis 2) to the prologue by taking the Fourth Gospel as the account of the new Genesis. Jesus, by an act, heals this man born blind, to make manifest the hand of God which shaped man at the beginning (5.15.2). Jesus returns to deny that the blindness was caused by sin and to claim that its only purpose was that the works of God should be manifest in him (Jn 9).

Jesus' actions repeat what he did at the first Genesis, 'displaying the hand of God to those who were capable of understanding, the hand by which man was modelled from mud'. What the creative word had overlooked in the intimacy of the mother's womb

---

[69] Ferlay confirms the position adopted above, that Irenaeus begins with the middle and looks back to creation and forward to the end: 'retrospectif sur la création et l'alliance'; 'Irénée de Lyon exégète', 225.

[70] See above, chapter two.

[71] Ferlay, 'Irénée de Lyon exégète', 226: 'éclosion totale d'un amour originel'.

[72] See Armenian version 18.70. SC 153, 244.

[73] The metaphors are not used in later theology because of their subordinationist flavour.

he now did in full day to demonstrate the works of God. The purpose of this display is that we should learn the immediacy of the only God and not go looking for intermediaries. The hand that formed us in the beginning, that shaped us in the maternal womb, is the hand of the shepherd who has sought and found us as sheep which were lost and who, 'regaining his own, hoists the lost sheep on his shoulders to carry it back rejoicing to the fold of life' (5.15.2).[74]

Further examples of John's heightened christology develop Jesus' claim that Moses had written of him (Jn 5:46) into the claim that the writings of Moses are Jesus' own words (4.2.3), for by word and theophany he has been present to men from the beginning. It was already the word who walked in the garden to prefigure that he would always be with men (*dem.* 12). By law and prophecy even more than by visible theophany, the word was present to prepare men for his coming.

Irenaeus also draws from John the link between spirit and church. Regeneration radiates from the incarnation as the church spreads through the world. There is a change of heart among the pagans now that the word has pitched his tent among men (*dem.* 94). This concept of salvation by contagion and participation will play a persistent role in Greek theology.

Entry into the kingdom is by water and the spirit (Jn 3:5). The mission of the church is driven by the spirit who was promised by the Baptist, received from the lord by the apostles, 'who shared and distributed it to the faithful, thereby instituting and founding the church' (*dem.* 41). Water and spirit run in parallel. The water offered by the Samaritan woman (Jn 4:14) springs to life eternal. This spring is identified (Jn 7:37) with the spirit who is not yet given, but who is to be given from the cross (Jn 19:30) when the water flows from his pierced side (Jn 19:34), and after resurrection when Christ gives the spirit to the apostles (Jn 20:22). So long as the gentiles were without the word and spirit, their calling was an arid desert: 'the word has made streams spring up abundantly and has sowed the holy spirit on the earth' (*dem.* 89). Outside the church,

---

[74] *suam lucrificiens et super humeros assumens ovem perditam et cum gratulatione in cohortem restituens vitae.* For Irenaeus, God finds joy in saving mankind. His words give new meaning to the prevalence of this image in early Christian art.

'those who do not share in the spirit . . . receive nothing from the purest source which flows from the body of Christ' (3.24.1).

No text says more about recapitulation than John 12:32, 'when I have been lifted up from the earth, I shall draw all to myself'. Irenaeus explains that the head of the church draws all to himself at the appropriate time (3.16.6). His concern for time, for the fitting time (*aptum tempus*), points to God's patience and temporal artistry (*zeithafte Kunst*).[75] A parallel concern for space looks to the universal spread of the gospel, beyond the borders of Israel, as a proof of the presence of the spirit. To the many mansions in the father's house (Jn 14:2) he adds, with his fusion of John and Paul, 'there are many members in the body' (3.19.3; cf. 1 Cor. 12:12).

Love dominates the accounts of trinity and incarnation that Irenaeus draws from the Fourth Gospel, and from love flows glory (Jn 17:22–6). This will be the subject of the following chapter.

8.8 PAUL

Irenaeus exhibits a complexity, which has made things difficult for historical theologians. Not least of his challenges is the interpretation of Paul which pervades his writing. While many had suggested where Irenaeus distorted Paul,[76] no one had taken the trouble to assess his contribution as the first great exponent of Paul. Progress has been made in a large recent work, which deals first with the use of Paul in each book of the *Against heresies*,[77] and then goes on to examine the influence of Paul on the three main areas of Irenaeus' thought: history of salvation, christology and anthropology.

Irenaeus transforms Paul's concept of continuity with a different idea of time and history. His many-sided development of the

---

[75] Von Balthasar, *Herrlichkeit* II, 76.

[76] Notably J. Werner, *Der Paulinismus des Irenaeus*, TU 6, 2 (Leipzig, 1889), 212–13. By the concept of natural law a unity between the two covenants is obtained. The specifically new and Christian salvation, the righteousness of God through faith alone, is suppressed in the interest of the continuity of saving history. The agreement of salvation in both covenants consists in the fulfilment of the natural law. This makes a striking difference from what Paul had said and means that any inner affinity between Paul and Irenaeus must be abandoned.

[77] Rolf Noormann, *Irenäus als Paulusinterpret* (Tübingen, 1994). The reader who finds this early detailed account 'etwas mühsam' may move to the second more systematic section which begins at p. 377.

Adam–Christ typology takes the restoration of divine sonship and immortality in new directions. His anthropology develops the Pauline defence of the flesh and of human creatureliness, against the spiritualising tendencies of enthusiasts.

As well as developments, there are clear differences between Irenaeus and Paul. Irenaeus takes Paul's Hellenistic Jewish ideas and blends them with classical and Hellenistic ideas such as the ideal of participation and assimilation to God. In anthropology, for example, Irenaeus uses against the Valentinians the same account of flesh and spirit which Paul used against Corinthian enthusiasts; yet here there is a new note which defends the flesh as part of God's creation and extends future hope into millenarian expectations.

The concluding negations of this study are important. Irenaeus built his theology on the rule of faith, not on Paul. His use of Paul was not governed by the Pastoral Epistles and Acts, but by Romans, 1 Corinthians and Ephesians. Matthew and Luke contribute to his theology. Yet Paul and John remain the chief sources of what is a new and different theology.

To this account a few points may be added in what is an ever widening question.[78] First, Irenaeus' use of Paul is not merely designed to control the damage caused by Gnostic interpreters, but rather to expound the central elements of his own theology. Secondly, Irenaeus infrequently attacks the heretical dualist interpretation of Paul, when it is used to support two gods or a determinist anthropology. More frequently he uses Paul to support his own insistence (against heretics) that there is one God, creator and supreme father, one Jesus Christ, the incarnate word of God, and one economy of salvation history.

When Irenaeus expounds his distinctive ideas on recapitulation and the economy of salvation he uses Paul persistently. In Book 1 the statements of the rule of faith (1.10.1 and 1.22.1) and of the key theological questions (1.10.3) use much Pauline thought and language. In Book 2, on the issue of Gnostic pride as the driving force of their theology, Irenaeus builds his case on Paul: knowledge puffs up, but love builds up (2.26.1). In Book 3 Irenaeus draws

---

[78] For example, the dissertation of E. Peretto, *La lettera ai Romani cc 1–8 nell'Adversus haereses di Ireneo* (Bari, 1971), covered only eight chapters of Paul.

heavily on Paul for his account of one God and the recapitulation of all things in Christ. That there is one incarnate Christ who summed up all things is proved through Paul (3.16–23). While Book 4 is concerned to prove from Christ's words what has been proved from the apostles, there is still reference to Paul to prove the unity of God's saving work in both testaments. In Book 5 he turns to Paul to show how wrong the heretics are about the resurrection which is God's strength perfected in our weakness (5.3.1; 5.3.3) (2 Cor. 12:9). The essence of Irenaeus' eschatology is drawn from 1 Corinthians 15:25–8.[79]

Irenaeus' central belief in one God is based on Paul (Eph. 4:5–6 (4.32.1; 2.2.6); Rom. 3:30 (5.22.1; 3.10.2)). His account of the kingdom of God is marked by Paul's respect for, and emphasis on, creation in general and the body in particular. The importance of body alongside of soul and spirit (1 Thess. 5:23) is paramount (5.6.1). The body is the image of God (5.6.1). The soul takes the shape of the body (2.19.6). The body is the temple of God (1 Cor. 3:16) (5.6.2). God is to be glorified in our bodies (1 Cor. 6:20), in our mortal flesh (2 Cor. 4:10) (5.13.3, 4). The members of the body should not be joined to a harlot (1 Cor. 6:15) (5.6.2). Bodies are part of the totality of things which is summed up in Christ (Eph. 1:10) and bodies will be raised from the dead (1 Cor. 6:14; Rom. 8:11) (5.7.1).

Irenaeus follows Paul in the place given to the Mosaic law. The law never prevented anyone from believing in the son of God (4.2.7) and the Decalogue is essential to salvation (4.15.1). He deviates from Paul in the place which he gives to ignorance rather than sin (5.12.5) as a cause of human disobedience. Above all, in the face of Gnostic determinism, he underlines the power of free will (4.37.1–4).

To conclude, Irenaeus' account of scripture has great relevance for biblical understanding and historical origins. He links scripture with his four concepts: the rational intimacy of the universal Intellect, the earthly pageant of the economy, the summit of

---

[79] This section draws on the useful summary in D. L. Balás, 'The use and interpretation of Paul in Irenaeus' five books *Adversus haereses*', *SecCent* 9 (1992), 27–39 which is a response to R. A. Norris Jr, 'Irenaeus' use of Paul in his polemic against the Gnostics', in *Paul and the legacies of Paul*, ed. W. S. Babcock (Dallas, 1990).

recapitulation and the grace of participation. He provides more data concerning the origin of a Christian bible than anyone else. Above all, he shows the mutual dependence of imagery and reason, of 'the unfettered images of apocalypse and the applied images of history and doctrine'.[80]

The fact that we have needed two chapters to explore Irenaeus' participation in truth is important, for it explains the remarkable way in which he argues, using both the rule of truth and the universe of scripture. Moving from centre to circumference, then back to the centre, through the whole range of biblical imagery and text, rubbing arguments and images together so that each is stronger, he manages to say and prove things. This is what Clement of Alexandria will call the true dialectic and it points, through its imagery, to the aesthetic element in Irenaeus' work, which is now to be our concern.

---

[80] Farrer, *A rebirth* 17. The opening pages of this book are extremely valuable for an understanding of Irenaeus.

CHAPTER 9

Aesthetics: participation in beauty

Irenaeus' demand for truth and reason is joined by his sense of perception. He is visually oriented (*homme du 'voir'*).[1] From the beginning we have found in Irenaeus the two criteria of truth and fitness, the logical and the aesthetic. Participation in truth, through the rule, ended in *consonantia*, a harmony at once logical and aesthetic, while the truth of scripture was governed by a rebirth of images. In this chapter we shall review the persistence of the aesthetic criterion, then note how a modern theologian used Irenaeus to support his claim that theology should be aesthetic rather than logical. Early Christian art echoes the imagery of Irenaeus. The manifestation of God enables participation in divine beauty. The vision of divine glory brings participation in life.

9.1 PERSISTENCE OF AESTHETICS

A rapid recall of earlier chapters indicates the persistence of perception in the thought of Irenaeus. When he speaks of his youth and Polycarp, he explains how visual and aural memories persist in the mind. He can go back to encounters with Polycarp with a clear recollection of where the master was teaching, how he spoke, and what he said. The freshness of the image underlines his power of perception.[2] On the other hand, Irenaeus' objection to gnosis is linked, from the beginning, to the need for vision and light. Despite

---

[1] Tremblay, *Manifestation et la vision*, 19.
[2] Eusebius, *H.E.* 3.20.4. The same priority of mental images is found in the account of the Gospels given by Erasmus, who claims that so vivid is the picture of Christ in the text that 'you would see him less clearly' if he were present to the eyes: 'Denique totum ita praesentem reddunt, ut minus visurus sis si coram oculis conspicias', Erasmus, *Novum Testamentum, Praefatio, Paraclesis, Opera Omnia*, VI (Lugduni Batavorum, 1705).

the visionary qualities of Valentinus, his followers love the darkness and wish to remain unseen. Irenaeus is concerned to spread light and to uncover what is hidden.

Irenaeus' account of God as cosmic Intellect (*nous*) stresses the perception of God. God is pure mind and consciousness (*sensus, sensuabilitas*). He is all eye, all light, all hearing, so that nothing is excluded from his perception. Creation is the work of God the wise architect. Everything has its distinctive place. As from the lyre different notes produce an unbroken melody, so in the variety of creation we listen to the melody, discern differences and admire the one artist who has produced the whole (2.25.2). Those who look down on the creator need to prove their superiority: they have produced nothing which can compare with the heavens, earth, stars, rains, frosts and snows, all in their special place. They have not ordered the variety of the innumerable parts of creation or tempered the oppositions of light and darkness, heat and cold, to form rivers, fountains, flowers, trees and the variety of animals 'all adorned with beauty' (2.30.3).

The intricacy of saving history reflects the plan of the divine architect to bring man to see his glory. The themes of the economy include the glory of creation and incarnation (4.20.7), the vision and knowledge of God (4.20.6), and the image and likeness which is perfected in man by the spirit. God works continually in time, speaking to his people and enlarging their vision.

Recapitulation unites a vast range of images in its correction and restoration of fallen humanity. The details of the first Adam are fulfilled in the perceived actions of the second Adam. Every event of the life of Jesus points beyond itself to a pattern of opposites and a fresh perception of God. He who hungered and thirsted was son of David and lord of David. He was from Abraham yet before Abraham. He was servant of God and also lord of the universe. He who was spat upon breathed holy spirit into his disciples. In his sadness he gave joy. Handled and touched, he passed through the midst of enemies and through closed doors. He whom the manger contained now fills all things (Irenaeus, frag. 52).

The new creation inaugurated by Christ raises his faithful people to heavenly places. While he was born in human fashion so that he might renew all mankind, the glory of the father is in the son and in this glory men may participate. The structure of his church spreads through the world as it offers a pure sacrifice with one soul and one heart. The final stage of his salvation on earth will be exuberant.

The tradition of truth is not abstract but visible in the church and the succession of the apostles. Secret tradition is suspect because it cannot be observed. The rule of faith guards against the folly of Gnostic myth and all truth is joined in concord (*consonantia*). The test of coherence is both aesthetic and logical. The bible is a work of typology, allegory and history to be interpreted by what is fitting (*to prepon*). The four Gospels, with their different symbols, express visible distinctions.[3]

9.2 A THEOLOGICAL AESTHETIC?

No one has argued more vigorously for aesthetic theology than has von Balthasar; he bases his case on Irenaeus as the first great Christian theologian[4] and illuminates the poetic and aesthetic elements in Irenaeus. Gnosticism, says von Balthasar, had presented a challenge through its myth, which later inspired poets like Shelley and Blake. The poetic response of Irenaeus proposed a fresh vision of the divine mystery and salvation history.

Vision grasps divine manifestation. Anyone who wishes can see the truth, for God never refuses his light. The prophets did not see God's face directly, but saw saving decrees and mysteries which were to give man a vision of God (4.20.10). From his own resources man cannot see God, but God chooses to make himself visible at a particular time (4.20). By his insistence on manifestation or display Irenaeus argued for the clarity of divine activity. Secret tradition must be public and the whole truth must be declared.

The idea of recapitulation is neither a piece of rhetoric nor a pretty picture, but a speculative achievement which is at the same time vibrant and poetic.[5] This central mystery both perfects and begins a new exposition where each part of creation is integrated

---

[3] See above, 8.4.

[4] H. U. von Balthasar, *The glory of the lord: a theological aesthetics* (Edinburgh, 1984), 31, ET of *Herrlichkeit*, vol. II.

[5] Ibid., 50. This claim, already established in chapters 5 and 6 above, shows the soundness of von Balthasar's achievement.

and renewed so that man might share the image and likeness of God. Both image and likeness point to an assimilation to God which transforms through divine presence the man who both carries and embraces the son of God (5.16.2).

What is it that God has manifested? First there is his own divine fullness, second is his relation to his creation, and third is the pattern of time and eternity. As rational spirit he is the source of all beauty, joining heaven and humanity. The centre of the universe is a humanity shaped by God and receptive of God's breath or spirit (5.6.1). The flesh shares in the artistic wisdom and power of the God who produces perfection from the weakness of his creature (5.3.3). The miracle of the human body enlivened by the soul is the clearest evidence of the hand of God – 'the flesh is devised to be receptive and to be able to contain the power of God, since in the beginning it received the art of God' (5.3.2). The eye gave sight, the ear gave hearing, the hand provided sensation, while arteries and veins produced the circulation of the blood, and nerves held the different limbs together. 'It is certainly impossible to describe the whole masterly structure of elements which constitute man; this did not come into being without greatness and wisdom. But what shares in the art and wisdom of God also shares in his power.' (5.3.2). Both body and soul grow in the image and likeness of God. The noble work of art which is man must be free to follow the gentle persuasion of God (4.37.1–4). The flesh is united with the spirit in the incarnate son of God so that flesh might be saved (5.14.2–4). The whole of creation is marked with the sign of the cross (*dem.* 34) because the essence of the mystery (3.12.9; *dem.* 25) is that the light of the father reaches us through the suffering flesh of Christ (4.20.2).

In all these details, von Balthasar discerns the artistic genius of Irenaeus, for whom proportion, order and beauty are to be found throughout the bible. The beauty of the bible and of the cosmos can only be seen through the mystery of recapitulation in Christ.

The demand that the created image should resemble the divine artist is the governing principle that orders the world. God must be allowed 'to draw out of himself the beautiful form of created things and the devising of the beautiful ordering of the world' (2.7.5). God can raise children of Abraham out of stones and his art never slackens.[6] God creates all things by his artistic logos (*dem.* 38; *dem.* 60). All is created in proportion and measure and nothing is without number (4.4.2). The design for creation comes from God's own power and from himself (2.16.1). The world of forms and numbers is not needed to give order to the world: we ourselves declare the harmony of created nature because in their relation to us, things are suitable, because their own rhythm is appropriate to the general rhythm for which they were created (2.15.3).

The Pythagorean heavenly and earthly numbers are unnecessary interpolations (2.14.6) for God has himself numbered the hairs of our head and given everything its own pattern of action, order, number and quantity, showing all the time his skill and intelligence in matching things together (2.26.2,3). God has brought all existing things into harmony. They are well proportioned, fitting and harmonious (4.38.3). The artist is the key to creation, just as the one harmonious melody is more important than the differences between notes (2.25.2). Scripture follows the pattern of the universe for its harmony is evident when we follow the rule of faith. Parables and plain speech fit together and interpret one another to produce from many words one harmonious melody (2.28.3).

The glory of man is to receive God's art and to become his perfect work in patient submission (4.20.2; 4.14.1). God's glory is the man who lives by the vision of God (4.20.7). Participation in God's glory comes through increasing love, devotion and gratitude (3.20.2) in those who stand before the face of the father (4.13.3). The glory which is found in the presence of God is marked by beauty in those who have struggled to attain it (4.37.6,7) and this glory is the proof of God's power in the presence of grateful, abiding and submissive love (3.20.2). Even the world is capable of receiving the glory of the father as it follows the divine decree and fulfils to perfection the work God has given (*dem.* 10).

God's artistry is shown, not in transcendent forms, but in the pattern of time where every point depends on him and looks to his glory. From the beginning, the son with the father made known prophetic visions in logical sequence and harmonious arrangement. Regular succession (*consequentia*) governs the timely

[6] Ibid., 71.

dispensations of salvation (4.20.7). The art of God is not in vain because the times and their fulfilment are appointed by his pleasure (3.23.1). His order and symmetry guide man towards his image and likeness (4.38.3). From the order of God's plan comes the mild peace of his kingdom (4.20.10) in which persuasion, not force, guides the hearts of men. The growth of man towards God is governed by the ideas of childhood, testing and habituation: the infant Adam rises to maturity (*dem.* 12), engages in a contest which ends in fellowship with God, and is made accustomed to God throughout his long pilgrimage. At the same time God is made accustomed to man and declares his goodness at every stage (3.20.1). God is not reluctant to share his goodness and guides his creature in a way which is everywhere harmonious.

God's artistry is supremely evident in the relation between the old and the new covenants. There is nothing out of order as God acts at each appropriate time (3.16.7). The different seasons (*kairoi*) reveal the rich multiplicity of one God who does all things in appropriate form, expression and communication. He is one God but rich in his gifts (3.16.7).

The artistry and harmony of the two covenants spring from the fact that despite their difference (3.12.12) they come from one God whose various acts of grace lead mankind to life incorruptible (4.9.3–4.11.1). The trinity was active from the beginning and there is no limit to the work of the divine artist. Before Abraham, God made his covenant with the whole world through Noah, pledging himself to all animals and men (*dem.* 22). In Abraham, God gave his word so that 'Abraham followed in generous faith, freely and without ties and so became the friend of God' (4.13.4). This natural law of freedom was given to the wandering Abraham through God's mercy (*dem.* 24).

The perfection of God's work from the beginning provokes the question: what could be new? Christ brought all novelty in himself when he fulfilled what had been foretold. Irenaeus answers this question with the fulfilment of Christ who brought renewal of all things by his own perfection (4.34.1).[7] God's temporal artistry in the divine economy conveys a mystery because on the one hand

---

[7] *omnem novitatem attulit, seipsum afferens qui fuerat annuntiatus.*

it is progress and growth (4.4.1; 4.9.3; 5.12.4), while on the other hand it is a return to childhood (*dem.* 46, 96) because God's word has become a child like us (*coinfantiatum*) (4.38.2).[8]

The church is governed by a tradition and order which gives it the same form throughout the world (5.20.1). In its beauty the faith is preserved forever young and fresh (3.24.1). The members of the church gain incorruption from baptism (3.17.2) and are fed in the eucharist with heavenly food (4.17.5). Yet the perfection of the church is eschatological and the pilgrim people finds fulfilment in heaven. Indeed the whole order of salvation on earth copies a heavenly original and the one God brings the image to the likeness of spiritual perfection (4.19.1). Both the tent of the covenant and the visions of the prophets pointed to heavenly things to come (*dem.* 26).

9.3 ART AND AESTHETICS IN EARLY CHRISTIANITY

The richness of imagery in Irenaeus invites attention to early Christian art and aesthetics. Early Christian art moves from images which were common to pagan art, such as the good shepherd, the philosopher and the praying figure, to the miracles of Christ as they manifest his glory and to biblical subjects which depict the triumphs of faith in saving history. As these are reflected in liturgy, so the figures appear in Christian art: Enoch, Elijah, Noah, Abraham, Job, Isaac, Lot, Moses, Daniel, the three Hebrews and Susanna. This art declares a simple message as the Christian addresses his lord:

You have come to us. You have been wonderfully present in our history. We wish to represent your presence in this picture. We have received these signs as constituting our history and our destiny. They are not a mere spectacle, they are our life and our truth. These things belong to the past, it is true. But you are lord of all time including our time. All that you have done is eternally present. The history of salvation is also a

---

[8] Novalis speaks of the man who has moved from childhood to manhood and back to childhood, the 'true synthetic child', as the ideal, much cleverer and wiser than an adult and at the same time ironic and playful. He links this with the movement of the true *Märchen* which must be prophetic. The teller of tales is prophet of the future. All of which is reminiscent of parts of Irenaeus; Novalis, *Schriften*, vol. III, ed. R. Samuel, H. J. Mähl and G. Schulz (Stuttgart, 1983), 281.

revelation. By this picture we must present it. Daniel and Jonah are not strangers to us. They are our brothers, our contemporaries in the faith. They form the cloud of witnesses which surrounds us with your grace.[9]

The earliest Christian art finds its beauty in such proclamation, not in classical excellence of form. It follows the popular tradition of Roman art which is best seen in the column at Adanklissi, the site of the Dacian campaign, in contrast with the classical beauty of Trajan's column, although both are concerned with the same subject. The first signs of classical influence on Christian art appear in the sarcophagus of Junius Bassus (AD 350), which is clearly more refined than the arch of Constantine (312). The classical beauty of Christian art develops in the latter part of the fourth century. Earlier Christians had found the unembellished events of the bible to be the revelation of divine glory. It was enough to tell the story.

The bible gave a limited account of beauty. The Greek environment joined beauty and goodness, but in the old testament goodness covered a much wider range of meanings to culminate in a conformity with the will of God. In the new testament, moreover, there is reference to beauty which is transcendent and eschatological (Rev. 21:11). This is the transcendence of divine glory and points back to the glory of God in the old testament; mystery surrounds this glory, but the work of God points to its creator. All this is clearly declared in the Greek books of the old testament. Wisdom 13:5 contemplates the creator through the beauty of his creatures. Sirach 43:9-11 indicates how the beauty of heaven, the stars and the rainbow leads man in wonder to God. There is a note of distrust in Wisdom 13:7 and Wisdom 13:3, for the beauty of the stars can lead to idolatry. This distrust will persist in Jewish and Christian tradition.

In the Synoptic Gospels the glory of God is seen in the transfiguration, the nativity stories, the entry to Jerusalem and the walk to Emmaus. The Fourth Gospel elevates divine glory to a central theme and the prayer of chapter 17 displays the ultimate glory in which the believer may participate. Paul has one striking reference in 2 Corinthians 3 where the transfiguration of Moses is

[9] P. Prigent, *Immagini Cristiane, immagini sacre, in arte e teologia* (Turin, 1997), 70.

reflected in the transfiguration of the believers. At all these points there is an attempt to declare, in language, the transcendent beauty of God.[10]

The visions of the apocalypse provide material for a theology of image or picture. They point to a reality which is higher than the earth. The revelation of this transcendent world is indicated by images which can only be approximate. Their meaning finds explanation in the hymns of the Apocalypse. These require that we consider the pictures as revelations which, so far from being remote, enable us to discover where we now are in the sight and according to the will of God. The approximate nature of the visions is evident in a common introduction: 'I saw as', 'which appeared', 'like to'. No image is able by itself to express its meaning. The Messiah is described as a lamb 'as it had been slain'. This ambiguity means that the visions are meant not to represent but to signify. Their meaning is an object of revelation. They speak through their symbolic force. All of which means that the most skilful visual representations of the visions of the Apocalypse fall far short of their meaning and power. The hymns indicate a link between image and cult and point to the presence of a reality. The images of the Apocalypse reveal a glory which is accessible only to the eyes of faith, the glory of a God who rules over the world.[11]

A fuller theology of the image can be gained from Irenaeus who supplements the concept of the word with the concept of vision. The frequency of the words 'see', 'vision', 'visible', 'invisible', 'show', 'manifestation' and 'light' (*video, visio, visibilis, invisibilis, ostendo, ostensio, lumen*) is striking. Moreover Irenaeus punctuates his writings with appeals to vision – 'You see' (1.9.1); 'See!' (1.14.3).

The appeal to vision is a principle of method, a way of argument. In order to refute heresy one must first see it and recognise it; for heresy is like a savage animal hidden in a thicket. Irenaeus brings it into the open so that it may be seen and attacked. Indeed mere *ostensio* or manifestation is enough to show how irrational Gnostic teaching is. The manifestation is followed by projecting the light of

[10] P. Prigent, 'Bible et beauté, Esthétique de l'éthique, De la morale comme art d'aimer', in Supplement, *Revue d'éthique et de théologie morale* 181 (1992), 129 44.

[11] P. Prigent, 'Pour une théologie de l'image: les visions de l'Apocalypse', *RHPhR* 59 (1979), 373 8.

scripture so that nothing is hidden and the heretic can only persist in his error because he is blind.

Vision governs the theology of redemption because life comes through the sight of God. Salvation consists in seeing God. God's glory is a living man and what makes man alive is the vision of God. Perception of God, however, presents a problem. How does Irenaeus handle the insistence of the bible on two different things: the pure in heart will see God (Matt. 5:8) and no one can see God and live (Exod. 33:20)? Irenaeus makes a distinction between the greatness of God and his love. Man cannot contemplate the exalted grandeur of God; but God's love makes God known at all times through Jesus Christ (4.20.4 and 4.20.1).

To reach the vision of God, the plan of salvation brings man from anticipation in the old testament to the visible divinity of Christ. God is seen by the spirit prophetically, by the son through adoption and he will be seen as the father in the kingdom of heaven. Degrees of participation in the divine splendour are degrees of participation in the divine vision and life.

From the many stages of the divine economy the climax is reached in the coming of the son. He is the father in visible form just as the father is the son in invisible form (4.6.5, 6). At present the believer finds in the scripture, which is inspired by the spirit, the possibility of seeing God. Also the eucharist presents the shape of heavenly things (4.19.1). Through these means the Christian is accustomed to see God in a vision which then expands until in the kingdom of heaven he sees God face to face.

In these and other ways the vision of God is integral to human salvation and represents the final goal of Christian revelation. Life eternal comes only through the vision of God.[12]

9.4 MANIFESTATION, VISION AND PARTICIPATION

Two themes dominate the aesthetic of Irenaeus: manifestation and vision (*manifestatio/ostensio* and *visio*). They contrast with Gnosticism, where all is concealed and secret. This concealment demands disclosure to be followed by exposition. The themes which

---

[12] A. Benoit, 'Pour une théologie de l'image: remarques sur le thème de la vision chez Irénée de Lyon', *RHPhR* 59 (1979), 379 84.

Irenaeus follows are both biblical and Greek, both visual and rational. Perception and vision mean everything to him.[13]

As a ruthless empiricist, he constantly appeals to evidence and demands respect for facts.[14] His repeated objection to the Gnostics is that they are wilfully blind and turn from the light of the gospel (2.27.2). He presents visible manifestation as a contrast; all, who have reached the smallest particle of truth can see who Christ is and what has been declared of him (3.19.2). The evidence of facts must be accepted without argument, whether these facts are proclaimed by scripture or observed in the world.[15]

In this light there is vision, disclosure, refutation and demonstration. The disclosure denounces both obscurity and error, together with those who deceive through this error. Their error once hidden is destroyed when it is brought to light and shown to be vacuous; their folly produces flagrant contradiction (2.12.3). On the other hand true doctrine is coherent: for example, a true incarnation is declared by eucharistic communion (5.2.2; 4.18.5). To see the truth of Christian proclamation we look at the clear, unambiguous words of scripture (3.11.8; 5.36.3), which offer the unique message of the church as something to be seen (5.20.1). The unity of this message is in contrast with the unending divisions of the heretics.

No one has seen more clearly than Irenaeus a marvellous unity in the divine economy.[16] His ideas were taken up again in the nineteenth century when Hegelian influence drew attention to the history of salvation.[17] The unity of the history of salvation derives from its one author who is the one God (4.2.1–7), and is expressed through the twofold formula of father/son and word/word-incarnate.[18]

What is the manner of the manifestation of God? It declares the invisible God. For the Gnostics the supreme father is both incomprehensible and invisible (1.1.1). Irenaeus does not deny that the father is invisible and that no one can survive the sight of his glory (4.20.5). Yet according to his love, his goodness and almighty

---

[13] Tremblay, *Manifestation et la vision*, 19.
[14] Ibid., 21.
[15] Ibid., 24.
[16] O. Cullmann, *Christus und Die Zeit* (Zurich, 1946), 48.
[17] See above, 4.1.
[18] Tremblay, *Manifestation et la vision*, 41 5.

power, God grants to those who love him the privilege to see him. So those who have pure hearts are blessed (4.20.5). This constant refrain of love's accessibility to God sets the divine vision within the communion of the believer and the father. Because the love is immense, immeasurable, aesthetics must take over from logic, and lead on to prayer.

Where God has been manifest, man has seen his glory, for the sight of God comes to those who love him. By Christ they are adopted and are able to carry (*portare*) and to lay hold of (*capere*) the son of God whom they embrace (*complecti*) (3.16.3).

What emerges from Irenaeus' account of adoption is that the vision of God is intimately spiritual, a mystical communion, a participation in the mystery of sonship. The vision of God granted to Simeon, the shepherds and the wise men has this inner perception of the son (3.16.3, 4; 3.20.2). A whole mass of terminology points to perception.[19]

There is no life without participation in God and no participation without a vision of God and the enjoyment of his goodness (4.20.5). The patriarchs saw God in the sense that they participated in him and prefigured a future indwelling and union. In Christ, this participation becomes a sharing in the divine sonship (4.14.1), and in the eschatological kingdom a still greater vision will come to those who lay hold of God (4.37.7). This final vision shares in the glory of God, as light can only be seen by those who are within light (4.20.5). The spirit, offspring of the father, joins man to God (4.7.4); for without the spirit no one can see the son of God and without the son no one can approach the father (*dem.* 7). Already we share joy through the spirit, who brings us to God whom we shall see finally face to face (5.7.2–5.8.1). The spirit is the pledge or earnest of our inheritance (Eph. 1:13–14) living within us and enabling us to address God as father (Rom. 8:15).

To conclude, the vision of God in Irenaeus, for all its unqualified vigour, is integrated with entry into the mystery of God. God is seen directly in his son who is the face of the father. The incarnation is ultimate and concrete. God will be seen by those who are adopted in Christ, whom they seize, carry and embrace. Irenaeus' passion

---

[19] Ibid., 138 9.

for the vision of God is not, as some have suggested, an alternative to conceptual thought: Irenaeus insists that both the truth and beauty, the logic and aesthetics of the Christian revelation can only be discovered through prolonged awareness of the saving presence of God in Christ.

9.5.1   GLORY

'The glory of God is a living man and the life of man is the vision of God' (4.20.7). This much-quoted aphorism can best be understood within the context of wider argument. The argument of Book 4 which precedes chapter 20 includes two points.

(i) *The wholeness of creation.* Irenaeus begins by a defence of the creator against the blasphemy of the Gnostics. They will not allow the salvation of the flesh, yet this flesh is made by God and sustained by him (4 pref.). In rejecting creation they reject the totality of God's dispensation in Christ, in creation and the economy of salvation (4.1). From creation to redemption there can be no break in the work of God (4.5). So Justin had claimed that if the only God were denied, he would not believe his source: if the lord himself had spoken of another God beside the creator and sustainer, Justin would have found his lord incredible. From this one God came the only son of God to sum up in himself his own handiwork (4.6.2). The word could be seen and touched. Announced by law and prophets, he proclaimed himself and the father to all (4.6.6).

(ii) *The wholeness of time.* Abraham rejoiced to see the day of Christ, as did his descendant Simeon who saw the salvation which God had prepared before the face of all people. The promised light had given revelation to the Gentiles and glory to the people of Israel (4.7.1). The vision of God expands, not because he changes, but as we love him more. We know in part but we shall see him face to face, and in that perfection of trust and love we shall not see another Christ, but only him who was born of Mary and who suffered for us (4.9.2). From one God comes ever greater grace, in many gifts (4.9.3). The love which fulfils the law and which alone makes man perfect never ends. The more we behold him the more we love him (4.12.2).

In chapter 20 Irenaeus brings together the wholeness of creation and the wholeness of time. All begins from the creation where God makes man after his image and likeness (4.20.1). The word becomes flesh that all things on earth might behold their king. From his glorious flesh, we reach immortality and are clothed with the light of the father (4.20.2). God joins those who now know him with their beginning in himself (4.20.4). The glory of God passes to those who from his love behold him and find life through the vision which joins them with the prophets (4.20.5, 6). Within the wholeness of time and the wholeness of creation, God's glory is a living man, and man's life is the vision of God. The life which the word gives is joined with the life which God bestows on all creation (4.20.7).

The word told Moses to stand on the ridge of the rock and to see his rear part but not his face. When he finally came as man, Moses was able to see him on the mount of transfiguration (4.20.9). In the wholeness of time the prophets and Moses saw the likeness of the glory of the lord in many forms and in many dispensations (4.20.11).[20] Daniel saw him as son of God, a crashing rock, and son of man. The revelation to John was so powerful that he fell to the earth as though dead; for no one looks upon God and lives. But the word renewed him to life and reminded him that he had leant on his bosom at supper. So he was able to endure the visions of the lamb and the white horse, of the king of kings and the lord of lords. These were forms of the dispensations of the father, given as visions to show what was to come (4.20.11). What was said and done by the prophets is fulfilled in the church. The scarlet sign of Rahab, which pointed to the redemption of the people from captivity, returns in Christ (4.20.12).

After chapter 20, Book 4 continues to speak of the unity of faith in patriarchs and in believers who look towards the inheritance of the kingdom which they now behold through faith. In all his dispensations God does nothing which does not point as a sign to the final reality.

The wholeness of time is ensured by the glory of God, when the word made flesh descends into the lower parts of the earth so that

---

[20] *utpote dives et multus exsistens, non in una figura neque in uno charactere videbatur videntibus eum, sed secundum dispensationum eius causas sive efficaciam* (4.20.11).

he might see the state of those who rested from their work and that they might see him and learn of his salvation (4.22.1). For he did not come simply for those who believed in him during his earthly life, nor did the providence of God cover those only who have lived since that time. For all who from the beginning have feared and loved God, who have lived in justice and piety with their neighbours, and who have longed to see Christ and to hear his voice, for all of these, at his second coming he shall speak to rouse them from their sleep so that they might take a place in his kingdom (4.22.2). Thus the scripture displays the wonderful dispensations which have preserved our faith in the one God who made us and have ever increased our love for the son of God who fulfilled the different dispensations of divine glory (4.26.5). The prophets remain secure, for they saw his glory at the right hand of the father and saw him coming on the clouds of heaven. They spoke of his pierced side on which men would gaze (4.33.11), of the fire which would burn up the chaff, of his beauty as he rode forth fairer than the children of men with his sword on his thigh. The splendour of his kingdom ensured that those who hear would desire that kingdom (4.33.11). He is the wonderful counsellor and mighty God foretold by Isaiah, the lord who speaks from Sion and the God who comes from the south, from Mount Pharan covered with leaves. At his coming the lame shall leap, the dumb shall speak, and the eyes of the blind be opened. The weak hands and the feeble knees will be strengthened and the dead in the grave will arise in the presence of him who takes our weaknesses and our sorrows upon himself. Throughout the wholeness of creation and the wholeness of time the glory of God brings life and salvation.

9.5.2 CRITICISM AND DIFFICULTIES

The striking formulae of Irenaeus may easily distract attention from the problems which emerge in his account of the glory of God. What are the strengths and weaknesses?

First, we may note the strength of his position.[21] Already in Book 2 Irenaeus has set the contrast between the transcendence of God and his providence. God cannot be known because of his

---

[21] E. Lanne, 'La vision de Dieu dans l'oeuvre de Saint Irénée', *Irén* 33 (1960), 311–20.

transcendence but he cannot be ignored because of his providence. No one can escape the awareness of his overruling power (2.6.1–3). In Book 4 the notion of providence is replaced by that of love. Meanwhile in Book 3 Irenaeus begins from Christ as the supreme source of knowledge of the father (3.11.5, 6) and goes on to speak of God as the glory of man and man as the receptacle of his wisdom and virtue (3.20.2). The incarnation enables man to see God and to lay hold of him. The word of God has lived in a man to accustom man to receive God and God to dwell in man.

Irenaeus follows on from this thought in his extended account in 4.20. The purpose of the incarnation is that all creation should see its king and that in the splendid flesh of the lord it should find and receive the light of the father and incorruptibility (4.20.2). The incarnation is the mixture and communion of God and man so that man may participate in God by seeing him and enjoying his goodness. This participation follows a progressive manifestation of the glories of the father at different times and to different people. The transfiguration on Mount Tabor is the climax where God is seen by Moses, Elijah and the disciples. The end of time has come through the incarnation and it is now possible for Moses to speak to God face to face.

What are the problems with this theology? First, is there a problem in Irenaeus' use of the negative attributes of God which were common to Valentinians? No: this kind of transcendence was attributed to God by philosophers and others who had little in common with Gnosticism. Secondly, is the primacy of the flesh of Christ consistent with divine transcendence? The light of God which is slowly revealed finds its perfection in the flesh of Christ, yet the glory of God is inaccessible (4.20.5). This difficulty can be resolved by the idea of progress which accustoms man to see God. The prophets have glimpsed his glories at different stages of the divine economy. Between the adoptive vision, which his children now enjoy, and the eternal vision of the kingdom there is a special point in the transfiguration where the king is seen and the promise to Moses is fulfilled. There is an anticipation here of the final vision of divine glory promised to men.

9.6 THE LIMITS OF BEAUTY

Aesthetics as perception 'pure vision, abstracted from necessity'[22] is everywhere in Irenaeus. This second criterion beside that of logic guides his thought. The term 'aesthetics' was coined by Baumgarten,[23] where he argued that the kind of knowledge which came from sense experience and feeling should be distinguished from the abstract knowledge of logic and reason. This difference could be joined to the distinction between aesthetic, logical, moral and religious values which in Irenaeus, as in subsequent Western tradition, are often difficult to separate. When they are confused, the Orthodox speak of the sin of aestheticism and iconoclasts destroy beauty in the name of God.

While aesthetics as perception and what is fitting are important for Irenaeus, the perceived glory of God is not only beautiful; it is also the source of truth, goodness and reality. Above all it is an object of religious faith. The subjection of all these elements to beauty, as found in the Romantic movement, finds no support in Irenaeus. While sharing a room in the Tübingen Stift, Hölderlin, Hegel and Schelling, a youthful and redoubtable trio, produced the *Systemprogramm*, which, by merging ethics, physics, religion and politics under aesthetics, could redeem the world. 'I am now convinced that the supreme act of reason, in which all ideas are embraced, is aesthetic, and that truth and goodness are joined together only in beauty.'[24]

Irenaeus finds God through reason and aesthetics just as Plato finds his first principle through the argument of the *Republic* and the aesthetics of the *Symposium*. There the similarity ends, for Irenaeus moves in two other directions. First, finality is found not merely in the first principle of truth, beauty, goodness and reality, but in

---

[22] R. Fry, *Vision and design* (London, 1920), 25.

[23] *Meditationes philologicae de nonnullis ad poema pertinentibus* (Halle, 1735). Taking Descartes' distinction between clear and confused ideas, he found sense data to be both clear and confused, able to be brought into an ordered structure by poetry as 'sensate discourse'.

[24] G. W. F. Hegel, F. Hölderlin and F. W. J. Schelling, 'Das älteste Systemprogramm des deutschen Idealismus'. It concludes 'Ein höherer Geist vom Himmel Gesandt, muss diese neue Religion unter uns stiften, sie wird das letzte, grösste Werk der Menschheit sein'; *Sturm und Drang. Klassik. Romantik. Texte und Zeugnissen*, ed. H. E. Hass, vol. II (Munich, 1966), 1654–6.

a God who is believed. Beauty is part of the glory of God and is subordinate to the object of faith. Second, and more startling, the glory of God is found not in transcendent forms but in the word made flesh. When we come to the end of all our pilgrimage our final vision shall be the face of him who was born of Mary.

For all its exuberance, the aesthetic of Irenaeus is only part of his theology. The glory of God is not merely beautiful, while the wholeness of creation and the wholeness of time point beyond aesthetic judgements. The glory of God is a living man and to that living humanity we now turn.

CHAPTER 10

Human growth from creation to resurrection: participation in life

Irenaeus' anthropology, his optimism for man, has long excited enthusiasm. At the Renaissance he inspired Erasmus. In the twentieth century he gave fuel to those who, like Teilhard de Chardin, were driven by science to see man's evolution to Christ as the Omega point. The dogma of original sin was to be discarded and there was hope for all. On examination, however, Irenaeus proved more complex. The great theme of man as the image of God seemed to lack cohesion. Sin was still an awesome evil. How could divine spirit be mixed with body and soul? Through it all Irenaeus argued his way to the triumph of resurrection and life eternal. He holds our attention because of his passionate enthusiasm that mortal man should participate in the life of God. Controversy has centred on four problems: image and likeness, sin and fall, breath and spirit of God, flesh and spirit.

10.1.1 IMAGE AND LIKENESS: THE PUZZLE

The terminology of image and likeness was widely present in Greek philosophy from Plato to the Stoics.[1] Here man's rational principle was the image of God, and likeness to God was acquired by perfection of this reason. Early Christian writers changed this and defined perfection by the gift of the divine spirit and salvation (4.20.6).

Recapitulation[2] restores the divine image and likeness which was lost in Adam.[3] Likeness to God is found in the incarnate word of

[1] See J. Fantino, *L'homme, image de Dieu chez S. Irénée de Lyon* (Paris, 1986), 5–7.
[2] Peter Schwanz, *Imago Dei* (Göttingen, 1979). The secondary literature on this topic is vast.
[3] Paul and John do not connect this concept of divine image with the creation story of Genesis 1:26–7. This connection is first found in Ignatius of Antioch.

God (*dem.* 32; 3.18.1), the image from which the creation of man was taken (*dem.* 22).

There is confusion among interpreters on the meaning of image and likeness in Irenaeus, because Irenaeus can differentiate between the two. The image plainly is the body, and the likeness comes through the spirit (5.6.1). The image includes the physical and intellectual qualities with which man is born. Image cannot be lost whereas likeness can. This explains the claim (3.18.1) that Adam lost the likeness but regained it in Christ. In general, the image and likeness of God can be distinguished into the image which is natural man (5.10.1, 2) and the likeness which comes from the son and the spirit (5.6.1).

Later fathers have two interpretations. Origen sees man as created in the image of God with the purpose of gaining the likeness of God. The image is the beginning and the likeness is the end. Other fathers, like Gregory of Nyssa and Augustine, do not distinguish between image and likeness. Irenaeus offers support to both positions, sometimes making the two terms interchangeable,[4] sometimes making the image visible and the likeness invisible.

10.1.2   IMAGE AND LIKENESS: INSEPARABLE CONJUNCTION

One careful study of this question[5] acknowledges that Irenaeus' striking formulae lead to problems. For example, in his account of creation, man is made *in* the image and likeness of God, whereas Christ *is* the image and likeness of God. Irenaeus denies the Valentinian interpretation, which separated God from man and higher from lower man through a distinction between image and likeness: some men had the image only, some also had the likeness. Irenaeus rejects this position and denies any such division.[6] God had said, '"For I made man in the image of God" (Gen. 9:6) and the image of God is the son according to whose image man was

---

[4] P. Beuzart, *Essai sur la théologie d'Irénée* (Le Puy, 1908), 69 73.
[5] Wingren, *Man and the Incarnation.*
[6] All accept Loofs' insistence on the future reference of Christ at creation. He is the *homo futurus*. This does not exclude, as Loofs believed, the importance of the pre-existence of Christ. Both are essential to Irenaeus.

made; and for this reason he appeared in the last days that he might show the image to be *like* himself' (*dem.* 22).

Those who are made after God's image and likeness gain man's original state (5.10.1). Yet only in the new humanity of Christ does man find the image and likeness towards which he was created, for Christ is like God and is the image of God. Also he is like Adam and possesses the shape or form of Adam. Christ is true God and true man. Other men are not true men because they have not yet reached the likeness of God. The new beginning in Christ is parallel to the creation of Adam, a second fashioning (*secunda plasmatio*) (5.23.2).

Image and likeness must be held together. Where Irenaeus distinguishes between the two (5.6.1; cf. 5.16.2), he is taking the Gnostic position in order to destroy it. He is arguing *against* the possibility that either the image or the likeness might be saved alone. If it were the case that the image could be saved alone, we should be speaking about the body, and if it were the case that the likeness could be saved alone we should be speaking about the spirit. Irenaeus rejects this separation. By sharing in the body of Christ, which is the church, man can grow in the image and likeness of God (3.17.3). Baptism and eucharist enable this process to take place. As Christ gives and men receive, so they move towards their destiny in Christ. All is the work of the spirit who transforms man into the likeness of him who became man that men might become divine.

10.1.3 IMAGE AND LIKENESS: DISJUNCTION

Irenaeus argues (against the Gnostics) that all men have a point of contact with God.[7] He therefore needs to distinguish what has been ruined by the fall and what subsists after the first sin. Where image and likeness are synonymous, as they are in the original biblical text (Gen. 1:26), the image-and-likeness was lost by Adam's fall and regained in Christ (3.18.1). However, elsewhere there is a distinction, as where the likeness is lost and restored by Christ, who in his flesh preserves the man who was made in his image and likeness (3.22.1).

---

[7] This paragraph is indebted to Beuzart, *Essai sur la théologie d'Irénée.*

Sometimes the difference is clear. The image of God is the body of the incarnate Christ, which is the model of the first creation and the final perfection.[8] The likeness may be identified as reason and freedom[9] or as the incorruption which flesh will finally receive.[10] It may even be identified as something visible which was lost because the word was not yet visible (5.16.2).

The likeness comes as the spirit makes man immortal and incorruptible through the paternal light which shines in the flesh of the glorified Christ (5.6.1; 5.7.2; 5.8.1). Man becomes like the unseen father through the word who has been made visible (5.16.2). In this way, the words 'let us make man in our image and likeness' extend beyond creation to the whole divine economy, which ends when mankind progresses from the kingdom of the son to the transforming vision of the father (5.16.2; 5.36.1–3).

10.1.4 SOLUTIONS TO THE PROBLEM: FANTINO AND SESBOÜÉ

Similitudo has two meanings in Irenaeus.[11] It can refer to the similarity (ὁμοιότης) which man bears to God, through the freedom he has always had, and to the intelligence which enables him to follow the purpose of God. *Similitudo* can also mean likeness (ὁμοίωσις), or growing like God through obedience to the holy spirit. The image (εἰκών) describes what is common between the incarnate son and every human being. Through the presence of the spirit, the son is the perfect image of God. Image and likeness bring man into unity with him who is the beloved image of the father (5.6.1; 5.36.3). In his incarnation he presents the archetypal image, making visible the invisible reality of God (4.6.6; 5.16.2). Here the perfection of God and man are joined.

Quite remarkably, the three concepts of similarity, image and assimilation link man to father, son and spirit respectively. Here we have another evidence of the deeper unity of Irenaeus' thought. God gives freedom to man, and this point of divine similarity is

---

[8] 4.37.7; 5.9.3; 5.12.4; *dem.* 11.   [9] *dem.* 11; *haer.* 4.4.3; 4.37.4; 4.38.4.
[10] *dem.* 32; *haer.* 3.18.1; 4.38.3; 5.1.3; 5.6.1; 5.8.1; 5.10.1; 5.16.1.
[11] Fantino, *L'homme, image de Dieu*, 68–81.

inalienable from man. Man's image of God is imperfect and needs to be made like the incarnate son, the archetypal image. It is essential to man and declares the bond between creation and salvation. Man exists in imperfection and needs to be transformed. This transformation is his salvation by assimilation to the son through the spirit. 'The likeness with the father is the basis on which the image of the incarnate son is constructed progressively by the action of the holy spirit . . . the father acts by his son in the holy spirit to bring to being the spiritual, perfect man.'[12]

In all this Irenaeus stands apart from his contemporaries by joining anthropology and soteriology – Christ mediates both image and resemblance/likeness/assimilation as the true archetype of both.[13] For Irenaeus, image is both form and substance, and likeness is the saving action by which the spirit raises man to God. Irenaeus and the Hermetic writers both see image as joining form and substance, but only Irenaeus allows the divine image a place in the created, lower world. The primacy of the physical also marks Irenaeus off from the Alexandrine fathers for whom image and likeness is an entirely spiritual matter: man's intellect is the image of God, and likeness is spiritual transformation by the holy spirit.

For Irenaeus, man as body and soul is the image of the incarnate son. Indeed 'because by his humanity he is the archetypal image, the incarnate son is the first-principle of creation; because as word of God he communicated the spirit, the incarnate son is likewise the first-principle of salvation'.[14] Because the son incarnate is the archetypal image, every human possesses similar shape and flesh. Every believer receives assimilation (likeness) from the holy spirit at baptism as a dynamic which gradually transforms the image until it is perfected by resurrection.

Adam was weak, incomplete, an infant, possessing by the spirit a likeness to God which he lost through disobedience. Yet God led Adam on the way of penitence (3.23.5), of life (3.23.7), of immortality (3.20.2; *dem.* 15), of communion with God (5.27.2). The possibilities, once lost by disobedience, were restored by Christ who offered adoption, perfection, deification, and liberation from

---

[12] Ibid., 178. [13] Ibid., 179. [14] Ibid.

sin and death. The fullness of Christ now excels what was given during his earthly life and makes men divine.

Irenaeus diverges from Paul and John in avoiding explicit reference to a new creation.[15] For him the first created humanity receives salvation and the gift of the spirit. The likeness in Adam is extended rather than replaced. Within the divine economy, there is no separation between creation and salvation. Christ comes to restore and to complete that perfection to which creation was called.[16]

Fantino's lucid account has been confirmed by Sesboüé's more recent analysis.[17] The divine initiative shows that the love of God is the source of creation. God made Adam in order to have a recipient for his benefits (4.14.1). He then chose the patriarchs with a view to their salvation, formed his people to teach them the ways of God and instructed the prophets 'making man accustomed on earth to carry his spirit and to possess communion with God' (4.14.2). Salvation presupposes creation and ends in participation.

10.2.1   SIN AND FALL, ORIGINAL SIN

The second problem in Irenaeus' anthropology concerns original sin. Irenaeus does not clearly state whether sin is hereditary or individual achievement, or a mixture of both. All views appear in his account. God requires obedience, and the opposite of obedience is sin (4.39.1). Disobedience to God is evil and brings death (*dem.* 16). Did Irenaeus consider sin as necessary to man's development (4.28.3; 4.29.1, 2; 5.29.2), or was it simply a disaster which God repairs by redemption (3.20.2)?

The conflict between truth and falsehood sets the stage.[18] God is true, the devil is a liar. In the form of the serpent, the devil lied to Eve and thereby obtained power or dominance over man (5.21.1)[19] – and the sin of Adam brought the death of the human race. Irenaeus identifies the devil with the serpent[20] who became God's enemy

---

[15] But note man's *secunda plasmatio* (5.23.2).

[16] Fantino, *L'homme, image de Dieu*, 181.

[17] Sesboüé, *Tout récapituler*, 85 9.

[18] Which is appropriate to *Against heresies*.

[19] *Per mulierem enim homini dominatus est ab initio.*

[20] Following Wisdom 2:24, John 8:44, Revelation 12:9. The cunning of the serpent is derived from 2 Corinthians 11:3.

(4.40.3), through envy of God's creation (5.24.4) and of man's gift of life (5.24.4). The lie which the devil told was similar to the falsehood of all heretics (5.21.2). The disobedience of Adam and Eve (3.22.4) caused them to eat (5.23.1) and to transgress the commandment of God.[21] This, for Irenaeus, showed their ingratitude towards God (4.37.6; 3.20.1; 5.3.1) in the face of God's exuberant goodness (3.20.1).

As a result of the fall, Adam was overcome by fear and tried to hide from the ever-present God, because in his confusion he knew himself to be unworthy of God's presence. The fear of the Lord is the beginning of understanding which leads to penitence, which attracts the kindness and mercy of God.[22] Nevertheless, Irenaeus does not see the sin of Adam as the worst sin: the sin of Cain, who killed a man, who acted without reverence or penitence and who persevered in his wickedness, drew the curse of God (3.23.3, 4). In contrast, Adam immediately felt a sense of shame and penitence, so God turned his fault along a way towards better things (4.39.1).

God, as a good father, could not turn away from his creation but mercifully gave salvation (5.21.3). After man had learned his fault and turned gratefully to his lord, God's magnanimity brought man on to resurrection and incorruption. Out of his largeness of heart God even permitted the fall (3.20.1, 2).[23] Adam was expelled from paradise not because God was jealous of his participation in the fruit of the tree, but because a merciful God wished to remove him from perpetual, incurable sin. God put a stop to man's sin by interposing death and the dissolution of the flesh, so that man might in the end cease to live in sin and commence to live for God (3.23.6). Man was not handed over to the devil permanently or entirely (3.23.3). He could take again his path of holiness through repentance, and with the help of God he could recover from the bite of the serpent (4.2.7). Otherwise Satan would appear to be the final victor.

Adam is the first man and the source of unity to the human race who are all his sons. We are guilty because we stem from Adam,

---

[21] Man's primal sin was disobedience as Paul (Rom. 5:19) had said.
[22] So when Adam took the fig leaves, he chose a penitential form of clothing which was exceptionally uncomfortable (3.23.5).
[23] Irenaeus' subtlety and clarity on this point show that the contrast between rise and fall theodicies is not appropriate to his account.

and inherit all from him. We are begotten in the same captivity which Adam endured and remain in servitude, as slaves to the devil, because we are Adam's sons (3.23.2). From the disobedience of one man, many became sinners and forfeited life (3.18.7). Similarly the disobedient Eve brought death on the human race (3.22.4). In the beginning we were led captive in Adam (5.21.1) and we committed the sin in the garden against Christ himself (5.17.1). Therefore Irenaeus understands original sin at least in the limited sense of *inherited guilt*.[24] A mass of imagery pours in. Because we have sinned in Adam and are descended from him physically, we are born as slaves, for all children who are born in slavery are legally slaves, however sad this sounds (3.23.2). Christ comes to save all from sin's captivity and to restore all to communion with God, whether they be infants, little children, children or men young or old (3.18.7). At the tree of paradise we incurred a debt to God which is remitted at the tree of the cross (5.17.3). We are all sick, suffering from the bite of the serpent with a disorder between our soul and our body; to heal this sickness God endured all things on our behalf (4.37.7). Slavery, birth, debt, two trees, sickness and healing – all the images tumble out.

One scholar[25] points also to *inherited mortality* (5.1.3), to natural origin as a *generatio mortis* (4.33.4) and to the captivity of the children of Adam (3.23.1), who need baptism for regeneration (3.17.1). However, sin is nowhere reduced to a consequence of Adam's sin.[26] Adam is the emblem of the human race; rejection of God is always possible because man may choose either good or evil. God himself is never responsible for, but magnanimously allows the apostasy of man, and this very apostasy, as the prophet said, will lead to healing under the grace of God (4.37.7).[27] Evil is something which is overcome within God's total scheme. Irenaeus wrote to Florinus

---

[24] While Irenaeus is the first to make Romans 5:12 central to his anthropology, he does not develop it metaphysically, but points to the incarnation and the purity of the Christ who was born from a pure mother to regenerate mankind (4.33.11). The purity of Christ and his mother is seen as the great exception within a fallen race.

[25] Duncker, *Des heiligen Irenäus Christologie*, 142. See also Duncker's inaugural dissertation, *Historiae doctrinae de ratione quae inter peccatum originale et actuale intercedit pars continens Irenaei, Tertulliani, Augustini sententias* (Göttingen, 1836).

[26] Ziegler, *Irenäus*, 220.

[27] Ibid., 223.

concerning the monarchy of God with the subtitle 'that God is not the cause of evils' (*H.E.* 5.20).

10.2.2 PERFECTION OF ADAM [28]

The primitive condition of man was one of innocence and child-hood (3.23.5), where Eve was wife to Adam but still a virgin (3.22.4). Their intellectual powers were undeveloped, for these are not necessary to please God (2.26.1). Adam was not perfect in himself, for only the unbegotten God is perfect (4.38.3). Adam's perfection consisted in his proximity to the perfect God (4.38.3), in the sense that God's spirit is in him. Through use of created things he must grow in maturity and find immortality (4.5.1) to end in eternal subjection to God (4.28.3). Man is forever marked by growth, as the child grows in the womb and the wheat grows on the stalk (2.28.1). Perfection for Irenaeus lies at the end, not at the beginning, of man's education by God, a process which takes account of the fall from the beginning.[29] Because the redeemer already existed, man was created to be redeemed, lest the redeemer become superfluous. Man possessed body and soul, reason and free will, unimpaired but imperfect and undeveloped. 'The fall and its consequence, death, did not disturb God's plan for the world and its salvation but contributed to its realisation, continuing the education of mankind which the plan already envisaged.'[30] The fall was a happy fault (*felix culpa*).

10.3.1 UNITY OF MAN AS BODY, SOUL AND SPIRIT

The third problem concerns man's grasp of breath and spirit. For the Gnostics, man is created by different powers at different times, and he begins as the work of an inept maker which is then passed over to a maker more skilled and more powerful. Not only does man have more than one maker, but he has more than one part; his parts are of unequal value and do not form a real unity. Against this account, *Irenaeus insists on the unity both of the creator and of the creation.*[31]

---

[28] Koch, 'Zur Lehre vom Urstand', 193–214.
[29] Ibid., 210, 'er rechnet schon den Sündenfall mit ein'.
[30] Ibid., 212.
[31] Beuzart, *Essai sur la théologie d'Irénée*, 54–84.

One God made man and made him in his entirety. The property
of God is to make and the property of man is to be made (4.39.2;
4.11.2). Yet there is no gap between them which can be filled by
intermediaries. The hands of God, his word and his spirit, are in
direct contact with man.

Valentinians divided men into three categories, spiritual, earthy
and psychic.[32] Irenaeus rejected this division of mankind into three
classes and man into three parts. The human race is one and the
individual is one. Neither body nor soul nor spirit is man but their
union forms a complete human person (5.6.1). The natural man
is composed of two parts, body and soul, equal in their dignity
because they are both created by God. The soul is the faculty of
sense, mind, thought or meditation: *sensus, mens, cogitatio, intentio
mentis* (2.29.3). To body and soul must be added the spirit which is
man's *participation* in the spirit of God so that man consists of flesh,
soul and spirit (5.9.1).

At one place, Irenaeus distinguishes between the breath of life
(*afflatus*) and the spirit. The first gift of life was bestowed by the
divine breath. The complete gift of life is bestowed by the spirit of
God. The breath is a temporal thing, the spirit is eternal (5.12.2).
Body and soul and spirit, while inseparable, have a hierarchy. The
soul is superior and the body is like an instrument in the hand of a
tradesman (2.33.4).

The soul comes from the breath of God and is his creature
(5.12.2). The soul is stronger than the body because it gives breath
and life and increase to the body (2.33.4). Indeed the soul teaches
the body which it possesses and governs (2.33.3, 4). Body and soul
explain the activity of man. Two parts, not three, are important.
The incorporeal soul possesses the shape of the body. Just as water,
when it is placed in a vessel, takes the shape of that vessel, so the soul
takes the shape of the body (2.19.6). The story of the rich man and
Lazarus shows how souls continue; they do not move from body to
body but possess without change the character of the body (2.34.1).

Irenaeus sees death as a terrible thing, when the body loses the
soul (5.7.2), for the departure of the soul is the loss of that which

---

[32] In this they simply carried over the Platonic division of spirit, soul and body into the
species of man as a whole.

gave a beginning to man's substance (5.7.1). What God has once made, and which has been decomposed back into the earth, he will again restore (5.3.2). Each man has his own body and his own soul through the wealth and power of God (2.33.5). There can be no basis for a belief in transmigration of souls, for body and soul are joined together.

The activity of the spirit is the clue to man's unity. God's spirit gives to man the breath of life and the gift of rationality (5.1.3). The spirit gives existence and life to man as an animate and rational being (5.3.2). But this does not happen through the rejection of the flesh, but by the communion of the spirit and flesh (5.8.1). Our substance, which is made of soul and flesh, receives the spirit of God to become spiritual man (5.8.2). God grants communion to those who need him (4.14.2). It is not possible to live without life and life only comes by participation in God, through seeing God and enjoying his goodness (4.20.5). The spirit opens to man the way of becoming like God.

10.3.2 BREATH OF LIFE

Irenaeus distinguishes the breath of life which made man an animated being from the life-giving spirit which made him spiritual (5.12.2). He quotes Isaiah, who speaks of the breath given to the people and the spirit to those who walk on earth, indicating that breath is common to everyone on earth but that the spirit belongs only to those who tread down, that is walk on, their earthly desires. Again, Isaiah distinguishes spirit from breath when he speaks about the spirit which will go forth from God and the breath which God has made (Isa. 57:16 and 42:5). Breath is something temporal while spirit is eternal. Breath increases for a short period and continues for a limited time; then it departs and its former habitation is without breath. In contrast, the spirit pervades man from within and from without, remaining there and not leaving him. The substance of the flesh dies when it loses the breath of life, but the spirit which the lord brings is of a different order.

In Christ, we all live a spiritual life given by God (5.12.3). Both breath and spirit are given to the same substance; the first does not last while the second endures for ever. In Adam we all die but in

Christ we live through the gift of the spirit (5.12.3). The breath of life belongs to the created nature of man whereas the spirit grants participation in God.[33]

The breath of life presents a puzzle which, like that of image and likeness, can only be solved by the concept of different levels of participation.[34] The breath of life is breathed into the face of man to produce a living soul. It cannot be called mortal because it is the breath of life (5.7.1). The soul is life to the body and also the source of reason (5.1.3); but it is not immortal because it depends on God for the breath of life. 'Life does not come from us, nor from our own nature, but it is bestowed according to the grace of God. Therefore he who shall have preserved the gift of life and given thanks to him who bestowed that gift will also receive length of days for ever and ever' (2.34.3). Participation governs body as well as soul. The body participates in the soul as God pleases and the soul participates in the life which God gives. This means that souls which once did not exist can continue by the will of God which brought them into being (2.34.4).[35]

Has the soul a natural immortality? Puzzle and controversy surround the question. An affirmative answer begins from 2.34.3. It is claimed that Irenaeus here uses the concept of life in connection with salvation and the life of the spirit.[36] It is this life which is lost and regained. The soul may continue to exist without participating in the life-creating spirit. For Irenaeus distinguishes between animation and vivification, but not between life lived in the flesh and other forms of life. The relationship between the present life and eternal life is a relation between different levels of participation.[37] The flesh can partake of life now in its animated condition and therefore may partake of life in its vivified condition (5.3.3). There is a direct continuity between present life and eternal life. The temporal is weaker and the eternal is stronger. 'There is no suggestion

---

[33] H-J. Jaschke, *Der heilige Geist im Bekenntnis der Kirche* (Münster, 1976), 253.

[34] See section 10.5.

[35] Contrary to the axiom that what comes into being must pass away.

[36] 'la vie supérieure qu'instaure en nous l'Esprit Saint par sa présence sanctificatrice et divinisante', A. Rousseau, 'L'éternité des peines d'enfer et l'immortalité naturelle de l'âme selon saint Irénée', *NRTh* 99 (1977), 854.

[37] Behr speaks of the difference between the living soul (Gen. 2:7) and the life-giving spirit (1 Cor. 15:45–6) as two modes from one source. J. Behr, *Asceticism and anthropology in Irenaeus and Clement of Alexandria* (Oxford, 2000), 109.

that they are two different types of life: physical/biological and spiritual/the presence of the Spirit. That the flesh has become accustomed in this present temporal life, to bear life, demonstrates that it is capable of being vivified by eternal life.'[38]

Those who rise to life eternal have their own body, their own soul and their own spirit. The others have their own souls and their own bodies but have stood apart from the goodness of God (2.33.5):

Here we see the same dynamics as are operative in Irenaeus' discussion of life in *AH* 2.34 and *AH* 5.3.3: those who have been thankful for the gift of life in this temporal life, and are thus pleasing to God, will be raised and maintained in eternal life. But now this thought is expressed in terms of the Spirit, which is given to each in a manner that makes the Spirit 'their Spirit'. Thus those who have pleased God in their body, soul, and Spirit will be raised in their body, soul, and Spirit. The parallel dynamics of these texts, and the fact that it is *in* their body, soul, and Spirit that they have pleased God, demand that it is also in their body, soul, *and* Spirit that the others have shown themselves worthy of punishment, and so are raised in their body and soul for the punishment of an existence without the Spirit, without participation in life.[39]

Indeed the whole creation subsists by the power, skill and wisdom of God (5.18.1),

For the Father simultaneously bears the creation and his own Word, and the Word borne by the Father bestows the Spirit on all as the Father wills, to some, who are in a created state, which is made, He gives the Spirit pertaining to creation, to others who are according to adoption, an engendering, he gives the Spirit of the Father. (5.18.2, Behr's translation)

Rousseau translates differently:

and the Word borne by the father gives the Spirit (spirit) to all in the manner which the father wills for us. To some according to their creation, he gives the spirit which belongs to creation, the spirit which is something made; to others according to their adoption he gives the Spirit which proceeds from the father, the Spirit which is his progeny.

Here the claim is that Irenaeus means two different things by the word *spiritus*: a created spirit which is the breath of life, and the holy spirit.

---

[38] Ibid., 97.
[39] Ibid., 101. Rousseau restricts possession of the 'Spirit' to those who have been justified; SC 293, 339 40.

Can we clarify the relation of the spirit to the breath of life? Irenaeus works back from 1 Corinthians 15:45. From Isaiah 57:16 he points out that the breath of life is something made, which will leave the body. 'But when the Spirit pervades man inside and out, it is permanent and remains with the man.'[40] Irenaeus then uses 1 Corinthians 15:46 to distinguish what is animated from what is spiritual and claims 'it was first necessary for man to be fashioned, and having been fashioned to receive the soul and then to receive communion with the spirit'. He concludes with the claim, 'therefore, just as the one who became a living soul, by turning to evil lost life, so again the same one by turning to what is better and receiving the life giving spirit finds life' (5.12.2). The breath of life produces animation while the holy spirit produces vivification.

In 4.20.5 the role of participation is made explicit: one cannot live without life and life comes from participation in God, which is to see God and to enjoy his goodness.[41] The one source of life is received in two ways – creation and vivification. All created things draw their life from God. Some receive a pledge of the spirit in anticipation of eschatological vivification. God and man are becoming accustomed to one another in the interim period. The process of growth – through creation, increase, adulthood, multiplication, strengthening, glory and vision of the lord – brings incorruptibility (4.38.3). Here is the economy of man, the anthropology of Irenaeus expressed in one sentence.[42] Each stage is a different level of participation. The anthropology of Irenaeus, like all his theology, requires the four concepts of intellect, economy, recapitulation and participation.[43]

Irenaeus (5.6.1) oscillates between the two meanings of spirit, which are two levels of participation. When man loses the spirit

---

[40] Behr, *Asceticism*, 106.

[41] ἡ δὲ ὕπαρξις τῆς ζωῆς ἐκ τοῦ θεοῦ περιγίνεται μετοχῆς. μετοχὴ δὲ θεοῦ ἐστι τὸ ὁρᾶν καὶ ἀπολαύειν τῆς χρηστότητος αὐτοῦ.

[42] 4.3.8.3: ἔδει δὲ τὸν ἄνθρωπον πρῶτον γενέσθαι, καὶ γενόμενον αὐξῆσαι, καὶ αὐξήσαντα ἀνδρωθῆναι, καὶ ἀνδρωθέντα πληθυνθῆναι καὶ πληθυνθέντα ἐνισχῦσαι, ἐνισχύσαντα δὲ δοξασθῆναι, καὶ δοξασθέντα ἰδεῖν τὸν ἑαυτοῦ Δεσπότην. Θεὸς γὰρ ὁ μέλλων ὁρᾶσθαι, ὅρασις δὲ Θεοῦ περιποιητικὴ ἀφθαρσίας, ἀφθαρσία δὲ ἐγγὺς εἶναι ποιεῖ Θεοῦ.

[43] Since participation is a mixture of affirmation and denial, there will always be ambiguities. A lucid note on the present discussion shows the persisting ambiguity and the triumphant certainty – man is not God, only man with God is man; Sesboüé, *Tout récapituler*, 90–9.

of God, he is still a man shaped by the hand of God in God's image, but the likeness is no longer there.[44] The paradox of God the spirit in whom man's spirit participates – where man's spirit does not belong to the initial definition of man as body and soul, but belongs to the definition of perfect man – corresponds with the difference between image (body and soul) and likeness (body, soul and spirit).

If the language fumbles, the intuition is profound and clear. The link of man to God is so intimate that it belongs to the being of man considered as a creature and considered as vocation. Man is not God; God is radically transcendent to man. Yet, nevertheless, one cannot speak of man completely without bringing in the connection to God which is part of him.[45]

One cannot divide the divine spirit which shapes and saves man from the spirit which is a constituent of man. The spirit of man participates in the spirit of God and thereby brings life to body and soul.

10.4.1 SPIRIT TRANSFORMS FLESH INTO INCORRUPTION

The fourth problem in Irenaeus' anthropology concerns the relation between flesh and spirit. In Book 5, where he argues for the resurrection of the body or the resurrection of the flesh, his argument is governed by two principles, one logical and the other theological. Logically, he is concerned to expose the inaccurate argument which has been levelled against the resurrection of the body. He compares his opponents to those who are not expert at wrestling and who gain a hold on their opponent which is not to their advantage, but which in their ignorance they will not abandon. In the end they tumble and become objects of ridicule. Their failure in argument is due to their refusal to analyse the meaning of the words they use (5.13.2).

The theological principle which lies behind Irenaeus' argument comes from Paul. For Paul, the one question to ask about a man is: what or whom does he serve?[46] Anthropology is a question of

---

44 Ibid., 95.
45 Ibid., 97.
46 Käsemann, *Perspectives on Paul*, 26 31; *Paulinische Perspektiven*, 53 60.

power. Those who serve flesh and blood cannot enter the kingdom of God. Those who are ruled by the spirit are transformed by divine grace into incorruptibility.

The argument begins with the theorem of participation: the lord brought immortality firmly and truly by bringing us into communion with God. This he achieved by the great exchange, giving his own soul for our souls, his flesh for our flesh, and pouring out the spirit of the father for the communion of God and man. The three elements of soul, flesh and spirit take their place in this constant theme of Irenaeus. Christ has attached man to God by his own incarnation (*imponente*) and he has imparted God to men (*deponente*) by means of the spirit (5.1.1). The whole economy of salvation points to the transformation of flesh into incorruption. Unless this regeneration be possible, then God has neither restored the work of his hands nor taken possession of that which is his own (5.2.1, 2).

Objections against resurrection and incorruptible flesh will not bear examination, says Irenaeus, for God created human bodies from what did not exist and all he has to do at resurrection is to put together the parts which he has previously formed. While the complexity of the human body is great, it is a simple matter for God to reassemble existing parts (5.3.2).

Nor can it be argued that these disparate members are not capable of receiving life, for they have already received temporal life as creatures upon earth. The eternal life of God is much more powerful than any temporal life and it can readily vivify the members which it brings together (5.3.3). Since the lord has shown himself able to bring life into what he has made, and since the flesh is clearly able to receive the gift of life, there is no barrier to the flesh receiving incorruption and eternal life (5.3.3).

The power of God to preserve bodies is clearly indicated in scripture, where some are shown to have lived seven, eight or nine hundred years. From the beginning God has been able to rule, order, sustain and move all that he made. The hands of God have ever been efficacious (5.5.1). There is no limit on what God can do with his creation. The unbelief of those who are sceptical does not affect the faithfulness of God (5.5.2).

The resurrection of Christ concerns the substance of his flesh. Our resurrection, like his, must be a resurrection of the flesh, for

he will raise us by the same power which he used in his own resurrection. The reality of his flesh was proved when he showed the
marks of the nails and the wound in his side. Our mortal bodies
will be raised as he was raised.

This is the work of the spirit, whose power we already know in
his pledge which prepares us for future incorruption. Those who
possess this pledge of the spirit are subject to the spirit and serve
the spirit rather than the flesh. The service of the spirit is the only
alternative to the service of the flesh, to a slavery which reduces
men to pigs and dogs (5.8.1, 2).

10.4.2 STRENGTH MADE PERFECT IN WEAKNESS

The flesh which cannot inherit the kingdom of God is the flesh
which is not joined to soul and spirit. By itself, flesh could never
reach incorruption, but flesh is joined to soul and spirit within
the perfect man, and the weakness of the flesh is taken up by the
strength of the spirit. Consequently the flesh is able to do things
which, without the spirit, it could never achieve (5.9.2). By this spirit
we now live in obedience to God (5.9.3). To speak exactly, the flesh
is not able to inherit the kingdom of God; but the spirit of God
takes the flesh as an inheritance into the kingdom of God. The
various parts of man which rot in the earth are inherited by the
spirit and translated into the kingdom of heaven. Flesh and blood
cannot inherit, but the word dwells within and the spirit comes
upon the flesh and the blood to give it life (5.9.4).

Irenaeus corrects Paul on the olive tree. The wild olive stands for
flesh and blood, the good olive stands for the spirit. The branch of
the good olive is grafted into the wild olive and the first nature of
man is restored as he becomes the image and likeness of God. No
longer is man mere flesh and blood, but a spiritual man, although
he still possesses flesh (5.10.2).

Paul sets out the difference between flesh and spirit. The works
of the flesh (fornication, uncleanness ... orgies (Gal. 5:19)) contrast with the fruits of the spirit (love, joy, peace ... self-control
(Gal. 5:22)). The flesh will die unless it produces the works of
the spirit and moves from corruption to incorruption when the
spirit of God grants the gift of life. This spirit is God's eternal

spirit which pervades the whole being of man and never leaves him (5.12.2).

The life-giving power of the word of God is seen in the healing by which he restored all kinds of illnesses and disabilities. When he raised Lazarus and others, his life-giving power was proved and he prophesied that the hour would come in which the dead in the tombs would hear the voice of the son of man and come forth (Jn 5:28). Paul gives no ground for objections against the body (5.13.2); he speaks of the body of Christ's glory and how the believer's body will be transformed into glory. When the mortal is swallowed up in life and the flesh is no longer dead but incorruptible, it will sing the praises of God; as Paul said to the Corinthians, 'glorify God in your body' (5.13.3).

There would have been no point in the incarnation if the flesh were not to be saved. For the flesh of the lord established his human nature and confirmed the salvation of our flesh. Unless he had himself been flesh and blood, as man was originally made, he could not have saved what had perished in Adam (5.14.1). By recapitulation his righteous flesh brought the flesh from slavery to sin into friendship with God (5.14.2).

From Irenaeus a whole theology of physical redemption arises. His insistence that human flesh is transformed by participation in the incorruption of divine life has lasting relevance.[47] Futility and pessimism belong to those who deny the salvation of the flesh (5.2.2).

There are five main proofs for the salvation of the flesh.[48] The first proof comes from the almighty power of God (5.3.2). If God cannot raise the dead, then he is not the almighty creator who calls things out of nothing. The second proof is the power of the flesh to participate in life. If flesh can share in weak and mortal human life, it can share in the stronger eternal life which God gives (5.3.3).

---

[47] The relevance of this theme was evident in Eastern Europe when materialism reigned but the individual was virtually destroyed. Joppich presents a pertinent account of this element of Christian theology and links it with the understanding of man as the image and above all the likeness of God. For the likeness of God is the gift of incorruption, whereby the flesh which is the image of God is transformed. Irenaeus opposes the Gnostic hostility to the body and the Gnostic denial of salvation for the flesh. G. Joppich, *Salus carnis. Eine Untersuchung in der Theologie des hl. Irenäus von Lyon* (Münsterschwarzach, 1965).

[48] Ibid., 68 9.

Thirdly, the goodness of God proves the divine gift of life; for if God did not give life to the body then he would be either neglectful or hostile (5.4.1, 2). The fourth proof comes from the old testament, where the long lives of the patriarchs show that God is able to extend the life of those who are joined to him by love (5.5.1, 2). The fifth and final proof comes from the eucharist; for if flesh cannot be saved then our Lord did not redeem us by his blood and we cannot share in his flesh and blood through the eucharist. We stand in need of communion with him (5.2.1), and that communion is possible because Christ was true man who possessed flesh and blood.

10.4.3 FLESH AND GLORY

God's glory is seen in the flesh of the incarnate word.[49] The narratives of the incarnation speak constantly of glory. Mary glorifies the lord at the annunciation (3.10.2) and the song of the angels gives glory to God as do the shepherds when they hear the message of the angels (3.10.4). Both Simeon and Anna glorified God when they saw Jesus the infant in the temple (3.10.5). The miracles which the incarnate Christ worked gave glory to God (5.17.1, 2). Indeed the light of the father shone in the real flesh of the son (4.20.2). The transfigured Christ fulfilled the promise to Moses that he would see God face to face on the rock (4.20.9). The reality of the flesh of Christ is tied to the communication of his grace and to the truth to which he bore witness (3.18.7). Had he not been real flesh then he could not have been truth.

In his account of final glory, Irenaeus unites 1 Corinthians 15 and John 17.[50] The glory of God is shown within the nature of the creation and the triumph of God is brought about by the union of the spirit of God with the substance of the flesh. Here, for Irenaeus, the glory is to be found, neither in exaltation above creation nor in any form of separation, but in the intimate joining of God with his creature to produce immortality (4.38.3).

The glory of God is revealed in the flesh (5.3.2, 3). The flesh which was produced by the skill of God at the beginning will once again receive the power of God to be transformed. The spirit

---

[49] Scherrer, *La gloire de Dieu*, 135. Also see above, 9.5.
[50] Scherrer, *La gloire de Dieu*, 249.

surrounds man within and without (*spiritus circumdans intus et foris hominem*) and remains always with man, never abandoning him (5.12.2). This is the action of the same creator God, the imprint of whose fingers is upon us. 'His hand created your substance. That hand will reclothe you with pure gold and silver, both within and without, and will adorn you so beautifully that the king will be moved by your beauty' (Ps. 44:12) (4.39.2).

Salvation, we have seen, is a thing of beauty.[51] The prophets have spoken of the glory which is to come for those who are fairer than the children of men, anointed with the oil of gladness above others, and who with beauty ride forth to rule in truth and meekness and justice. These things and other things 'of a like nature are spoken concerning him to indicate the beauty and splendour which exist in his kingdom, together with the transcendent and pre-eminent exaltation given to all who are under his sway' (4.33.11). The transformation of the flesh is the work of the spirit who makes the flesh his temple (5.9.4). The spirit is given as the seed of life which comes from Christ upon the cross. From him who slept on the cross, the spirit is mediated to the flesh so that the work which he had shaped is joined and mixed to produce living sons for the living God (4.31.2).

10.5 GROWTH THROUGH PARTICIPATION

Irenaeus' four untidy problems (image and likeness, sin and fall, breath and spirit, flesh and spirit) show that human life depends on participation in God. We become immortal by our vision of God and participation in him (4.20.6). Life springs neither from us, nor from our nature, but is given by the grace of God (2.34.3). Participation defines Irenaeus' account of the life which will grow to all eternity.

It is the characteristic of humanity to become. Man's growth to maturity is gradual through the benefits of God's love until he finally sees and lays hold of God (4.37.7). He begins as a child (4.38.1, 2) and is fed on infant food. In his weakness he falls prey to the tempter. He moves beyond immaturity because he has the

[51] For the aesthetic dimension of Irenaeus' thought, see especially the previous chapter.

gift of freedom to choose the way of assimilation to God. His own freedom is matched by the sovereign freedom and liberality of God's grace.[52] This means that he may begin as man and end as God. Divine providence leads him towards the goal of incorruption. His increase is entirely the work of the spirit, who is the bread of immortality and gives nourishment for growth (4.38.1, 2). Only from him who is before all things do men, the recent creatures of his grace, receive increase towards perfection (5.1.1).

Dostoevsky claimed that truth was never found at either extreme but only in the middle; hence come the difficulty and debate in Irenaeus' anthropology. Man is not God but he can grow in the likeness of God. Man is, by his own choice, a sinner; but God takes him and draws him upwards to perfection in Christ. Man is mere body and soul, incomplete until he shares in the divine spirit. Immortality is never a property of man in his own right. He must constantly receive this gift by participation in the God who grants him life through a continuing act of creation (5.3). The body is included in this reception of life. He who raised up Jesus from the dead now gives life to our mortal bodies through his spirit dwelling in us (Rom. 8:11). It is the triumph of God's goodness, not our survival, which we celebrate in the resurrection of the body (3.20.1).

Within all the complexity of Irenaeus' anthropology, God's goodness shines. While some have doubted whether Irenaeus coordinated (and not merely juxtaposed) his ideas, theocentric optimism pervades all. It matters to man to know that he is a copy of the incarnate Christ, that God's first loving concern after the fall was to put Adam into more comfortable clothes, that life is a sign of God's gift and that the weakness of flesh is the correlate of God's strengthening grace and goodness. To that goodness and man's share in it we now turn.

---

[52] See the rich development of this theme in R. Berthouzoz, *Liberté et grâce suivant la théologie d'Irénée de Lyon* (Fribourg, 1980).

CHAPTER 11

Goodness and truth: ethics of participation

Irenaeus begins with a robust ethic of self-determination, an athletic contest for the eternal crown, with prolonged negative provision for losers. Freedom, he knows, is less straightforward because man's range of choices is limited by many factors. Adam fell captive to sin and only after many divine moves did he become free in Christ. Love unites with a passion for truth, affirms the values of natural law and rejects the lusts of the flesh which have no place in God's kingdom. Within a martyr church, Irenaeus finds perfection in the martyr who reproduces the perfect action of Christ. A long-standing objection to Irenaeus (that perfection in Christ removes ethics) is examined. Finally, the highest good is known as truth in the love of enemies.

11.1.1 FREE WILL AND FREEDOM

Irenaeus insists upon the self-determining choice of every human person.[1] All are free to choose or to reject. The same insistence is found earlier in Justin and Theophilus. Irenaeus, like Clement, joins Plato on the responsibility of the individual,[2] and moves from free will to that perfect free obedience where God's goodness is possessed and preserved (4.12–16; 4.37–9).

Irenaeus' account of freedom is expressed most succinctly in four chapters (4.37–40). He begins from 'the ancient law of liberty' which God granted to man, that man from the beginning should have his own power of choice. He is able to follow God's good

---

[1] This is for Erbkam the basis of all his ethics. H. G. Erbkam, *De sancti Irenaei principiis ethicis* (Königsberg, 1856), 6.
[2] Rep. 617e: 'The blame is on the one who chooses, God is without blame.'

counsel without compulsion. God does not use violence. Those who choose the way of obedience find righteousness, while those who reject the good and spit it back against God, justly incur the judgement of God. For, as Paul has said, they despise the riches of divine goodness, patience and forbearance.

God has given what is good and those who do good are honoured, for it is possible for all either to do or refrain from good. If men were good or evil by nature there would be no honour in right action (4.37.2).[3] Therefore the prophets exhorted men to act justly lest they tumble into forgetfulness of God's good counsel. They must let their light shine before men, and glorify their father in heaven[4] as they choose and fulfil God's will. Similarly Paul presupposes free will when he calls his readers away from evil and their former darkness. As man is free to act rightly, so he is free to believe. The lord says 'according to your faith so be it to you', preserving man's free power of choice. A God who predetermined the moral life of men would make himself powerless and irrelevant, while his ethical robots would gain no virtue.

Earlier in Book 4 Irenaeus has set out the importance of free will. Christ comes to separate the wheat and the chaff which are made by the one God who is maker and judge. But while wheat and chaff cannot change their nature, rational man is self-determining. He chooses to be either wheat or chaff, and for this reason he will be justly judged if he rejects right reason (4.4.3).

Man's free will even extends to choosing his own parents, for he has two kinds of sonship: that into which he is born, and that which he chooses by obedience to a teacher who becomes his father. All are indeed sons of God their maker, but in obedience and doctrine they are not his sons. The disobedient cease to be his sons; but those who believe and obey the teaching of God are indeed his sons (4.41.2, 3).[5]

Irenaeus refers his account of double sonship to an unnamed source. This source is possibly Polycarp, who speaks in his letter

---

[3] W. A. Löhr, 'Gnostic determinism reconsidered', *VigChr* 46 (1992), 381–90. While naming the argument a 'heresiological cliché', Löhr shows the contrary, namely that it is developed in a wider scheme of thought.

[4] Matthew 5:16 is part of the explanation why a living man is the glory of God.

[5] See Armenian variants for this passage; SC 100 (1965), 984.

to the Philippians of faith as the mother of us all (*Philippians* 3). Irenaeus tells how Polycarp addressed Marcion as the first-born of Satan and refers to Polycarp's letter to the Philippians where those who choose may learn the truth and the faith (3.3.4).[6]

God calls for violence from men as he denies violence to himself. Those who choose freely are athletes who strive for an imperishable crown. Costly obedience teaches the love of God, which grows to maturity when we lay hold of God (4.37.7). Irenaeus (4.38) faces the question 'Why did God not make man perfect at the beginning?' Certainly God had the power to give man perfection from the beginning but man, because of his recent origin, could not have received this perfection. A time of development (the divine economy) and a crowning act (recapitulation) had to intervene. No criticism can be levelled against God, for he showed at all times power, wisdom and goodness. His wisdom was displayed in the proportion, measure and harmony of his creation. The immensity of his goodness is evident in the way in which he is always adding something more to man. As the one uncreated being, God enables man to progress to immortality. If, by definition, absolute perfection was not possible for a creature, the best option for God was a creature who could grow to a derived perfection. Man's immortality establishes the goodness of the God who gives it. All this happens in the order and rhythm by which God moves man ever closer to his own image. The fruitfulness and multiplication ordained by God to be the lot of man (Gen. 1:28) concerns mankind's ability to grow and to move towards God in the ethical contest where he competes.

Man's knowledge of good and evil and his ability to choose between them make him twofold where God is simple (4.39). He who would become God must first fulfil the obedience of a created being. Then he will be perfectly formed by God's hands, while those who remove themselves from the light of God the father go to darkness and punishment. They are themselves the cause of their eternal dwelling in regions of darkness. The one God the father prepares good things for those who persevere in fellowship and submission (4.40.1–3) and eternal fire for those who do not.

---

[6] Satan, of course, will never accept responsibility for his apostasy and puts the blame on his maker. This is a typical falsehood and a refusal to recognise responsibility for his own choice (5.26.2).

The Christian message of redemption or liberation only makes sense if man, despite free will, is not free. In Irenaeus, as in Clement of Alexandria and Augustine, there is a distinction between free will and freedom. Irenaeus' understanding of freedom moves with the changing dispensations of God's gift of salvation.[7]

The simplest approach to freedom has already been noted in the anthropology of 4.37.1–7. Here there is one stage only. Against the Valentinian claim that the perfect few are free without qualification and whatever they do is right, Irenaeus argues that free will, the ability to choose, is part of being human and that all may choose or reject. Man's autonomy existed from the beginning and was never threatened by God, for it was part of the divine image. In free and frail humanity God brings to righteousness the free will which he had placed in man as he leads him on towards immortality and eternal obedience (5.29.1).

A two-stage account follows the parallel between Adam and Christ. In the garden, Adam, by disobeying the will of God, becomes a captive and suffers in his captive state (3.23.2). A slave through disobedience, he becomes a slave of sin which wounds and works against him (3.18.7). Transgression dominates his life. Slavery to sin brings slavery to death, and man is captive under the power of death. In a three-part account the divine economy brings man from free will and slavery to freedom, acting through the whole history of the slavery which followed Adam's sin (3.19–23). Then, in the fullness of time, God sends the second man, the word of freedom (3.19.1), to bind the strong man who enslaved Adam and his posterity. The second Adam delivers man and gives him life (4.22.1).

In 4.16.1–5 Irenaeus introduces a seven-part account of slavery and freedom. From Adam to Moses, the patriarchs Enoch, Noah and Abraham lived without the law. They were righteous men (1.27.3) because they had the Decalogue inscribed on their hearts and they loved their maker who kept them from all injustice (4.16.3). As free men they shared and followed 'natural precepts' (4.16.5).[8]

---

[7] R. Tremblay, *Irénée de Lyon, 'L'empreinte des doigts de Dieu'* (Rome, 1979), 35–62.

[8] V. E. Hasler, *Gesetz und Evangelium in der alten Kirche bis Origenes* (Zürich and Frankfurt, 1953), 48–57.

In Egypt this righteousness and love disappeared. God, in his love, led his people out of Egypt that they might hear his voice and become his disciples again. He taught them love and justice and gave them the Decalogue. All these things helped man to friendship with a God who required nothing more from him (4.16.3). But the Decalogue was not enough, for the children of Israel made and worshipped a golden calf (4.15.1), turning back to the captivity which they had known in Egypt. Therefore God introduced all the cultic prescriptions as a yoke of servitude to restrain Israel from sin. This yoke remained until in Christ's new covenant God abolished the precepts of servitude. Christ replaces the law of slavery with the law of liberty: that man should love God with all his heart and follow his word, abstaining from evil deeds and desires (4.16.5).

So the economy of human freedom moves from Adam to the patriarchs with natural precepts, to the darkness of Egypt, to Exodus and restoration to the natural precepts of the Decalogue; but when the people fall again into apostasy, God imposes prescriptions appropriate to the slavery they have chosen. Finally, the covenant of freedom abolishes all these prescriptions except for the ten commandments. In this account Irenaeus is concerned to refute the Marcionites, who divide the whole law and indeed creation from the work of redemption in Christ. For one God works through six stages (Adam, patriarchs, Egypt, Exodus, Decalogue, law of servitude) until the final liberty of Christ.

The progress of free will to freedom goes beyond the power of choice to an inner submission which spontaneously obeys God. How are we to understand the progression (4.16.1–5) from slaves to free men, to sons of God? The captives turn from God to the golden calf and are placed under the slavery of the law in the hope that they may regain inner obedience to God. The free men of whom Irenaeus speaks are the just men and patriarchs who lived before and after Abraham and before the time of Moses (4.16.2). They had the ten commandments written on their hearts (4.16.3) and followed these natural precepts (4.15.1). At the end of the progression come those who are 'sons', set free through inner submission to God, his children by adoption, to follow, through the spirit, what God wants them to do. For the others, God recalls the ten commandments and inscribes them as an inner law. The external law is for education, to train people for freedom and sonship. The sons of God follow him without chains (4.13.2), of their own choice observing the inner law which Christ intensifies and applies.

To sum up, Irenaeus begins (4.37.1–7) with an account of the self-determination to accept or refuse the gift of God, for liberty can only be given if man can accept or refuse it (4.15.2). The power to choose is essential (4.37.1, 2), free from all necessity (4.37.6) and linked with the gift of reason or judgement. It is part of the divine likeness, for God himself is also free (4.37.4), and is amply established from scripture, not merely a construction of human reason. In the second place, Jesus Christ is the author of our liberty. Only by the word and son of God made flesh, dying and rising again, is our freedom possible. His coming in the flesh (4.16.4, 5) replaced slavery with freedom. He widened natural laws through his new covenant of liberty which gave to all the adoption into sonship, where through knowledge and love of God, those who are no longer slaves reject evil desires as well as evil acts. In this new power of freedom, testing is severe, but faith shows itself triumphant.

11.2.1 LOVE OF TRUTH

Like Justin, Irenaeus writes from love of truth.[9] His concern is to attack those who have falsified the good word (1 pref. 1). Here he is following Paul's 'love which rejoices in the truth' and Plato's love of truth for which Socrates gave his life. There is a moral obligation to expose error in the interests of truth (1 pref. 2), in opposition to those who have invented reckless and wretched falsehood. Marcus, for example, has reduced the truth to mere appearance. He scatters the letters of the alphabet over his fabrication to make falsehood appear impressive (1.15.4). Heretics literally wallow in falsehood, or to use a different metaphor, they tumble into emptiness and shadow. The dog of Aesop snapped at the reflection of a piece of bread in the water and lost the real bread which was in his mouth. This is what heretics are doing all the time (2.11.1) with their fanciful pile of mental moves, which they transfer to God, to produce implausible falsehood (2.13.10). Ignorantly, they patch together opinions of the

---

[9] See my *Justin Martyr*, 77–86.

philosophers and claim the patchwork as their own work (2.14.2). Even if this were well done it would be inappropriate, because if the philosophers whom they cite had known the truth, there would have been no need for an incarnation – the truth would have been there already.[10] Since the philosophers did not know the truth, what the Gnostics call knowledge is ignorance, and what they call truth is falsehood (2.14.7). In contrast to this abyss of error the truth of God is accessible in safety and accuracy (2.16.3). How different from his abiding truth is the inconsistency, folly and irrationality of the blind guides and the blind, who fall into the abyss of ignorance (2.18.7)! They ignore the proper order of knowledge and try to surpass God (2.26.3). They take the parables and handle them with no sense of propriety or logic[11] to produce fantastic falsehoods (2.20.1).

We have noted some of these logical failures earlier; Irenaeus wants us to see also that they are ethical failures and that their avoidance constitutes moral excellence. Irenaeus contrasts sophistry and falsehood with truth and love which surpass all knowledge (2.36.1). The marks of the church are sympathy, compassion, steadfastness and truth (2.31.2). Love which moves towards communion with God moves through God to life and light (5.27.2). The light of truth is linked with love; but when Christ shone in the world, men loved darkness rather than light (Jn 3:18, 21) (5.27.2). Love and truth define Christian living. He who does not do all the good he can is foreign to the love of the lord (Iren., frag. 4; cf. James 4:17). He who loves will always speak well of those who deserve well, and refrain from speaking evil of those who do not so deserve (frag. 6; frag. 9).

Irenaeus divides his audience into two groups: those who react reasonably and may possibly be convinced, and those who react with unreason and empty verbosity (2.31.1). The latter claim miracles, which are magical illusions, and are not effective remedies. They neither prove the power of God nor show human concern. These magical tricks destroy, harm and deceive mankind (2.31.2). By contrast the church, with steadfastness and truth, declares its concern for those in need.

[10] Justin sees spermatic logos in philosophers and prophets. Clement sees philosophy as the paidagogos for the Greeks to lead them to Christ.
[11] *improprie et inconsequenter.*

Truth has its enemies. Heretics are slippery serpents and hopeless partners in argument. Yet it is always possible for a lost soul to return to truth, when truth is set out before that soul (3.2.3). Error leads the ignorant to deface the shape of the gospel (3.11.9), to poison their hearers and to replace the milk of the gospel with a mixture of lime and water which destroys rather than gives life (3.17.4). Sincerity and truth stand in contrast to the vainglory (4.33.6) of those who reject truth, divide the church (4.33.7) and avoid the light (5.13.2). Blasphemy and sophistry lead away from truth (5.20.2) to instability. Murder and avarice follow from Adam's fall (5.24.2). When the love of truth is rejected and salvation ignored, God hands over those who have rejected him to error (2 Thess. 2:8–12) (5.25.3), wilfully to wander like blind mice (5.29.1).

11.2.2 LOVE AND NATURAL LAW

In his blend of love and truth, Irenaeus joined Paul and Plato. In his blend of love and natural law, he united Paul and the Stoics. Both moves will have lasting consequences. Love does not stand solitary. Goodness includes justice, for whatever is good is just, and whatever is just is good (3.25.2). The two great commands point to the perfection and necessity of love (4.12.2). Natural law has its place and the natural man has been justified by natural law and by faith. Natural law, as observed by the patriarchs, was extended and fulfilled in the Sermon on the Mount. Our righteousness is to exceed that of the Pharisees because we believe in the son as well as in the father, because we do not merely say, but actually do the good, and because we avoid evil desires as well as evil acts. Here love fulfils and extends the law (4.13.1). The finality of love surpasses the power of evil. It condemns evil desires along with evil acts (2.32.1).

The Mosaic law had educational value. Making use of physical things and teaching the way of service it drew men on to the commandments of God. When the word came he replaced servile obedience with glorious freedom. God's slaves became God's friends.[12] The perfect liberty of the new covenant did away with the law of

---

[12] The Jews had the law, the discipline and prophecy but the natural law had earlier been planted in all to embody the truth of the ten commandments (4.15.1). The law looked

Moses (4.16.5). All things move towards the perfection of love.
The earthly commands of the law of Moses were types of spiritual
things; but we must not add types of types as the heretics incessantly
do (4.19.1). The grace of the father has worked in different ways
and dispensations (4.20.7). Here, as in his account of freedom,
Irenaeus responds to Marcion through an economy of ethics which
enriches the concept of love with moral content and defends the
creator.

11.2.3 LUSTS OF THE FLESH

The power of carnal lust is shown in the heretics who claim to be
free from all evil. They think they are gold in the mud; however
messy the mud is, they remain undefiled. Yet, says Irenaeus, their
behaviour points in a different direction and reveals contamina-
tion: sexual indulgence, gladiatorial shows, heathen festivals and
eating sacrificial meat (1.6.3). Only the psychics, they claim, need
the virtue of continence, while pneumatics may indulge in every
way (1.6.4). For example, Marcus is rewarded by the prophetess
with the gift of sexual union (1.13.3), and his followers make lib-
eral use of love potions (1.13.5). Regrettably, those who look at
the church from the outside imagine that all Christians are like
the Carpocratians (1.25.3).[13] While Tatian and others reject marriage as fornication (1.28.1), Basilides and Carpocrates advocate
promiscuity (1.28.2). The Cainites teach that salvation comes to
him who has experienced everything, and an 'angel' guides the
seeker to try all kinds of sin (1.31.2). Enlarged experience of this
kind leads to lust and abomination not to wider understanding
(2.32.2). By contrast, the light of the true believer rejects luxury,

---

forward through signs such as circumcision (4.16.1). But the patriarchs had the law written
in their heart, and they were fed with manna to prepare them for rational or verbal food,
since man should not live by bread alone, but by the word which proceeds from the
mouth of God (Deut. 8:3) (4.16.3).

[13] This indicates that moral accusations against Gnostics have substance. Irenaeus would
not raise harmful rumour for the sake of scoring a point against his opponents. Further
there is a basis for this behaviour in the ideas of the Gnostics described. Those who
know that they are pure gold will enjoy a dip in the mud. Clement of Alexandria sets out
the Gnostic metaphysical basis for indulgence. Plotinus raises the same objection against
Gnostic morals.

pleasure and lust, because such things lead to forgetfulness of God
(4.2.4).

Carnal lusts, which prohibit entry into God's kingdom, are described by Paul as 'flesh and blood' (5.9.1). The works of the flesh
are contrasted with the fruits of the spirit (5.11.1). Getting rid of
our old humanity simply means preserving our God-given bodies
from the lusts of the flesh (5.12.3). It is not part of a total asceticism for ascetic injunctions are absent because they have dualist
overtones.[14] Rather, the power of evil may be traced to Satan who
first took humanity captive and was then justly taken captive himself (5.21.3). Yet our need of earthly rulers shows that the power of
evil continues. Men would eat one another like cannibal fishes if
there were no secular authorities to punish evil-doers (5.24.2). The
devil is more determined than ever to overcome humanity (5.24.4)
and the Antichrist is the recapitulation of the apostasy of Satan
with every impiety and lawlessness (5.25.1). Yet, through his own
humanity, the word conquers him and shows him to be an apostate
(Lk. 10:19) and gives believers the power to tread on snakes and
scorpions (5.24.4).

11.3 MARTYRDOM

For the first Christians, especially those at Lyons, martyrdom was
the peak of moral excellence because it most clearly reflected the
ultimate goodness of the cross, which the disciple must carry after
his lord. It was also the fulfilment of Plato's philosophical ideal:
the practice of death. Erasmus saw Irenaeus as a candidate whose
temper of mind was fixed by the thought of martyrdom. What
does martyrdom mean for Irenaeus? To begin with, martyrdom
requires two things.[15] First, it means death, not just confession of
faith. Second, this death must be marked by love (4.33.9). The
martyr takes the place within the church of the persecuted, spirit-
filled prophet (4.33.9). Yet martyrdom is not exclusively spiritual,
but includes the participation, indeed the transformation, of the
flesh. As the spirit absorbs the weakness of the flesh and bestows

---

[14] 'We find no clear evidence of asceticism in Irenaeus', Erbkam, *De sancti Irenaei principiis
ethicis.*
[15] Tremblay, *Irénée de Lyon,* 89 115.

on it the strength of the spirit (5.9.2), so weakness is swallowed up, and the glorious power of the spirit is displayed.

What does the martyr achieve? He gains the cross in the world, which proves that the cross is not transcendent above the world as the Gnostics claim (3.18.5). The martyr imitates Christ concretely as he conquers, endures, displays God's goodness and ascends to heaven (3.19.3). Stephen copies the master of every martyr when he prays for the forgiveness of those who kill him (3.12.13). In his perfection, when Christ is struck he does not hit back, when he suffers he does not threaten, and oppressed by violence he asks the father to forgive his murderers. 'It is he who has truly saved us, the word of God, the only son who has come from the father, Christ Jesus our Lord' (3.16.9). By this perfection we are saved, for we cannot be saved by an empty cross or by a saviour who escapes to the pleroma when faced with suffering and death. The martyrs come closest of all to God; the church shows the presence of the spirit in a new way through its martyrs (4.33.9, 10). For the act of the martyr is never an isolated act, but always the act of a member of the church, which stands like Lot's wife, unchanging, although it continues to have members removed from it. It strengthens the children it sends on to the father (4.31.3). Martyrdom belongs to the church and the church is enriched by the martyrs, who point beyond all things to their final triumph in the presence of God. Tribulation is necessary to those who are saved, that they might be ground into fine flour for the feast of the king. Irenaeus quotes the words of Ignatius (*Rom.* 4.1), who speaks of himself as the grain of Christ, to be ground by the teeth of wild beasts and to become the pure bread of God (5.28.4).

So Irenaeus has a complex theology of martyrdom, which derives from his fusion of John with Paul in a theology of the cross and offers yet another link with Plato whose just man is crucified. It could only come from within a martyr church.[16] A martyr who forgives his enemy is the final form of Christian vocation which seeks to become God. The martyr displays the presence of the crucified God. He points to the cross as the glory of the love of God, to the son of the father as the lamb eternally slain. The church

---

[16] See 6.1.2 above, and Scherrer, *La gloire de Dieu*, 180–206.

rejoices in its children who gain the privilege of martyrdom, for they are the fruit of the spirit who dwells in the church, and the living images of the one whom the church loves.

Two disparate elements in the theology of Irenaeus[17] are his belief in deification on the one hand and his moral exhortation on the other. In the first element, all was given in the physical redemption of the believer, in the other element, all was to be acquired by the believer through his moral struggle. The different strands of Irenaeus' thought were a preoccupation of the past. Today, the worthwhile pursuit in the study of Irenaeus is to see ways in which he brings together these apparently disparate elements. Here, in the interpretation of apparently conflicting views, we find his own authentic thought.[18]

We begin from the difference between God and man as the difference between the maker and what is made (4.11.2).[19] God's goodness makes and man is made. To complete his definition of man, we must add that man is a creature defined by growth and improvement (4.11.1) and a receptacle who receives from God. While God is always the same, man is always changing and must always move forward to God. God never ceases to do good to man and to enrich him, and man never ceases to receive from God and to be enriched by him (4.11.2). Participation joins creation as the second part of human definition. The Johannine prologue begins, 'All things were made by him' and ends 'of his fullness have we all received and grace upon grace'. These clear definitions of God and man have important consequences. Obedience to God is neither a law to be fulfilled in pursuit of life eternal, nor an attempt by man to find his own fulfilment. Only because God gives and shares his glory can man find salvation in obedience to him (4.14.1). 'For to follow the saviour is to participate in salvation and to follow the

---

[17] According to A. von Harnack, *Lehrbuch der Dogmengeschichte*, vol. I (5th edn; Tübingen, 1931), 559–60, 588.

[18] B. Aland, 'Fides und subiectio. Zur Anthropologie des Irenäus', in *Kerygma und logos*, FS for Carl Andresen, ed. A. M. Ritter (Göttingen, 1979), 12. This section is indebted at several points to this study.

[19] It is also the difference between what is participated in and what participates.

light is to embrace the light' (4.14.1).[20] So we share in the glory of God. Our part is obedience and this obedience is immortality. 'Subjection to God is incorruption' (4.38.3). Man's subjection is his answer to his mortal and weak condition. His love, subjection and gratitude to God (*dilectio, subiectio, gratiarum actio*) (3.20.2) are descriptions of authentic human being. They are not commands, but a process by which man moves to perfect submission in God (4.16.4). For in this submission the true glory of God is seen (3.20.2). God gives and man receives.

In contrast, the power of Satan is the power which sets itself up as God in revolt against God (5.21.3). Satan embodies evil because he demands divinity and denies the difference between God and man. But how is man who is under the power of Satan to achieve his proper position as a creature under a beneficent creator? Through Christ, God makes man whole (*redintegrans*) and grants the gift of immortality (5.21.3). Ethical behaviour is only possible to those who are free, and we have seen that freedom for Irenaeus, as for the Christian tradition in general, has two elements. First there is self-determination, the free will which belongs to all mankind (4.37.1). Then there is real freedom, the ability to exercise choice over a wide range. In the absolute sense, only God possesses sovereign freedom (4.38.3). Through Christ, however, freedom is granted and it is possible (especially for the martyr) to follow God without chains (4.13.2).

Freedom cannot be a possession of man by himself (4.37.1). Irenaeus speaks of human perfection as something which, in subjection to God, becomes God's perfect work (4.39.2). The incarnate word of the father and spirit of God, joined to the ancient substance of Adam, made man living and perfect in virtue of his reception of the perfect father (5.1.3). Man, who learns from his own weakness that God is immortal and powerful, finds the strength of God made perfect in his weakness (5.3.1; 5.3.3). Perfect man is the mixture of soul with the spirit of the father, and with the flesh which was moulded after the image of God (5.6.1). Recapitulation finds the perfection of man in Christ with whom he is embodied and conformed. Yet man is always man and never God, always receiving,

---

[20] *Sequi enim salvatorem participare est salutem et sequi lumen percipere est lumen.*

always becoming, always flesh, flesh which must be redeemed and reformed (5.9.1), but flesh which can live by the participation of the spirit as well as its own substance.

Life in the *eschaton* is life through the spirit and in the flesh.[21] In the present those who display the life of the spirit most powerfully are the martyrs. They are the men who are fully alive, as they show how the weakness of the flesh is absorbed by participation in the power of the spirit (5.9.2). So the antithesis beween perfection in the spirit and moral exhortation is overcome. As in other puzzles, the crucial move is that of participation.

11.5 LOVE OF ENEMIES AS CRUX OF RECAPITULATION

The word 'recapitulate' is used in early Christian literature in two ways: to describe either the perfection of all being in Christ (Eph. 1:10) or the perfection of all law in the love command (Rom. 13:9–10). Is there any relation between these two applications (ontological and ethical) of the word? The answer must lie in Irenaeus, who quotes Romans 13:10 to the effect that love is the pleroma of the law.[22] Closely related is the Sermon on the Mount, which talks about fulfilment as the work (ontological) of Christ and as the perfection (ethical) required of his followers.[23] Jesus' correction and perfection of old testament law culminate in the distinctive love of the disciples which reflects the divine perfection of the father in heaven. Matthew 5:48 is cited at least five times: 'Be ye perfect as your father in heaven is perfect!' The two ideas (ontological perfection and ethical perfection) are juxtaposed in 3.18–20.[24] Irenaeus sees the love of enemies and the recapitulation of all things in Christ as converging where Jesus says 'Father, forgive them, for they know not what they do.'

Book 3 of *Against heresies* falls into two main parts.[25] The first part (6–15) expounds the unicity of God. The second part (16–23)

---

[21] *vivens . . . propter participationem spiritus, homo autem propter substantiam carnis.*

[22] He does not quote Romans 13:9 where ἀνακεφαλαιόομαι is used.

[23] See the magisterial essay 'Fulfilment-words in the New Testament: use and abuse', in C. F. D. Moule, *Essays in New Testament interpretation* (Cambridge, 1982), 3–36.

[24] Also in *haer.* 4.13–16, 20.

[25] Following A. Rousseau and L. Doutreleau, *Contre les hérésies*, III,2 (Paris, 1974), SC 211, 493–5. See also III,1 (SC 210), 190–205.

expounds the unicity of Christ, the son of God made man in order to sum up his own creation, under three theses: Jesus is truly man, truly God and true renewer of Adam. The passage 3.18–20 bridges the first and second theses, declaring Christ to be true man and true God, changing reality with a new creation and changing man's morality from servitude to sonship. The movement is from theology to ethics and shows that for Irenaeus the centre of each is identical: forgiving love, which redeems and perfects mankind upon the cross. In the words of the man Jesus ('Father, forgive them'), the divine image is perfected and restored in mankind. The same words express the perfect goodness of the father in heaven who sends his sun and rain on good and evil men alike. His sovereign love is not conditioned by the moral frailty of those who benefit. The supreme ethical act of love is needed to transform man ontologically from death to life.

Irenaeus turns to a much-quoted statement of recapitulation. The word who was in the beginning with God, was always present to the human race and, at a time fixed by the father, then joined his creation to himself by becoming a man who was capable of suffering. The long history of man was summed up by Christ briefly in himself, who gave an epitome of salvation to provide an inclusive recovery and a new beginning for mankind. What was lost in Adam, God's image and likeness, may now be recovered in Christ (3.18.1). The image of God meant life and goodness to which the sin of man brought death and moral corruption. Fallen man could neither be remade nor receive salvation; but the word of God through his incarnation and death did both for him (3.18.2).

This happened at the cross. Irenaeus quotes Romans 10, where salvation comes to him who confesses Jesus as crucified and risen lord.[26] He died and rose to be lord of the dead and the living. Christ crucified is the sum of Paul's proclamation. The cup of blessing is communion in his blood.[27] Christ's death brought together those who were far away (Eph. 2:13), freed those who were under the

---

[26] See E. Käsemann, 'The Spirit and the Letter', *Perspectives on Paul*, 155–66, ET of 'Geist und Buchstabe', *Paulinische Perspektiven*, 267–85, where Romans 10:5–13 is taken as a test case.

[27] Rom. 10:6–9 and 14:9, 15; 1 Cor. 1:23 and 10:16 and 15:3–4, 12, 21. 'Après quelques lignes très denses relatives au pourquoi de cette incarnation, voici de nouveaux textes de Paul, dans lequels celui-ci répète inlassablement que le Christ en personne a souffert la

curse of the law (Gal. 3:13) and transformed their relationship with others for whom Christ died (1 Cor. 8:11). There never was an impassible Christ, as heretics claim. The sovereign good of crucified love is necessary to bring man from death to life (3.18.3).

When Christ speaks of the necessity that the disciple's cross should follow his, we have the second link of ontology with goodness. Love crucified must be repeated in the disciple who takes up his cross and follows, losing his life in order to find it (3.18.4). His confession points to yet another consummation where Christ will confess those who have confessed him. 'They try to follow the footsteps of the passion of the Lord and to be martyrs of him who was passible' (3.18.5). Those who despise the martyrs will be rejected by the same Christ who receives the martyrs into glory (3.18.5). Existence under the cross, manifest in the martyr, is part of the central mystery.

For the cross displays the ultimacy of love. The reconciling act is declared in 'Father, forgive them, for they know not what they do.' A new epoch begins as he who taught the forgiveness of enemies now makes real his precept.[28] From his long suffering, patience, mercy and goodness, the word who told us to love our enemies and pray for those who hate us, 'himself did this very thing on the cross, loving the human race so much that he prayed for those who were putting him to death'. If there were a second Christ who avoided the cross, we should prefer without hesitation the one who suffered and who bore no grudge against those who did evil to him. He is truly good (3.18.5).

Truth and goodness must go together. If Christ did not really suffer, so far from thanking him we should blame him. He told us to suffer gladly by turning the other cheek, but he himself (heretics claim) avoided suffering and was inferior to his followers. Even our salvation is undone for unless his obedience has really replaced our disobedience, sin has not been destroyed. However, our lord is the one true master and is truly good,[29] fighting and defeating

---

Passion, a été suspendu au bois, a versé son sang, est mort, a été enseveli et est resuscité', Rousseau and Doutreleau, SC 210, 194 5.

[28] 'Tout cela exclut la thèse hérétique d'un "Christ" demeuré étranger à la Passion', Rousseau and Doutreleau, SC 210, 195.

[29] *sed quoniam solus vere, magister Dominus noster, et bonus vere Filius Dei et patiens Verbum Dei Patris Filius hominis factus* (3.18.6).

the devil, redeeming disobedience by his obedience, freeing his own creation and destroying sin. All this he did out of supreme goodness and love (3.18.6). The spring of recapitulation is ultimate goodness which cannot lack truth. Human salvation depends on the truth of the incarnation, where man is joined to God. Only a real union of God and man could enable man to share in incorruption. This final union consists of love and friendship. The mediator of God and man had to belong on both sides 'in order to bring each into friendship and concord and to ensure that God should welcome man and man should offer himself to God' (3.18.7).[30] Those who deny the reality of Christ's incarnation, which embodies this communion of love, are still under the sway of sin and death. He was what he appeared to be and his works are true (3.18.7).

Irenaeus' argument follows the themes: from death to life, love crucified, goodness and truth, inauguration of filial freedom. The movement is intricate but clear. As often elsewhere, he can move between a central simplicity and the circumference of a circle of ideas, then move from a different point on the circumference through other ideas to the same centre. In the centre, Christ as true man and true God, sums up and renews humanity. This he does on the cross when he forgives his enemies out of infinite love. This is the keystone of recapitulation.[31] The ethics of Irenaeus bring together the first half of this book. They begin from the goodness of God who makes man free, first with free will and finally with perfect freedom. This he does through the many steps of his economy and through the perfect work of Christ in recapitulation. Participation holds all together, for in Christ and the martyrs who forgive as they suffer on earth, the ultimate goodness of God is accessible to humans. In the words 'Father, forgive them' mercy and truth are met together.

---

[30] *per suam ad utrosque domesticitatem in amicitiam et concordiam utrosque reducere, et facere ut et Deus adsumeret hominem et homo se dederet Deo.*

[31] The ultimacy of divine love recurs in the European tradition. When Lessing makes his famous claim that the accidental truths of history can never become the necessary truths of reason, he rejects the fulfilment of prophecies in history except, quoting Origen, for the traces of them which remain in the lives of those who live according to the word. He moves from the Gospel of John to the Testament of John: 'Little children, love one another' which is apocryphal, but no less divine. See *Lessing's Theological Writings*, selected and translated by Henry Chadwick (Stanford, 1957), 51–61; *Lessings-Werke*, 3rd edn, ed. K. Lachmann, revised by F. Muncker, vol. XIII (Leipzig, 1897), 1–8.

PART V

Conclusion

When a poet's mind is perfectly equipped for its work, it is
constantly amalgamating disparate experience.

T. S. Eliot, *Selected Essays, 1917–1932*

For none is perfect but the uncreated who is God. As far as
man is concerned, he must be created and when created he
must receive growth, and having grown he must become
adult, and being adult he must abound, and having aboun-
ded he must grow strong, and having grown strong he must
be glorified, and being glorified he must see his lord: for it is
God who must one day be seen and the vision of God produces immortality and 'immortality brings one close to God'
(Wisdom 6:19).

(4.38.3)

CHAPTER 12

The glory of God and man

Any book on Irenaeus will have a reluctant conclusion, for his ideas and images go on and there is always something new to be seen. The apparent confusions in his thought (*doctor confusus*) may be overcome by conceptual stamina or poetic imagination. Yet his daily immersion in the bible (2.27.1) piles image upon image, thought upon thought (*doctor constructivus*). Our paths through the Irenaean jungle do not deny exuberance, but give strength to his claim that scripture is a garden where every fruit is to be eaten (5.20.2). This chapter will show how these paths merge in his dynamic humanism, his creative use of argument and imagery, his optimism and, through participation, his sense of the immediacy of God.

Irenaeus has a sense of order which is common to the culture of the West, but adds to it a fresh zest. He enriches classical humanism with a joy in the human condition and an admiration for man. His God is the good shepherd who rejoices in the work of salvation. Gnostics, with their denigration of creation, are in his opinion atheists. The wonder of God the creator and of man the creature go together, for the glory of God is man fully alive (4.20.7) and God is the glory of man who receives his wisdom and power (3.20.2).

Irenaeus deepened the classical tradition by the value which he placed on the human self. The salvation of the flesh is the goal of Irenaeus' gospel, so that paradise is better seen at the end than at the beginning and chiliasm is a prelude to incorruptibility (5.32.1). One

251

writer has seen contemporary relevance in Irenaeus' concentration on 'flesh'[1] through which there is a way to the glory of God (4.39.2). Man remains clay in the hand of the potter. The Gnostic claim to perfection ignores the fact that man is a developing creature within a process which runs from creation to consummation.[2]

For Irenaeus the Gnostic man is 'a monstrous mixture of the superhuman and the inhuman'.[3] Gnostic pessimism denies the co-operation of body and soul, because the body is dilapidated and preparing for combustion.[4] Like gold in a furnace, the pneumatic element is untouched by any physical experience, so that a pneumatic person may eat and do what he will. Irenaeus opposes this 'monstrous liturgy of self-celebration',[5] because it destroys the contingent human self.

Gnosticism has a cognitive system which submits reality to egocratic fantasy.[6] The soul is in prison in the body and will not be released until it has paid the last farthing (Lk. 12:58; Matt. 5:25–6) by committing every impiety. Those who have consummated all sins break the cycle of transmigration and soar to angelic bliss (1.25.4). This is a negation of humanity, of natural law, of any boundary between God and man. The Gnostic 'total man' accomplishes all in one *parousia*: he lacks nothing, absorbing all difference in himself. The body is irrelevant, a relic of the evil demiurge.

Inevitably, all Gnostics wish to be teachers and invent something new (1.28.1). They dislocate the text of scripture, over which they set themselves by abandoning any rule of truth (2.27.1). Irenaeus' chief concern is not with details of any particular heresy but with dogmatic irrationality, 'utter incurable stupidity' (2.30.5), and demonic deception and fantasy (2.31.3), where there is no differentiation between reason and unreason. What bothers him is that, for Gnostics, there can never be a difference

---

[1] Verweyen, 'Frühchristliche Theologie', 397: 'Das durch Gottes Hände nach seinem Bilde modellierte (plasmare!) Fleisch des Menschen als Grund und Ziel der gesamten "oikonomia", des gesamten Heilsplanes Gottes.'

[2] Ibid., 399: 'wo alles Fleisch unter dem Haupt Christi "rekapituliert", in das leuchtende Bild Gottes wieder eingeholt sein würde'.

[3] G. Vincent, 'Le corps de l'hérétique (la critique de la gnose par Irénée)', *RHPhR* 69,4 (1989), 411: 'l'économie anthropo-théologique de l'humain'.

[4] Ibid., 412.

[5] Ibid., 413.

[6] Ibid., 414: 'du fantasme de totalisation égocratique'.

'between reason and folly, between faith in God and a passion for absoluteness'.[7]

Resurrection is not an event for the body, says the Gnostic, but is the knowledge of the truth (2.31.2). Modernity has offered a similar certitude of instant truth, the destruction of what Irenaeus calls 'economy' (*dispositio*) which 'disposes us when we cannot dispose it'.[8] Recently the passion for novelty, for horror, for the sensational, reduces experience to one elementary stimulant. The subject is decomposed. In contrast, Irenaeus has a deep concern for a humanity which recognises God and creation and rejects fantasy. Eve was 'bound' by lack of faith, Mary was freed by her faith. Christ delivers humanity by binding the strong man and robbing him of his possession (3.23.1). The Gnostic offers a real identity with God, with all the mystery of his being, an identity which precludes death and separation, which rejects the world and the body as ephemeral and irrelevant. This claim to identity is a fantasy, from which Irenaeus offers deliverance through the incarnate Christ.

12.2 TWO CRITERIA: ARGUMENT AND IMAGERY

Koch's objections against Irenaeus (*doctor constructivus et confusus*)[9] are met by Irenaeus' double criterion – logic and aesthetic. Argument and imagery are the keys to his thought. Irenaeus presents a clear coherence of many images. Categories of later controversy cannot be projected on him, and the analysis of Loofs is now hypercritical and outmoded.[10] Whatever the influences on Irenaeus, his originality provides 'the extraordinary power of a theological vision, rich and harmonious, veiled in simplicity of expression. Each element fits together as part of an ever wider doctrinal synthesis.'[11]

---

[7] Ibid., 420: 'la toujours possible indifférenciation, de la raison et de la folie, de la foi en Dieu et de la passion pour l'absolu'.

[8] Ibid., 420.

[9] See above, 1.3–1.4.

[10] Ruiz, 'L'enfance d'Adam', 97, quoting Benoit, 'Irénée et Justin', *Actes des journées irénéennes des 9–10–11 mai 1984. La foi et la gnose hier et aujourd'hui: Irénée de Lyon*, CICL 15 (Lyon, 1984), 64. At best, source criticism discovers what Irenaeus began from. It is more rewarding to discover what he did with the material to hand and his own originality.

[11] Ruiz, 'L'enfance d'Adam', 114.

For one reader the synthesis stems from the concept of God as the unique source of life.[12] Light has meaning as life (Jn 1:4), which shines in creation and in incarnate glory. Light has logical and aesthetic force. Light points logically to the discovery of fresh meaning or hidden fallacies, and aesthetically to glory.

The thought of Irenaeus lived on in reason and imagination. The rebirth of biblical images which marked the beginning of Christian thought gave access to the all-embracing mind of the good God. The imagery was governed by the twin criteria of truth and fitness, by logic and aesthetic. The multiplication of Gnostic aeons was as much an offence against poetry as it was against the logic of Plato's third man. The images have logical content. They are 'configurations of the economies' of divine activity. They describe what God is doing and what he will do and what man should do and know.

In Justin and Irenaeus, the prophetic visions serve in place of Plato's forms, and function as mathematics in their constancy. When Trypho complains that Justin repeats his prophetic evidence too frequently, the reply comes that there is nothing wrong with the repetition of simple equations such as $2 + 2 = 4$ (*dial.* 85.5). The prophets, for Irenaeus as well as for Justin, hold a relation not unlike that of mathematics to the material world. The Gnostics separated mathematics from the physical world. Today scientists do not. 'These are not disjoint realms but they are parts of an interlinked complementary created reality, as our "amphibious" experience as embodied thinking reeds testifies, and as is also witnessed to by the "unreasonable effectiveness" of mathematical pattern as the clue to the structure of physical law.'[13]

Both imagery and logic, poetry and argument find a first principle or the thing itself. A modern poet writes:

> The important thing is to build new sentences
> to give them a new shape,
> to get acquainted with grammar like a new friend . . .
> I would like to go right back
> devising a sentence
> unlike any such creature in creation,

---

[12] Ibid., 115.
[13] J. C. Polkinghorne, *Belief in God in an age of science* (Yale, 1998), 129.

like nothing on this planet . . .
It would glitter, articulate,
strum and diversify.
It would be the thing itself.[14]

Certainly, Irenaeus' recapitulation in the ultimate reality of Christ glitters, articulates, strums and diversifies, yet belongs to this planet.

Some will stumble at the claim that Irenaeus has a Platonic paradigm and the denial that he is a Platonist. The distinction is simple. Our environment determines the categories in which we think. In a post-Christian world, people still think in terms of guilt and charity. An illuminating incident occurred in the 1950s when a conservative theologian unwittingly mimicked an eminent atheist philosopher, John Anderson. The conservative insisted with much argument that all revelation was propositional.[15] The philosopher had argued at length that truth must be propositional and his ideas dominated the environment where both lived.[16] The parallels were detailed and exact. Yet the theologian had never heard a lecture or read a line of the philosopher. Had he done so he would have disagreed. He had simply lived and worked in a city dominated by the philosopher's ideas. Contrary beliefs were expressed in identical categories. Similarly Irenaeus, living in a Platonic world, for all his biblical content, set three of his concepts in a Platonic mould of divine Intellect, recapitulation into the form of the good, and participation. He had to bend the mould for the economy of saving history, but even this economy became simultaneous as well as linear. The patriarchs became contemporaries. Therefore the use of the term 'Platonic paradigm' is illuminating, although it may be misunderstood.

In the end, the chief influence of Gnosticism on Irenaeus was that it forced him to take Athens seriously. Gnosticism was inaccessible except through the Platonism which it caricatured. Picture-book Platonism could best be challenged by the Socratic tradition of argument. In this way Gnosticism (theosophy) stimulated

[14] Chris Wallace-Crabbe, 'The thing itself', in *I'm deadly serious* (Oxford, 1988), 10.
[15] D. B. Knox, 'Propositional revelation, the only revelation', *RTR* (1960). See my discussion, 'Realism and revelation', *ABR* (1960), 29–37.
[16] John Anderson, 'The knower and the known', *PAS* (1926–7), 61–84. See also 'Empiricism', *AJPP* (1927), 241–54.

its opposite (philosophy) to produce Christian theology. When we have seen this, we have begun to understand the second century.[17]

12.3.1 OPTIMISM AND GROWTH THROUGH PARTICIPATION

Of the four great concepts of unity – divine Intellect, economy, recapitulation, participation – the first and last point to optimism and growth, while the middle concepts show the way in which growth is achieved.

Irenaeus links the concept of divine Intellect with active goodness to make a 'theocentric optimism'. God's goodness is prior to his action (4.39.2). He is the rich source of all good things (1.12.2; 4.39.4). Optimism springs from confidence in the goodness of creator and creation.[18] Irenaeus finds Gnostics to be restless and dissatisfied; they are always seeking but never finding (5.20.2). In contrast, Irenaeus puts forward a love of being and a good sense which sees in the opposites which the Gnostics reject a ground for admiration. The diversity of the world is a splendid harmony from the composer of a wonderful universe (2.26.3; 2.25.1; 4.4.2).

Because of God's goodness it is right to follow nature. One must respect the nature of each object. The Gnostics want to adulterate, abuse, transform, or destroy the object which is in front of them, whereas Irenaeus wishes to relate to it. One must respect the mind and its limited knowledge (2.25.4). One must grow in knowledge; development is the rule for the human mind. These three principles express the method of Irenaeus and are compatible with Stoic veneration of nature. Gnostics find salvation in evading nature, but Irenaeus finds it among existing things (5.36.1). He notes with wonder the rich natural beauty in which Adam was placed (*dem.* 12). He speaks harshly of the sins which are against nature. The jealous murder of Cain is worse than the incest of the daughters of Lot who wished to maintain the human race. Against the contempt of Gnostics for the mass of humanity, Irenaeus is concerned that

---

[17] The line between theosophy and philosophy in the second century was not as clear as it has been since the Enlightenment; but it was there.

[18] D. B. Reynders, 'Optimisme et théocentrisme chez Saint Irénée', *RThAM* 8 (1936), 225–52.

every human being should find incorruption and life eternal, as he turns from the emptiness of carnal things to the new order of the flesh which God gives (5.10.2).

The word heals all human decay in man and restores humanity (5.12.6). He brings in himself all that is new and all that was promised (4.34.1). Here God triumphs in his work and man rediscovers his nature under the sovereignty of spirit (3.10.2). Restored to his first condition (5.32.1), he rejoices in the vision of God (5.7.2). So divine Intellect, the first concept of Irenaeus, as 'theocentric optimism', flows into the second concept of divine economy which points to growth.

In his optimism concerning man and God, Irenaeus stands in the second-century Christian tradition. He owes most to Justin whose good creator made the world for the sake of man (*1 apol.* 10.2) The father of all things has guided his people in every age that they might share in his life and immortality. God loves all men with justice and goodness (*dial.* 23.2). Christians imitate the good God who sends rain and sun on both holy and wicked men (*dial.* 96.3). 'None is good but God alone who made all things' is Justin's embellishment of the Gospel saying (*1 apol.* 16.7; *dial.* 101.2). God's goodness is his favourite theme. Optimism is further indicated in his account of spermatic logos which is present in every human being (*2 apol.* 8). All who have lived with logos are Christians (*1 apol.* 46).

The same optimism concerning man and God is found in Tertullian. The testimony of the soul naturally Christian springs from the deepest level of human consciousness, for all men know the goodness of the one God (*apologeticum* 17.5–6). Faith is the recognition of a well-known God. Revelation confirms what is known from creation, Christ confirms what is known from prophecy. God is commended by nature and daily life, and less known only because his unicity has been concealed by a variety of names (*adversus Valentinianos* 3.2). The goodness of the creator is shown supremely in the making of man.

12.3.2 PARTICIPATION AND EXCHANGE

The verb 'to participate' is used by Irenaeus to report and criticise Gnostic doctrine, to criticise false doctrine and to expound true doctrine. We may note typical examples. First, Nous pondered how he might communicate to the other aeons the greatness of the Father (1.2.1); a woman thanks Marcus for having dubiously communicated to her his own grace (of prophecy) (1.13.3).[19] Secondly, how can the twelfth aeon participate in passion when the other eleven aeons, who are all derivative from one source, did not (2.23.1)? How can docetic Ebionites truly participate in salvation if he whom they believe was no more than an imaginary being (4.33.5)?

The concept is used in positive exposition. Participation is the life of the church. Where the church is, there is the spirit of God; but the spirit is truth and those who do not participate in the spirit, are not nourished into life from their mother's breasts, and do not receive that purest fountain which flows from the body of Christ (3.24.1). Participation is personal: the advent of the king brings joy and liberty to his subjects who participate by seeing and hearing him, enjoying the gifts which he confers (4.34.1). To follow the saviour is to participate in salvation, as to follow the light is to participate in the light (4.14.1). Such participation is not automatic, for while some choose light others choose darkness and participate in its calamities (5.28.1). Body participates in divine wisdom and power (5.3.2), and the flesh which now participates in life from God will participate in life eternal (5.3.3).[20] Only in faith and obedience can one participate in what is good. The devil promises all things to those who fall down and worship him; but what pleasant or good things can he who has fallen share (5.22.2)? There are degrees of participation. As an artist begins with an idea but takes time to execute it, so the body, as instrument of the soul which it participates, slows it down (2.33.4). Finally, participation is reciprocal: from man to God and from God to man. To fulfil all the conditions of human nature, the son participates and is made incarnate in man for the sake of man (3.18.7).

Irenaeus does more than any other earlier Christian writer to establish participation as a category of Christian thought.[21] On the one hand, the concept belongs to Plato,[22] where it describes the

---

[19] See also 1.30.8 and 2.17.4.

[20] On bodily participation in God see also 5.4.2; 5.6.2; 2.29.1,2; 2.34.4.

[21] See D. L. Balás, *ΜΕΤΟΥΣΙΑ ΘΕΟΥ. Man's participation in God's perfections according to Saint Gregory of Nyssa* (Rome, 1966), 1–9; D. L. Balás, 'Participation', *Encyclopedia of early Christianity*, 2nd edn (New York, 1997), 873–6.

[22] μετέχω, μέθεξις, κοινωνία, μίμησις.

participation of particulars in forms. The particular thing shares in but is not identical with the form. Aristotle rejected Plato's forms but retained the notion of participation to describe the difference between the imperfect and perfect possession of a quality.

On the other hand, in the new testament the words are used in a different way. μετέχω is most frequent; Christ shares our mortal nature (Heb. 2:1), we share in him (Heb. 3:14), sharing his sufferings (Phil. 3:10; 2 Cor. 1:7) and his glory. Philippians 3 is built around this theme and influences Irenaeus strongly. We share in the eucharist (1 Cor. 10:16–18) and the communion of the spirit (2 Cor. 13:13). κοινωνία dominates the first epistle of John and participation in the divine nature is the end of salvation (1 Pet. 1:4).

Irenaeus joins the biblical with the philosophical account through Justin, who had used participation on two central issues. The spermatic logos is shared in varying degrees by all men. The soul finds life only by participation in God who is life. The second point is central to Irenaeus (2.34.4), where the difference between participation and identity, established by Plato, elucidates the problems of image and likeness, breath and spirit.[23]

Participation retains a dialectic. Just as Plato joined the One and the One-Many in the form of the good, so the divine economy belongs to a God who joins darkness and light. In creation, participation points to pied beauty.

> Glory be to God for dappled things –
> For skies of couple-colour as a brinded cow;
> For rose-moles all in stipple upon trout that swim;
> Fresh-firecoal chestnut-falls; finches' wings;
> Landscape plotted and pieced – fold, fallow, and plough;
> And áll trádes, their gear and tackle and trim.[24]

On the cruel cross, glory shines. Even to eternity the one light of God is shared by those who remain his creatures and are not swallowed up in his being but are always going on.

---

[23] See discussion in chapter 11 and the differing solutions of Behr and Sesboüé; also see Spanneut, *Le stoïcisme des pères de l'église*, 148: 'Comme chez les auteurs précédents, on trouve, greffées sur un système de base héllenique, des données chrétiennes bibliques, plutôt juxtaposées que coordonnées.'

[24] 'Pied beauty', G. M. Hopkins, *Poems and Prose of Gerard Manley Hopkins*, ed. W. H. Gardner (Penguin Books, 1953), 30.

Participation means communion with God and with Jesus Christ.[25] The Gnostics have separated father, word and spirit, but Irenaeus holds them together so that man might live a life of union with God. From creation where God, immediately present, makes man in his own image, by the presence of the word throughout the economy to the incarnation, man is joined to God. 'How could we have shared in adoption if the word of God had not entered into communion with us and become flesh himself?' (3.18.7). Between God and man unity is restored (3.18.7). Communion means participation, so incorruptibility follows union with God. The corruptible is absorbed by incorruption and the mortal by immortality (3.19.1). Participation in God's glory comes through the vision of his splendour (4.14.1). At the eschatological banquet men will share at God's table (4.16.1), until God's final gift of himself (5.36.3).

In every chapter of the second half of this book, there has been a place for participation and the reciprocity of 'exchange-formulae'. Irenaeus' link of participation with exchange [26] begins from Paul's account of Christ who became poor that we might be rich (2 Cor. 8:9). In the hymn of Philippians 2:3–11, the believer shares in the humility of Christ and his exaltation. The Adam–Christ parallel (Rom. 5:2–21) exchanges life for death. In Ephesians, redemption from sin brings near those who were once far off; they become members of the body of Christ. The exchange motif goes back to Moses at the burning bush, where Christ came down to confront Moses and to save his people just as he later came down and then ascended for the salvation of men (3.6.2). He sums up humanity in himself, exchanging invisible for visible, incomprehensible for comprehensible, impassible for passible, the word becoming man, drawing things together in himself to be ruler in the invisible, spiritual realm, as well as in the visible and corporeal realm, assuming primacy and making himself head of the church, 'so that he might draw all things to himself at the right time' (3.16.6). The pattern is constant: descent/ascent, the great exchange and participation.

[25] R. Winling, 'Une façon de dire le salut: la formule "être avec Dieu être avec Jésus-Christ" dans les écrits de Saint Irénée', *RevSR* 58 (1984), 105–35.

[26] Teilhabe und Tausch. See F. Normann, *Teilhabe — ein Schlüsselwort der Vätertheologie* (Münster, 1978), 90–2.

The theme of exchange begins and ends Book 5.[27] In the preface Irenaeus asks that he be read carefully. There is one true teacher, the word of God, the Lord Jesus Christ. The act of truth is an act of exchange:

> because of immeasurable love,
> he became what we are
> to bring us to be even what he is himself.
>
> (5 pref.)

Knowledge works through exchange (5.1.1). There is no other way to learn the mind of God than through our teacher who is the word of God made man. We may know what he is by seeing, hearing and imitating our teacher. The exchange produces participation and, in a single stroke, destroys the dualism of the heretics.

Therefore because it is through his own blood that the lord has redeemed us, since he has given his soul for our souls and his flesh for our flesh, since he has also poured out the spirit of the father to effect the union and communion of God and man, making God descend into men by the spirit, and making man ascend up to God by his own incarnation, and since certainly and truly in his coming he has given us incorruption by the communion which we have with him – all the doctrines of the heretics are destroyed. (5.1.1)

Participation is for Irenaeus the argument before which all dualism tumbles into ruins.

Participation is brought about through the descent of God's first-born word to grasp the creature, and by the ascent of the creature who grasps the word and ascends beyond the angels to become the image and likeness of God. Mutual participation assimilates the creature to the divine likeness. The great exchange is achieved by the descent of the word and the ascent of man (5.36.3).

The same note of a descending son of God who restores the divine image and likeness is found at the end of the *Demonstration*. The words of the scripture[28] point to that universal divine wisdom whose light goes out and returns from the stars, and who then descends to earth to communicate the divine likeness to his creature

---

[27] See the relevant commentary of Orbe, *Teología de San Ireneo*, and the fine work of W. Overbeck, *Menschwerdung* (Bern, 1995).

[28] Baruch 3:29–4:1, attributed to Jeremiah.

(*dem.* 97). Participation means growth. God makes; man is made. But man who is found in God will advance to God (4.11.2).

12.4 THE IMMEDIACY OF GOD

From the divine Intellect who contains all but is not contained, who creates from nothing, who has held Adam in his hands throughout the economy, and who has summed up all things in Christ, Irenaeus is ruled by a sense of the immediacy of a God in whose truth, beauty, life and goodness he now participates.

This immediacy joins time with simultaneity and the human with the divine. For Irenaeus the movement of time is real, since the economy of God belongs within God himself. When the prophets gaze on the mind of God, they see no abstract forms but a plan spread over time. Yet the economy is summed up in Christ, and recapitulation is projected back so that the living word speaks with Moses at the burning bush. The same immediacy goes on in the life of the believer, who lives with his lord in past and present and thereby with patriarchs and prophets[29] as he prays, 'All that you have done is eternally present. The history of salvation is also a revelation. By this picture we must present it. Daniel and Jonah are not strangers to us. They are our brothers, our contemporaries in the faith.'[30] By this immediacy 'the past and future / Are conquered and reconciled'.[31] Time and simultaneity belong to God and to all who participate in God. Simeon found the divine immediacy as he took in his hands a child who was the salvation of all, 'the son of God, the light of all, the glory of Israel, the peace and refreshment of those who had fallen asleep' (3.16.4).

Immediacy marks God's grasp on created reality when Irenaeus insists that Adam never left the hands of God. For God does not belong to a transcendent world of forms or aeons. Since creation, God without man is as unthinkable as man without God. There is no equal music which transcends the parts and voices of the divine

---

[29] See above, 9.3, for the immediacy of prophets and patriarchs in early Christian art.
[30] Prigent, *Immagini Cristiane*, 70.
[31] 'Here the impossible union of spheres of existence is actual / Here the past and future / Are conquered and reconciled.' T. S. Eliot, 'The dry salvages', *Four Quartets* (London, 1944), 33.

economy. The voice of the son of man is as the sound of many waters. Only because God is immediate within the world among its changes and chances, folly and brilliance, earthquake and fire, can his voice be heard. Irenaeus turned from Gnostic abstractions to the place where the kingdoms of this world become the kingdoms of God and his Christ.

For Irenaeus, Athens and Jerusalem meet at Patmos, as surely as the two great rivers meet at Lyons and flow on as one stream. The transcendent realities of Athenian philosophy are transmuted by the prophets and patriarchs of Jerusalem. Greek love of truth and beauty remains; but the Platonic scaffolding comes down. It is *not* the case that 'The One remains, the many change and pass; / Heaven's light forever shines, earth's shadows flee';[32] but rather 'Behold the tabernacle of God is with men, and he will dwell with them, and they shall be his people, and God himself shall be with them and be their God' (Rev. 21:3),

For the glory of God is a living man and the life of man is the vision of God. (4.20.7)

To advance from the image of the horizontal hourglass, where we began,[33] and to join his argument and his imagery, his logic and aesthetic, Irenaeus brings his reader into a place like the Sistine Chapel.[34] On each side and above him are the economies of prophets and apostles which make up the one economy of the divine Intellect. Before him is the recapitulation of all things in Christ, through whom prophets and apostles are joined. Yet divine Intellect, economy and recapitulation cannot be seen in abstract. The beholder must fall to prayer and by faith share, participate, in the glory which God gives in exchange for the humanity which God shares in Christ.

---

[32] P. B. Shelley, 'Adonais', *Shelley's poetical works* (Oxford, 1935), 438.

[33] See above, 1.6.2.

[34] When we have analysed the logic, aesthetic and ethic of Irenaeus, we can turn to *une théologie á genoux* as exemplified in P. Ferlay, *Saint Irénée de Lyon, la symphonie du salut* (Paris, 1982). Such a theology cannot solve the complexity to which Koch pointed; but it can hold together the mass of argument and aesthetic.

Appendix: Gnosticism

While the differences between so-called 'Gnostic' groups present a permanent problem,[1] there have been useful and concise accounts. Gnosticism is 'a doctrine of redemption, which appeared among Christians and pagans in late antiquity'.[2] Six common characteristics of various types of Gnosticism have been claimed:

1. a cosmic dualism, according to which the world is evil and ruled by evil powers. Matter and spirit are sharply opposed, but all things fall under the dominion of one or the other;
2. a clear distinction between the most-high, unknown God, and the God who created this world, usually identified with the creator God of the old testament;
3. some humans are naturally like God, bearing a spark of heavenly light, although their body belongs to an evil world;
4. the human condition and desire for freedom are explained by a myth of a pre-cosmic fall;
5. humans are liberated by knowledge of their true nature and heavenly origin;
6. only an elect few have the spiritual seed which determines by its presence or absence the destiny and the moral choices of each person.

---

[1] Irenaeus had plenty of information on the magical antics of the followers of Marcus, but they are best kept separate from the Valentinians, in spite of their juxtaposition in Book 1, which may well be due to a displacement of the text; D. H. Tripp, 'The original sequence of Irenaeus *Adversus haereses* 1: a suggestion', *SecCent* 8 (1991), 157–62.

[2] *TRE* 13, 519.

Today even such a summary has been questioned; earlier gener-
alisations are challenged and replaced by other vulnerable claims,
which may be set out briefly.[3] It may be argued that exegesis by
Gnostics was not governed by a pattern of protest or reversal;[4] that
their ideas were not parasitic;[5] that as a group, they were averse
neither to the body nor to the world, neither ascetic nor libertine,
neither determinist nor elitist.[6] It is even claimed that Gnostics
emerge as 'sanguine sociable creatures . . . judging by the ways in
which they often seemed intent precisely on pursuing a lessening
of sociocultural tension between their religious movement and the
larger social world.'[7] This popular approach turns to the market
place. 'Gnosticism' is no longer a brand name with a secure market.
'And in any case I wonder if the record of product performance
does not indicate that it is time for scholars as responsible modern
"producers of knowledge to issue a massive recall, and to focus collective attention on developing not merely a repackaging program
but a new model altogether".'[8] The Gnostic is an indescribable in
pursuit of the incompatible. Beyond marketing, however, questions
of historical investigation remain.

SCHOOLS OF PHILOSOPHY?

How did Gnostic groups behave? The category 'school' is not just
a device of heresiologists, but part of the self-understanding of (at
least) Ptolemy and the group around him, as shown by Irenaeus,
the Letter to Flora, and other texts of the church fathers. People
from the group around Ptolemy called themselves 'members of the
school of Valentinus' and from the beginning of the third century (at
the latest) the Valentinians themselves distinguished themselves as
two schools. There is a succession of teachers and a teacher–pupil
relation through the normal continuity and discontinuity of any

---

[3] See M. A. Williams, *Rethinking 'Gnosticism'. An argument for dismantling a dubious category*
(Princeton, 1996).

[4] Ibid., 77.

[5] Ibid., 94.

[6] Ibid., 96 212.

[7] Ibid., 264.

[8] Ibid., 266. The cultural attraction which derived from American nature mysticism, in
Emerson and Thoreau, is here rejected.

school.[9] Clement's *Excerpta* set out a well-known series of questions. There was sometimes a common life with sacraments and cult; Flora is a 'sister'. A claim has been made for Valentinianism as a philosophical school.[10]

What kind of philosophy might be envisaged?[11] Philosophy could be a domestic matter with the paterfamilias leading in the manner caricatured by Lucian. It could be popular, as in Musonius Rufus and Epictetus, with little logical argument. Also popular are the lectures of Maximus of Tyre who discussed great themes like the nature of philosophy, God, the origin of evil, and moral life, as well as practical problems like enduring injustice and avoiding anxiety. Persius, a student of the Stoic, Annaeus Cornutus, lists these subjects (*Satires* III.66–72).

More professional was Calvenus Taurus who held regular lectures, discussions on texts, chiefly in public places or rented buildings. For such lectures there were rooms in the *Athenaeum* of Hadrian.[12] Authority derived from a founder whose teachings should be accepted; but there was little continuity of teaching in late antiquity. For example, there was nothing in common between Carneades (213–129 BC) and Calvenus Taurus (fl. AD 145). There was a strong component of myth which found a starting point in philosophical and religious questions. Pupils of Valentinus and Ptolemy used myth, and seem to be poorly educated.[13]

WAS VALENTINUS A GNOSTIC?[14]

From the fragments which we possess it appears that Valentinus did not share the views of those who subsequently were known as his

[9] C. Markschies, *Valentinus Gnosticus?* (Tübingen, 1992), 395–6.

[10] B. Layton, *The Gnostic scriptures: a new translation with annotations and introduction* (New York and London, 1987), 267. His claim that Valentinus was a Christian reformer of a classical Gnostic system 'cannot be too strongly denied'. Markschies, *Valentinus Gnosticus?*, 405.

[11] J. Hahn, *Der Philosoph und die Gesellschaft: Selbstverständnis, öffentliches Auftreten und populäre Erwartungen in der hohen Kaiserzeit* (HABES 7; Stuttgart, 1987).

[12] K. Gaiser, 'Das Philosophenmosaik in Neapel. Eine Darstellung der platonischen Akademie' (AHAW.PH 2/1980, Heidelberg, 1980), esp. 8–23.

[13] C. Markschies, 'Valentinian Gnosticism: toward the anatomy of a school', in *The Nag Hammadi Library after fifty years*, ed. J. D. Turner and A. McGuire, Nag Hammadi Studies 44 (Leiden, 1997), 401–38.

[14] Markschies, *Valentinus Gnosticus?*

followers. In modern times we have seen stark contrasts among the pupils of Bultmann and marked divergence from the conclusions of their founder. Similar discontinuity is apparent between Valentinus and the Valentinians.

Six points of divergence may be noted. According to Valentinus, angels made humans from an ideal pre-existing pattern and gave them spirit from the highest God. According to the Valentinian school, the demiurge, in ignorance of a higher pattern, made humans who received spirit from Achamoth. According to Valentinus there is but one God the father, who is accessible to all, while for the school, the unknown father has a variable accessibility.

Valentinians have three 'Christs', while for Valentinus the one Jesus is both God and human. For Valentinus the goodness of the world derives, as for Plato (*Tim.* 29e), from the ideal pattern; for the school, the myth of the aeons presents a different picture. The golden chain of Valentinus has no place for the fall of Sophia. Valentinus restricted the Platonic interpretation of the biblical text while Valentinians multiplied texts.

It may therefore be argued that Valentinus was in no sense the reformer of a classic Gnostic system and that he stands somewhere between Philo and Clement as part of the Alexandrine thought world.[15]

IRENAEUS' ACCOUNT OF VALENTINIAN GNOSTICISM (1.1–8)

Contemporary scepticism concerning the Gnostic phenomenon need not bring us to join Tertullian in the 'duty of derision' against Gnosticism. Over the last fifty years very useful work has been done on newly discovered documents. Since the purpose of this book is to elucidate the thought of Irenaeus, the lack of a synthesis of Gnostic ideas is less important than Irenaeus' account of the stimulus to his thought. What forced Irenaeus to struggle towards a unified statement of Christian thought? Here there is no mystery. Irenaeus sets out what has stirred him to action in Book 1 and refutes it in Book 2. The remainder of his work shows that his response goes beyond the stimulus.

[15] Ibid., 404.

Irenaeus begins with a detailed account of a Valentinian myth which is the work of a generation after Valentinus and Ptolemy.[16] The attribution to Ptolemy (*et Ptolemaeus quidem ita*) is a gloss; but the authors were most likely Valentinians who, while calling themselves pupils of Valentinus, were in fact pupils of Ptolemy.[17] The work displays four movements (extension, dispersion, concentration in saviour, and return to unity by saviour) and falls into six episodes:[18]

(a) The first principle and first emanations;
(b) The passion of Sophia and the new emanations;
(c) The formation of Achamoth;
(d) Three substances;
(e) Creation of the cosmos;
(f) Christ and consummation.

(a) *The first principle and first emanations*

All things begin from the perfection of the pro-father, pro-first principle, abyss, who is incomprehensible, beyond apprehension, invisible, eternal, unbegotten, tranquil in profound repose. With him exists indivisibly thought (*ennoia*) who is also silence (*sige*) and grace (*charis*). From this beginning derive three pairs (*suzugiai*) of emanations (*probolai*) to the glory of the Father and to form the Ogdoad: Nous (or Monogenes) and Aletheia, Logos and Zoe, Anthropos and Ecclesia. Further emanations continue to the glory of the Father. From Logos and Zoe proceed five pairs of aeons (the Decad) and from Anthropos and Ecclesia six further pairs (Dodecad). These thirty form the Pleroma, or fullness of the Godhead.

(b) *The passion of Sophia and the new emanations*

(i) Passion of Sophia, emanation of limit: The only-begotten Nous alone beholds and rejoices in the Father. The other aeons long peaceably to see him. But the last of the thirty aeons, Sophia, yields to an ungovernable intention to apprehend his infinite greatness which transforms her through passion. Her passion is both a

---

[16] C. Markschies, 'New research on Ptolemaeus Gnosticus', *ZAC* 44 (2000), 225–54.
[17] Markschies, 'Valentinian Gnosticism'.
[18] The following account is indebted to the lucid summary of F. M. Sagnard, *La gnose valentinienne et le témoignage de saint Irénée* (Paris, 1947), 140–98.

disorder and a suffering, both physical and moral. She so strains towards the sweetness of the Father that she would have been dissolved into the All had not Horos (limit, or stauros, cross), appointed as consolidator of the Pleroma, convinced her that the Father is incomprehensible and confirmed her. So Sophia is converted and persuaded that the Father is incomprehensible, separated from her intention and passion through wonder, healed and purified. She is finally restored to her partner. What she has shed is a spiritual substance, without form, feeble and feminine, explicable from the story of the woman with an issue of blood who was healed by touching the garment of the son. The son is partner of truth and his garment is truth. The power which proceeds from him is Horos (limit). Limit is also known as cross, redeemer, absolver, definer and guide. Cross consolidates, confirms, establishes on the one hand and separates, defines, purifies on the other hand. All that is material is separated like straw from wheat and consumed in fire.

(ii) Emission of Christ and holy spirit, formation of the saviour: So that none of the aeons will ever be smitten by a passion like that of Sophia, the only begotten (Mind) now emits a new pair of aeons: Christ and Holy Spirit. Like the earthly Christ, the heavenly Christ will teach. He will reveal knowledge, teaching the nature of the *suzugia*, granting knowledge that the Father is incomprehensible and that the only way to him is through his only son. The eternal permanence of the aeons is due to incomprehensible transcendence of the Father; by contrast their birth and formation is caused by what is comprehensible in the father, which is the son. The holy spirit has a different teaching mission to the aeons: he makes them all equal, instructs them how to give thanks and leads them to the true rest. Equality of form and thought is achieved by uniting the masculine aeons with nous, logos, anthropos, Christ, and uniting the feminine aeons with truth, life, spirit, church. The abandonment of co-education is spectacularly successful: the choir of aeons, established firm in perfect rest and joy, blissfully sing to the Father. Still more they bring their distinctive best to produce an aeon of perfect beauty, Jesus, Saviour, Christ, Logos, All, who will play the decisive role outside the Pleroma. A string of texts and numbers justify the teaching concerning the saviour's formation.

(c) *The formation of Achamoth*

(i) Formation 'according to substance' by Christ: The extra-pleromatic Sophia, now called Achamoth, is in a pitiable state, bubbling from passion in darkened emptiness without shape or form. From the cross (limit) the pitying Christ forms Achamoth by his power, then ascends, leaving her with a scent of incorruptibility, formed and conscious but deprived of his presence. She is driven to seek the light she has lost but Horos bars her way and she is afflicted by sorrow, fear, anxiety and ignorance (1.4.1). While her mother has been altered, the fallen Sophia submits to the conflict of opposites and from this disposition comes the constitution and the substance of matter from which the world is made (1.4.2). She carries her mother's name 'patronymically' and also the name of holy spirit who is the feminine partner of Christ. She will in turn become the mother of spiritual (pneumatic) Gnostics and will be joined to the masculine Saviour. She may be called 'second Ogdoad' or simply 'Ogdoad', preserving the number of the fundamental and primitive Ogdoad of the Pleroma (1.5.2). Other names are 'earth', 'Jerusalem', 'mother' and 'lord'.

(ii) Formation 'according to gnosis' by the saviour: Outside the Pleroma, the saviour plays the decisive role. Endowed with all power, he is sent with his angels to Achamoth who receives power or virtue from his appearance. Her passions are healed through separation into those which are bad and those which are converted. In joy, Achamoth produces spiritual fruits (1.4.5).

(d) *Three substances*

There are now three substances: spiritual, which comes direct from Achamoth; passible or psychic, which comes from conversion (the demiurge is of psychic substance); material, which comes from passion. Hence come three races of men, three places (intermediate between Pleroma and demiurge, the seventh heaven whence the demiurge commands the lower heavens, and the world below under the cosmocrator) with the distinctive numbers of seven, eight and six. Achamoth orders the two lower substances which are not of the same substance with her. The demiurge and the psychics (on the right hand) are intermediary between the pneumatics and the material hylics (on the left). The soul of the world and the demiurge come from conversion. The lowest substance comes from passions: fear, sorrow and *aporia* (or *ekplexis*). From fear come the souls of men and animals, from sorrow come evil spirits and from *aporia* come the physical elements of the world. More explicitly (1.5.4) the four elements may be traced: earth from stupor (*ekplexis*), water from the movement of fear, air from sorrow, and fire from the ignorance which is hidden in the three other passions. Fear produces both matter and psychic substance, sorrow produces malignant spirits of the air, and *aporia* produces physical elements (or in one place, demons). The theme is not easy to set out.

(e) *Creation of the cosmos*

(i) The demiurge forms, under the secret influence of the mother, those beings which come after him. Enthumesis produces images of the aeons, while remaining unknown by the demiurge who is the image of Monogenes (the angels being images of the other aeons). The demiurge is Father and god of all things outside the Pleroma, self-imagined creator of beings psychic and material (1.5.2), which in reality are the productions of Achamoth. Not being spiritual, the demiurge cannot know what is spiritual and declares himself to be the only god (1.5.4).

(ii) When the demiurge has made the earth, he forms earthy man, from an invisible damp matter, and breathes into him the psychic element so that he is in the image and likeness of his maker. The hylic man is in his image, near to him but not of the same substance with him. Man is wrapped in his coat of flesh.

(iii) The demiurge is ignorant of the spiritual seed which has been implanted in him and sows it in the souls which he produces so that the pneumatic man escapes the demiurge to form the church which is the image of the aeon called Ecclesia. He receives his soul from the demiurge, his body from the mud, his envelope of flesh from matter, and his spiritual being from Achamoth his mother.

(iv) The three elements are distinct. The hylic man can never receive the breath of incorruptibility. The psychic man can turn either way to spirit or to matter. The pneumatic man is the salt and light of the world. The psychic is endowed with free will and capable of education in the world which was made for this purpose.

He needs good works and faith. The pneumatic simply because he is pneumatic will be absolutely and entirely saved, immune from the perishable earthy element in which he is clothed.

(f) *The Christ and the consummation*

The Christ of the Gospels is a special case, for he has received spirit from his mother, a psychic element from the demiurge, and a psychic body which appears but is not of flesh because flesh cannot be saved (1.6.1). For some, the saviour from the Pleroma descended on the Christ of the Gospels at baptism to contribute a fourth element to his constitution. The suffering Christ, psychic and organised by the economy of incarnation, suffers mysteriously, manifesting the shape of the Christ who is extended on the limit and who forms Achamoth according to substance. Indeed all that happens down here is a copy of things above.

Souls with spiritual seed are given special treatment by the demiurge who makes them (for reasons he does not know) prophets, priests and kings. Prophecies may speak of the mother Achamoth, of the spiritual seed and of the demiurge. The words of Jesus come from the saviour, the mother or the demiurge who nevertheless knows of nothing above him.

When the saviour comes the demiurge receives him with joy and learns all that he has not known before. He fulfils all that the economy of our world requires and before the final consummation he passes into the place of the mother Achamoth.

The final consummation divides the several seeds. Achamoth leaves her intermediate place to enter the Pleroma and marry the saviour, to form another *suzugia*. The pneumatics discard their psychic souls and enter the Pleroma to receive angelic brides. The demiurge passes into the intermediate place held by his mother Achamoth. Here too the souls of the righteous find their rest, for nothing psychic can rise higher.

All things material, through the fire hidden in them, will burst into flames and self-destruct. The psychics who have chosen the good will find their rest in the intermediate place; but those who have chosen what is evil will be sent to evil like that which they have chosen (1.7.1).

Select bibliography

TEXTS AND TRANSLATIONS

Irenaeus, *Against heresies*, text, W. Harvey, 2 vols. (Cambridge, 1857).
Against heresies, text, R. Massuet (Paris, 1710), *PG* 7 (Paris, 1882).
Against heresies, trans. A. Roberts and W. H. Rambaut, ANCL, 5,9 (1883–4).
Contre les hérésies, text and trans., SC,
    I: 263, 264 (1979): A. Rousseau, L. Doutreleau
    II: 293, 294 (1982): A. Rousseau, L. Doutreleau
    III: 210, 211 (1974): A. Rousseau, L. Doutreleau
    IV: 100; 2 vols. (1965): A. Rousseau, B. Hemmerdinger, L. Doutreleau, C. Mercier
    V: 152, 153 (1969): A. Rousseau, L. Doutreleau, C. Mercier.
Contre les hérésies, trans. A. Rousseau (Paris, 1984).
Des heiligen Irenäus Schrift zum Erweis der apostolischen Verkündigung in armenischer Version entdeckt herausgegeben und ins Deutsche übersetzt von K. Ter-Mekerttschian and E. Ter-Minassiantz, TU, 31,1 (Berlin, 1907).
The demonstration of the apostolic preaching, trans. J. Armitage Robinson (London, 1920).
Proof of the apostolic preaching, trans. J. P. Smith (New York, 1952).
Démonstration de la prédication apostolique, trans. A. Rousseau (SC, 406, 1995).
Proof of the apostolic preaching, trans. J. Behr (New York, 1997).
Justin, *Apologies*, text, A. W. F. Blunt (Cambridge, 1911).
The dialogue with Trypho, trans. A. Lukyn Williams (London, 1930).
Numénius, text and trans. E. des Places (Paris, 1973).
Philo, text, ed. L. Cohn and P. Wendland, 6 vols. (Berlin, 1896–1915).
    text and trans. F. H. Colson, G. H. Whitaker and R. A. Markus, LCL, 12 vols. (London, 1929–62).
Plotinus, text, P. Henry and H. R. Schwyzer (ed. minor), 3 vols. (Oxford, 1966, 1977, 1988).
    text and trans. A. H. Armstrong, LCL, 7 vols. (1966–88).

Vitruvius, *Ten books on architecture*, trans. and commentary, I. D. Rowland, T. N. Howe and M. J. Drewe (Cambridge, 1999).

REFERENCE WORKS

Aland, B., 'Gnosis und Kirchenväter. Ihre Auseinandersetzung um die Interpretation des Evangeliums', in Gnosis, FS for Hans Jonas, ed. B. Aland (Göttingen, 1978), 158–213.

'Fides und subiectio. Zur Anthropologie des Irenäus', in *Kerygma und Logos, FS für Carl Andresen zum 70. Geburtstag*, ed. A. M. Ritter (Göttingen, 1979), 9–28.

Alès, A. D', 'La doctrine de la récapitulation en S. Irénée', *RSR* 6 (1916), 185–211.

'Le mot οἰκονομία dans la langue théologique de S. Irénée', *REG* 32 (1919), 1–9.

'La doctrine eucharistique de S. Irénée', *RSR* 13 (1923), 24–46.

'La doctrine de l'Esprit en S. Irénée', *RSR* 14 (1924), 497–538.

Altendorf, H. D., 'Zum Stichwort: Rechtgläubigkeit und Ketzerei im ältesten Christentum', *ZKG* 80 (1969), 61–74.

Ammundsen, V., 'The rule of truth in Irenaeus', *JThS* 13 (1912), 574–80.

Audet, Th-A., 'Orientations théologiques chez saint Irénée. Le contexte mental d'une ΓΝΩΣΙΣ ΑΛΗΘΗΣ', *Trad* 1 (1943), 15–54.

Bacq, P., *De l'ancienne à la nouvelle alliance selon S. Irénée. Unité du livre IV de l'Adversus haereses* (Paris, 1978).

Balás D. L., *ΜΕΤΟΥΣΙΑ ΘΕΟΥ. Man's participation in God's perfections according to Saint Gregory of Nyssa* (Rome, 1966).

'The use and interpretation of Paul in Irenaeus' five books *Adversus haereses*', *SecCent* 9 (1992), 27–39.

Baltes, M. *Die Weltentstehung des platonischen Timaeus nach den antiken Interpreten*, 2 vols. (Leiden, 1976–8).

Balthasar, Hans Urs von, *Herrlichkeit. Eine theologische Ästhetik*, vol. II (Einsiedeln, 1962).

Barrett. C. K., *The signs of an apostle* (London, 1970).

Bauer, W., *Orthodoxy and heresy in earliest Christianity*, ed. R. A. Kraft and G. Krodel (Philadelphia, 1971), translated from the second German edition, ed. G. Strecker (Tübingen, 1964).

Behr, J., 'Irenaeus *AH* 3.23.5 and the ascetic ideal', *SVTQ* 37 (1993), 305–13.

Asceticism and anthropology in Irenaeus and Clement of Alexandria (Oxford, 2000).

Bengsch, A., *Heilsgeschichte und Heilswissen. Eine Untersuchung zur Struktur und Entfaltung des theologischen Denkens im Werk 'Adversus Haereses' des hl. Irenäus von Lyon*, EThSt 3 (Leipzig, 1957).

Benoit, A., *Saint Irénée, introduction à l'étude de sa théologie* (Paris, 1960).
'Ecriture et tradition chez saint Irénée', *RHPhR* 40 (1960), 32–43.
'Pour une théologie de l'image: remarques sur le thème de la vision chez Irénée de Lyon', *RHPhR* 59 (1979), 379–84.
'Irénée et l'hérésie, les conceptions hérésiologiques de l'évêque de Lyon', *Aug* 20 (1980), 55–67.
'Irénée et Justin', in *Actes des journées irénéennes des 9–10–11 mai 1984. La foi et la gnose hier et aujourd'hui: Irénée de Lyon*, CICL 15 (Lyon, 1984), 59–73.
Berardino, A. di and B. Studer, *Storia del metodo teologico*, vol. 1 (Casale Montferrato, 1992).
Berthouzoz, R., *Liberté et grâce suivant la théologie d'Irénée de Lyon* (Fribourg, 1980).
Beuzart, P., *Essai sur la théologie d'Irénée* (Le Puy, 1908).
Bianchi, U. (ed.), *Le origini dello gnosticismo* (Leiden, 1967).
Birrer, J., *Der Mensch als Medium und Adressat der Schöpfungsoffenbarung* (Bern, 1989).
Blanchard, Y-M., *Aux sources du canon, le témoignage d'Irénée* (Paris, 1993).
Böhlig, A., *Mysterion und Wahrheit* (Leiden, 1968).
Zum Hellenismus in den Schriften von Nag Hammadi (Wiesbaden, 1975).
Bonwetsch, G. N., *Die Theologie des Irenäus* (Gütersloh, 1925).
Boulluec, A. Le, *La notion d'hérésie dans la littérature grecque IIe–IIIe siècles*, 2 vols. (Paris, 1985).
Bousset, W., *Jüdisch-christlicher Schulbetrieb in Alexandria und Rom* (Göttingen, 1915).
Broek, R. van den, Baarda, T. and J. Mansfeld (eds.), *Knowledge of God in the Graeco-Roman world* (Leiden, 1988).
Brox, N., 'Charisma veritatis certum (zu Irenäus adv. haer. IV 26, 2)', *ZKG* 75 (1964), 327–31.
'Γνωστικοί' als Häresiologischer Terminus', *ZNW* 56 (1965), 105–14.
Offenbarung, Gnosis und gnostischer Mythos bei Irenäus von Lyon (Salzburg and Munich, 1966).
'Zum literarischen Verhältnis zwischen Justin und Irenäus', *ZNW* 58 (1967), 121–8.
'Rom und "jede Kirche" im 2. Jahrhundert. Zu Irenäus, adv. haer. III 3, 2', in *Festgabe Hubert Jedin zum 75. Geburtstag*, ed. W. Brandmüller and R. Bäumer (Paderborn, 1969), 42–78.
'Selbst und Selbstentfremdung in der Gnosis: Heilsaussicht durch Erkenntnis: die Religion Gnosis', in *Geschichte und Vorgeschichte der modernen Subjektivität*, ed. R. L. Fetz, R. Hagenbüchle and P. Schulz (Berlin, 1998), 298–318.
'Die biblische Hermeneutik des Irenäus', *ZAC* 2, (1998), 26–48.
Bultmann, R., *Theology of the New Testament*, 2 vols. (London, 1952, 1955).

Campenhausen, H. von, 'Irenäus und das Neue Testament', *ThLZ* 90 (1965) 1–8.

'Marcion et les origines du canon néotestamentaire', *RHPhR* 6 (1966), 213–26.

Ecclesiastical authority and spiritual power (ET; London, 1969).

'Die Entstehung der Heilsgeschichte', *Saeculum* 21 (1970), 189–212.

The formation of the Christian bible (London, 1972).

Chadwick, H., 'Justin Martyr's defence of Christianity', *BJRL* 47,2 (1965), 275–95.

Daniélou, J., 'Saint Irénée et les origines de la théologie de l'histoire', *RSR* 34 (1947), 227–31.

'Philosophie ou théologie de l'histoire?', *DViv* 19 (1951).

'La charrue symbole de la croix (Irénée, *Adv. haer.* 4.34.4)', *RSR* 42 (1954), 193–203.

Théologie du Judéo-christianisme (Tournai, 1958); ET, *The theology of Jewish Christianity* (London, 1964).

Message évangelique et culture héllenistique (Tournai, 1961); ET, *Gospel message and Hellenistic culture* (London, 1973).

de Andía, Y., 'Matt. 5.5, La beatitudine dei miti nell'interpretazione di San Ireneo', *RSLR* 30 (1984), 275–86.

'L'hérésie et sa réfutation selon Irénée de Lyon', *Aug* 25,3 (1985), 609–44.

Homo vivens: incorruptibilité et divinisation selon Irénée de Lyon (Paris, 1986).

'Irénée, théologien de l'unité', *NRTh* 109 (1987), 31–48.

Diels, H. (ed.), 'Aristotelis qui fertur de Melisso Xenophane Gorgia libellus', Philosophische und historische Abhandlungen der königlichen Akademie der Wissenschaften zu Berlin. Aus den Jahren 1899 und 1900 (Berlin, 1900).

Dillon, J., *The Middle Platonists* (London, 1977); revised edn (London, 1996).

Doignon, J., 'Le salut par le feu et le bois chez saint Irénée. Notes de philologie et d'exégèse sur *Adversus haereses* 4.34.4', *RSR* 43 (1955), 535–44.

Donovan, M. A., 'Irenaeus in recent scholarship', *SecCent* 4,4 (1984), 219–41.

'Insights on ministry: Irenaeus', *Toronto Journal of Theology* 2,1 (1986).

'Alive to the glory of God: a key insight in St Irenaeus', *TS* 49 (1988), 283–97.

One right reading? (Minnesota, 1997).

Doutreleau, L. and L. Regnault, Art., 'Irénée de Lyon', *DS* 7 (1971), 1923–69.

Duncker, L., *Historiae doctrinae de ratione quae inter peccatum originale et actuale intercedit, pars continens Irenaei, Tertulliani, Augustini sententias* (Göttingen, 1836).

Des heiligen Irenäus Christologie im Zusammenhange mit dessen theologischer und anthropologischer Grundlehre (Göttingen, 1843).

Erbkam, H. G., *De sancti Irenaei principiis ethicis* (Königsberg, 1856).

Escoula, L., 'Le verbe sauveur et illuminateur chez S. Irénée', *NRTh* 66 (1939), 385–400; 551–67.

Evieux, P., 'Théologie de l'accoutumance chez saint Irénée', *RSR* 55 (1967), 5–54.

Eynde, D. van den, *Les normes de l'enseignement chrétien, dans la littérature patristique des trois premiers siècles* (Gembloux and Paris, 1933).

Faivre, A., 'Irénée premier théologien "systématique"?', *RevSR* 65 (1991), 11–32.

Fantino, J., *L'homme, image de Dieu chez S. Irénée de Lyon* (Paris, 1986).

La théologie d'Irénée (Paris, 1994).

'L'origine de la doctrine de la création ex nihilo. A propos de l'ouvrage de G. May', *RSPhTh* 80,4 (1996), 589–602.

'Vérité de la foi et vie des communautés chrétiennes selon Irénée de Lyon', *RevSR* 70 (1996), 240–53.

'Le passage du premier Adam au second Adam comme expression du salut chez Irénée de Lyon', *VigChr* 52 (1998), 418–29.

Farkasfalvy, D., 'Theology of scripture in St Irenaeus', *RevBen* 78 (1968).

Farrer, A., *A rebirth of images* (London, 1949).

Ferlay, P., 'Irénée de Lyon exégète du quatrième évangile', *NRTh* 106 (1984), 222–34.

Fermandois, R. P., *El concepto de profecía en la teología de san Ireneo* (Madrid, 1999).

Festugière, A. J., *La révélation d'Hermès Trismégiste*, 4 vols. (Paris, 1944–54).

Gächter, P., 'Unsere Einheit mit Christus nach dem hl. Irenäus', *ZKTh* 58 (1934), 503–32.

Galtier, P., 'La rédemption et les droits du démon dans saint Irénée', *RSR* 2 (1911), 1–24.

'Les droits du démon et la mort du Christ', *RSR* 3 (1912), 344–55.

'La vierge qui nous régénère', *RSR* 5 (1914).

Gibson, A. Boyce, *Muse and thinker* (London, 1969).

Gorringe, T. J., ' "Not assumed is not healed": the *homoousion* and liberation theology', *SJTh* 38 (1985), 481–90.

Grant, R. M., 'Irenaeus and Hellenistic culture', *HThR* 42 (1949), 41–51.

'Carpocratians and curriculum: Irenaeus' reply', Essays in honor of Krister Stendahl, *HThR* 79,1–3 (1986), 127–36.

Irenaeus of Lyons (London and New York, 1997).

Grossi, V., 'Regula veritatis e narratio battesimale in sant'Ireneo', *Aug* 12 (1972), 437–63.

Haacker, K., 'Creatio ex auditu. Zum Verständnis von Heb 11:4', *ZNW* 60 (1969), 279–81.

Hackenschmidt, C., S. *Irenaei de opere et beneficiis domini nostri Jesu Christi sententia* (Strasbourg, 1869).

Hägglund, B., 'Die Bedeutung der "regula fidei" als Grundlage theologischer Aussagen', *StTh* 12 (1958), 1–44.

Harl, M., *Origène et la fonction révélatrice du verbe incarné* (Paris, 1958).

Harnack, A. von, 'Der Presbyter-Prediger des Irenäus (IV, 27,1–32,1)', in *Philotesia. Paul Kleinert zum 70. Geburtstag*, ed. A. von Harnack et al. (Berlin, 1907), 1–37.

Hasler, V. E., *Gesetz und Evangelium in der alten Kirche bis Origenes* (Zürich and Frankfurt, 1953).

Hefner, P., 'Theological methodology and St Irenaeus', *ChH* 44 (1964), 294–309.

Hitchcock, F. R. M., *Irenaeus of Lugdunum. A study of his teaching* (Cambridge, 1914).
  'Loofs' Asiatic Source (IQA) and the Ps-Justin De Resurrectione', *ZNW* 36 (1937), 35–60.
  'Loofs' theory of Theophilus of Antioch as a source of Irenaeus I/II', *JThS* 38 (1937), 130–9; 255–66.

Hoh, J., *Die Lehre des hl. Irenaeus über das Neue Testament* (Münster, 1919).

Holstein, H., 'Les formules du symbole dans l'oeuvre de S. Irénée', *RSR* 34 (1947), 454–61.
  'L'exhomologèse dans l'*Adversus haereses* de S. Irénée', *RSR* 35 (1948), 282–8.
  'Propter potentiorem principalitatem (Saint Irénée, *Adversus haereses* 3.3.2)', *RSR* 36 (1949), 122–34.
  'La tradition des Apôtres chez saint Irénée', *RSR* 36 (1949), 229–70.
  'Les témoins de la révélation d'après saint Irénée', *RSR* 41 (1953) 410–20.

Houssiau, A., *La christologie de saint Irénée* (Louvain and Gembloux, 1955).
  'Le baptême selon Irénée de Lyon', *EThL* 60,1 (1984), 45–59.

Hunger, W., 'Weltplaneinheit und Adameinheit in der Theologie des heiligen Irenäus', *Schol* 17,2 (1942).

Jaschke, H-J., *Der heilige Geist im Bekenntnis der Kirche, eine Studie zur Pneumatologie des Irenäus von Lyon im Ausgang vom altchristlichen Glaubensbekenntnis* (Münster, 1976).
  'Das Johannesevangelium und die Gnosis im Zeugnis des Irenäus von Lyon', *MThZ* 29 (1978), 337–76.

Jay, E. G., 'From Presbyter-Bishops to Bishops and Presbyters', *SecCent* 1 (1981), 125–62.

Jonge, M. De, 'The pre-Mosaic servants of God in the *Testaments of the Twelve Patriarchs* and in the writings of Justin and Irenaeus', *VigChr* 39 (1985), 157–70.

Joppich, G., *Salus carnis. Eine Untersuchung in der Theologie des hl. Irenäus von Lyon* (Münsterschwarzach, 1965).

Jossua, J. P., *Le salut: incarnation ou mystère pascale* (Paris, 1968).

Jouassard, G., 'Le "signe de Jonas" dans le livre IIIe de l'*adversus haereses* de saint Irénée', in *L'homme devant Dieu. Mélanges offerts au Père Henri de Lubac* (Paris, 1963), vol. I, 235–46.

Käsemann, E., *Exegetische Versuche und Besinnungen*, 2 vols. (Göttingen, 1960, 1965); ET, *Essays on New Testament themes* (London, 1964); *New Testament questions of today* (London, 1969).

Jesu letzter Wille nach Johannes 17 (Tübingen, 1967); ET, *The testament of Jesus* (London, 1968).

Paulinische Perspektiven (Tübingen, 1969); ET, *Perspectives on Paul* (London, 1971).

An die Römer (Tübingen, 1973); ET, *Commentary on Romans* (Grand Rapids, 1980).

Kereszty, R., 'The unity of the church in the theology of Irenaeus', *SecCent* 4,4 (1984), 202–18.

Klebba, E., *Die Anthropologie des hl. Irenaeus. Eine dogmengeschichtliche Studie* (Münster, 1894).

Koch, H., 'Zur Lehre vom Urstand und von der Erlösung bei Irenaeus', *ThStK* 96–7 (1925), 183–214.

Koschorke, K., *Die Polemik der Gnostiker gegen das kirchliche Christentum* (Leiden, 1978).

Krämer, H. J., *Der Ursprung der Geistmetaphysik* (Amsterdam, 1964).

Kunze, J., *Die Gotteslehre des Irenaeus* (Leipzig, 1891).

Lanne, E., 'Cherubim et Seraphim', *RSR* 43 (1955), 524–35.

'La vision de Dieu dans l'oeuvre de Saint Irénée', *Irén* 33 (1960), 311–20.

'La "xeniteia" d'Abraham dans l'oeuvre d'Irénée. Aux origines du thème monastique de la "peregrinatio" ', *Irén* 47 (1974), 163–87.

'L'église de Rome "a gloriosissimis duobus apostolis Petro et Paulo Romae fundatae et constitutae ecclesiae" (Adv. haer. III, 3, 2)', *Irén* 49 (1976), 275–322.

'Le nom de Jésus Christ et son invocation chez saint Irénée de Lyon', *Irén* 48 (1975), 447–67 and 49 (1976), 34–53.

'La règle de la vérité. Aux sources d'une expression de saint Irénée', FS for Cipriano Vagaggini, *StudAns* 79 (1980), 57–70.

'Charisme prophétique, Martyre et amour parfait', in *Pléroma*, FS for A. Orbe, ed. E. Romero Pose (Santiago de Compostela, 1990), 299–305.

'Saint Irénée de Lyon, artisan de la paix entre les églises', *Irén* 69 (1996), 451–76.

Lassiat, H., *Promotion de l'homme en Jésus Christ d'après Irénée de Lyon* (Tours, 1974).

Lawson, J., *The biblical theology of St Irenaeus* (London, 1948).

Lebeau, P., 'Koinonia, la signification du salut selon S. Irénée', in *Epektasis*, FS for J. Daniélou, ed. J. Fontaine and C. Kannengiesser (Paris, 1972), 121–7.

Lebreton, J., 'La connaissance de Dieu chez s. Irénée', *RSR* 16 (1926), 385–406.

Histoire du dogme de la Trinité, 2 vols. (Paris, 1928).

Löhr, W. A., 'Gnostic determinism reconsidered', *VigChr* 46 (1992), 381–90.

Loewe, W. P., 'Irenaeus' soteriology: Christus Victor revisited', *AThR* 17,1 (1985), 1–17.

Logan, A. H. B., *Gnostic truth and Christian heresy* (Edinburgh, 1996).

Loofs, F., *Theophilus von Antiochien Adversus Marcionem, und die anderen theologischen Quellen bei Irenaeus*, TU 46,2 (Leipzig, 1930).

Lubac, H. de, ' "Typologie" et "allégorisme" ', *RSR* 34 (1947), 180–226.

Histoire et esprit (Paris, 1950).

Lührmann, D., 'Confesser sa foi à l'époque apostolique', *RThPh* 117 (1985), 93–110.

McCullagh, C. B., *The truth of history* (London, 1998).

Mambrino, J., 'Les deux mains de Dieu chez S. Irénée', *NRTh* 79 (1957), 355–70.

Markschies, C., *Valentinus Gnosticus?* (Tübingen, 1992).

'Valentinian Gnosticism: toward the anatomy of a school', in: *The Nag Hammadi Library after fifty years*, ed. J. D. Turner and A. M. McGuire, Nag Hammadi Studies 44 (Leiden, 1997), 401–38.

'New research on Ptolemaeus Gnosticus', *ZAC* 44 (2000), 225–54.

Markus, R. A., 'Pleroma and fulfilment. The significance of history in St Irenaeus' opposition to Gnosticism', *VigChr* 8 (1954), 193–224.

May, G., *Schöpfung aus dem Nichts* (Berlin, 1978); ET, *Creatio ex nihilo* (Edinburgh, 1994).

Mees, M., 'Die Heilung des Kranken vom Bethesdateich aus Joh 5.1–18 in frühhristlicher Sicht', *NTS* 32 (1986), 596–608.

Meijering, E. P., 'Zehn Jahre Forschung zum Thema Platonismus und Kirchenväter', *ThR* 36 (1971), 303–20; reprinted in *God, being, history* (1975), 1–18.

'Die "physische Erlösung" in der Theologie des Irenäus', *NAKG* 53 (1972), 147–59; reprinted in *God, being, history* (1975), 39–51.

'Irenaeus' relation to philosophy in the light of his concept of free will', in *Romanitas et Christianitas. In memoriam J. H. Waszink*, ed. W. Den

Boer, P. G. van der Nat, C. M. J. Sicking and J. C. M. van Winden (Amsterdam, 1973), 221–32; reprinted in *God, being, history* (1975), 19–30.

'Some observations on Irenaeus' polemics against the Gnostics', *NedThT* 27 (1973), 27–33; reprinted in *God, being, history* (1975), 31–8.

God, being, history: studies in patristic philosophy (Amsterdam, Oxford and New York, 1975).

'Bemerkungen zum Nachleben des Irenäus im Streit der Konfessionen', *VigChr* 53 (1999), 74–99.

Merki, H., *ΟΜΟΙΩΣΙΣ ΘΕΩΙ. Von der platonischen Angleichung an Gott zur Gottähnlichkeit bei Gregor von Nyssa* (Freiburg CH, 1952).

Minns, Denis, *Irenaeus* (London, 1994).

Moltmann, J., *The trinity and the kingdom of God* (London, 1981).

Das Kommen Gottes (Gütersloh, 1995).

Molwitz, G., *De ΑΝΑΚΕΦΑΛΑΙΩΣΕΩΣ in Irenaei theologia potestate* (Dresden, 1874).

Mondésert, C., *Clément d'Alexandrie. Introduction à l'étude de sa pensée religieuse à partir de l'Ecriture* (Paris, 1944).

Mondésert, C. (ed.), *Le monde grec ancien et la Bible*, vol. I: *Bible de tous les temps* (Paris, 1984).

Moule, C. F. D., *The birth of the New Testament* (London, 1972).

'Fulfilment-words in the New Testament: use and abuse', *Essays in New Testament interpretation* (Cambridge, 1982), 3–36.

Nautin, P., 'L'*Adversus haereses* d'Irénée, livre III. Notes d'exégèse', *RThAM* 20 (1953), 185–202.

Lettres et écrivains chrétiens des IIe et IIIe siècles (Paris, 1961).

Nielsen, J. T., A*dam and Christ in the theology of Irenaeus of Lyons* (Assen, 1968).

Noormann, R., *Irenäus als Paulusinterpret* (Tübingen, 1994).

Norelli, E., 'Paix, justice, intégrité de la création: Irénée de Lyon et ses adversaires', *Irén* 64,1 (1991), 5–43.

Normann, F., *Teilhabe – ein Schlüsselwort der Vätertheologie* (Münster, 1978).

Norris, R. A., Jr, 'Irenaeus and Plotinus answer the Gnostics: a note on the relation between Christian thought and Platonism', *USQR* 36,1 (1980), 13–24.

O'Brien, Denis, *Théodicée plotinienne et théodicée gnostique* (Leiden, 1993).

Ochagavía, J., *Visibile Patris Filius. A study of Irenaeus' teaching on revelation and tradition*, OrChrAn 171 (Rome, 1964).

Oppel, H., 'KANON', *Ph*, Suppl. vol. 30 (1937).

Orbe, A., 'El hombre ideal en la teología de s. Ireneo', *Greg* 43 (1962).

Antropología de San Ireneo (Madrid, 1969).

'La revelación del Hijo por el Padre según san Ireneo (*adv. haer.* IV 6) (para la exégesis prenicena de Mt. 11.27)', *Greg* 51 (1970), 5–86.

' "Ipse tuum calcabit caput" (San Ireneo y. Gen. 3.15)', *Greg* 52 (1971), 95–150; 215–71.

'San Ireneo y la doctrina de la reconciliación', *Greg* 61 (1980), 5–50.
'Cinco exégesis ireneanas de Gen 2, 17b *adv. haer.* V, 23, 1–2', *Greg* 62 (1981), 75–113.
'La virgen María abogada de la virgen Eva (en torno a s. Ireneo, *adv. haer.* V, 19, 1)', *Greg* 63 (1982), 455–506.
'A propósito de dos citas de Platón en san Ireneo', *Haer.* 5, 24, 4, *Orpheus* N.F. 4 (1983), 253–85.
'San Ireneo y el régimen del milenio', *StMiss* 32 (1983), 345–72.
Visión del Padre e incorruptela según san Ireneo, *Greg* 64 (1983), 199–241.
San Ireneo adopcionista? (en torno a *adv. haer.* III, 19, 1), *Greg* 65 (1984), 5–52.
'Cristo, sacrificio y manjar', *Greg* 66 (1985), 185–239.
Teología de san Ireneo. Comentario al Libro V del 'Adversus haereses', 3 vols., BAC maior 25/29/33 (Madrid 1985/1987/1988).
'El "Descensus ad inferos" y san Ireneo', *Greg* 68 (1987), 485–522.
Introducción a la teología de los siglos II y III, 2 vols. (Rome, 1987).
'Deus facit, homo fit (un axioma de san Ireneo)', *Greg* 69 (1988), 629–61.
Espiritualidad de san Ireneo (Rome, 1989).
'Gloria dei vivens homo (análisis de Ireneo, *adv. haer.* IV, 20, 1–7)', *Greg* 73 (1992), 205–68.
'Los hechos de Lot, mujer e hijas vistos por san Ireneo (*adv. haer* IV, 31, 1, 15/3, 71)', *Greg* 75 (1994), 37–64.
'Sobre los "Alogos" de san Ireneo (*adv. haer.* III, 11, 9)', *Greg* 76 (1995), 47–68.
'El Espíritu en al bautismo de Jesús (en torno a san Ireneo)', *Greg* 76 (1995), 663–99.
'El signo de Jonás según san Ireneo', *Greg* 77 (1996), 637–57.
Teología de san Ireneo, vol. IV: *traducción y comentario del Libro V del 'Adversus haereses'* (Madrid, 1996).
Osborn, Eric, *Justin Martyr* (Tübingen, 1973).
The beginning of Christian philosophy (Cambridge, 1981).
'Paul and Plato in second century ethics', *StudPatr* 15 (1984), 474–85.
(with Colin Duckworth), 'Clement of Alexandria's Hypotyposeis: a French eighteenth century sighting', *JThS* 36 (1985), 67–83.
'Irenaeus and the beginning of Christian humour', in 'The idea of salvation', *Prudentia*, Supplement (1989), 64–76.
'Reason and the rule of faith in the second century AD', in *The making of orthodoxy*, FS for Henry Chadwick, ed. R. Williams (Cambridge, 1989), 40–61.
The emergence of Christian theology (Cambridge, 1993).
Tertullian, first theologian of the West (Cambridge, 1997).
'Love of enemies and recapitulation', *VigChr* 54, 1 (2000), 12–31.

Overbeck, W., *Menschwerdung* (Bern, 1995).

Payne, A. A., *The architectural treatise in the Renaissance* (Cambridge, 1999).

Pelland, G., 'Une étape importante des études irénéennes (à propos d'une nouvelle édition de l'*Epideixis*)', *Greg* 78,1 (1997), 139–45.

Peretto, E., *La lettera ai Romani cc 1–8 nell'Adversus haereses di Ireneo* (Bari, 1971).

'Criteri di orthodossia e di eresia nella Epideixis di Ireneo', *Aug* 25 (1985).

'La conversione in Ireneo di Lione. Ambiti semantici', *Aug* 27 (1987), 137–64.

Perkins, P., 'Irenaeus and the Gnostics. Rhetoric and composition in *Adversus haereses* Book One', *VigChr* 30 (1976), 193–200.

'Ordering the cosmos: Irenaeus and the Gnostics', in *Nag Hammadi, Gnosticism and early Christianity*, ed. C. W. Hedrick and R. Hodgson, Jr (Massachussetts, 1986), 221–38.

Petrement, S., *Le Dieu séparé. Les origines du gnosticisme* (Paris, 1984).

Pfeil, H., 'Die Frage nach der Veränderlichkeit und Geschichtlichkeit Gottes', *MThZ* 31 (1980), 1–23.

Pohlenz, M., '*τὸ πρέπον*, ein Beitrag zur Geschichte des griechischen Geistes', NAWG.PH 1 (1933), 53–93.

Polkinghorne, J. C., *Belief in God in an age of science* (Yale, 1998).

Pourkier, A., 'Epiphane témoin du texte d'Irénée (note critique sur Irénée, *Adv. haer.* I, 24, 6)', *VigChr* 38 (1984), 281–4.

Prigent, P., *Justin et l'ancien testament* (Paris, 1964).

'Pour une théologie de l'image: les visions de l'Apocalypse', *RHPhR*, 59 (1979), 373–8.

L'Apocalypse de saint Jean (Paris, 1981); 2nd edn (Geneva, 2000).

'Bible et beauté, Esthétique de l'éthique, De la morale comme art d'aimer', Supplement, *Révue d'éthique et de théologie morale* 180 (1992), 129–44.

Immagini Cristiane, immagini sacre, in arte e teologia (Turin, 1997).

'Art et révélation, réflexions théologiques su l'iconographie de l'Apocalypse', *1900 ΕΤΗΡΙΣ ΤΗΣ ΑΠΟΚΑΛΥΨΕΩΣ ΙΩΑΝΝΟΥ* (Athens, 1999), 383–406.

Prümm, K., 'Göttliche Planung und menschliche Entwicklung nach Irenäus' *Adversus haereses*', *Schol* 13 (1938), 206–24; 342–66.

Christentum als Neuheitserlebnis (Freiburg, 1939).

'Zur Terminologie und zum Wesen der christlichen Neuheit bei Irenäus', in *Pisciculi*, FS for F. J. Dolger, ed. T. Klauser and A. Rücker (Münster, 1939), 192–219.

Purves, J. G. M, 'The Spirit and the *Imago Dei*: reviewing the anthropology of Irenaeus of Lyons', *EvQ* 68 (1996), 99–120.

Quinn, J. D., ' "Charisma veritatis certum": Irenaeus, *Adversus haereses* 4.26.2', *TS* 39 (1978), 520–52.

Reynders, D. B., 'Paradosis. Le progrès et l'idée de tradition jusqu' à saint Irénée', *RThAM* 5 (1933), 155–91.

'La polémique de Saint Irénée. Méthode et principes', *RThAM* 7 (1935), 5–27.

'Optimisme et théocentrisme chez Saint Irénée', *RThAM* 8 (1936), 225–52.

Lexique comparé du texte grec et des versions latine, arménienne et syriaque de l'Adversus haereses de saint Irénée, CSCO 141, 142, *Subsidia*, 5,6. 2 vols. (Louvain, 1954).

Vocabulaire de la 'Démonstration' et des fragments de Saint Irénée (Chevetogne, 1958).

Rist, J. M., 'Plotinus on matter and evil', *Phron* 6 (1961), 154–66.

Plotinus, the road to reality (Cambridge, 1967).

Rizzerio, L., 'La nozione di ἀκολουθία come "logica della verita" in Clemente di Alessandria', *RFNS* 79 (1987), 175–95.

'Clemente di Alessandria e la "φυσιολογία veramente gnostica" Saggio sulle origini e le implicazioni di un epistemologia e di un'ontologia "cristiane" ', *RThAM*, Suppl. vol. 6 (Leuven, 1996).

Rose, M., *Parody: ancient, modern and post-modern* (Cambridge, 1993).

Roulet, J. de, 'Saint Irénée évêque', *RHPhR* 73,3 (1993), 261–80.

Rousseau, A., 'La doctrine de saint Irénée sur la préexistence du Fils de Dieu dans *Dém* 43', *Mus* 89 (1971), 5–42.

L'éternité des peines d'enfer et l'immortalité naturelle de l'âme selon saint Irénée, *NRTh* 99 (1977), 834–64.

'Le traité d'Irénée "Contre les hérésies": la cohérence d'une oeuvre', *Actes des journées irénéennes des 9–10–11 mai 1984. La foi et la gnose hier et aujourd'hui: Irénée de Lyon*, *CICL* 15 (Lyon, 1984), 13–31.

Ruiz, G., 'L'enfance d'Adam selon Saint Irénée de Lyon', *BLE* 89 (1988).

Runia, D. T., *Philo of Alexandria and the* Timaeus *of Plato*, 2 vols. (Leiden, 1986).

'Philo of Alexandria and the Greek *haeresis*-model', *VigChr* 53 (1999).

Sagnard, F. M. M., *La gnose valentinienne et le témoignage de saint Irénée* (Paris, 1947).

Scharl, E., 'Der Rekapitulationsbegriff des heiligen Irenäus', *Orientalia* 6 (1940), 376–416.

Recapitulatio mundi. Der Rekapitulationsbegriff des heiligen Irenäus und seine Anwendung auf die Körperwelt (Freiburg, 1941).

Scherrer, T, *La gloire de Dieu dans l'oeuvre de Saint Irénée* (Rome, 1997).

Schoedel W. R., 'Philosophy and rhetoric in the *Adversus haereses* of Irenaeus', *VigChr* 13 (1959), 22–32.

'Theological method in Irenaeus (*Adversus haereses* 2. 25–28)', *JThS* 35 (1984), 31–49.

Schoedel W. R. and R. L. Wilken (eds.), *Early Christian literature and the classical intellectual tradition*, FS for R. M. Grant, ThH 54 (Paris, 1979).

Schwager, R., 'Der Gott des Alten Testaments und der Gott des Gekreuzigten. Eine Untersuchung zur Erlösungslehre bei Markion und Irenäus', *ZKTh* 102 (1980), 289–313.

Schwanz, P., *Imago Dei* (Göttingen, 1979).

Sesboüé, B., 'La preuve par les écritures chez saint Irénée. A propos d'un texte difficile du livre III de l'*Adversus haereses*', *NRTh* 103 (1981), 872–87.

'Quatre entrées pour un discours', *Penser la foi, Mélanges Joseph Moingt* (Paris, 1990), 373–90.

Tout récapituler dans le Christ, christologie et sotériologie d'Irénée de Lyon (Paris, 2000).

Siegwalt, G., 'Introduction à une théologie chrétienne de la récapitulation', *RThPh* 113 (1981), 259–78.

Simonetti, M., 'Per typica ad vera', *VetChr* 18 (1981).

'Il problema dell'unità di Dio da Giustino a Ireneo', *RSLR* 22 (1986), 201–40.

Skarsaune, O., *The proof from prophecy, a study in Justin Martyr's proof-text tradition: text-type, provenance, theological profile*, *NT* Suppl. vol. 56 (Leiden, 1987).

Skeat, T. C., 'Irenaeus and the four-gospel canon', *NT* 34,2 (1992), 194–9.

Skinner, Quentin, 'Meaning and understanding in the history of ideas', *HTh* 8 (1969), 3–53.

Slate, C. P., 'Two features of Irenaeus' missiology', *Miss* 23 (1995), 431–42.

Smith, C. R., 'Chiliasm and recapitulation in the theology of Irenaeus', *VigChr* 48 (1994).

Smith, D. A., 'Irenaeus and the baptism of Jesus', *TS* 58 (1997), 618–42.

Soskice, J. M., *Metaphor and religious language* (Oxford, 1985).

Spanneut, M., *Le stoïcisme des pères de l'église* (Paris, 1957).

Permanence du stoïcisme (Gembloux, 1973).

Stanton, G. N., 'The fourfold Gospel', *NTS* 43 (1997), 317–46.

Strecker, G., *Eschaton und Historie* (Göttingen, 1969).

Striker, G., 'Κριτήριον τῆς ἀληθείας', NAWG.PH 1 (1974), 47–110.

Torrance, A. J., 'Creatio ex nihilo and the Spatio-Temporal dimension with special reference to Jürgen Moltmann and D. C. Williams', in *The doctrine of creation*, ed. Colin E. Gunton (Edinburgh, 1997).

Torrance, T. F., 'The deposit of faith', *SJTh* 36 (1983), 1–28.

'Kerygmatic proclamation of the gospel: the demonstration of apostolic preaching of Irenaios of Lyons', *GOTR* 37,1–2 (1992), 105–21.

Tortorelli, K. M., 'Balthasar and the theodramatic interpretation of St Irenaeus', *DR* 111 (1993), 117–26.

Tremblay, R., *La manifestation et la vision de Dieu selon Saint Irénée de Lyon* (Münster, 1978).

'La signification d'Abraham dans l'oeuvre d'Irénée de Lyon', *Aug* 18 (1978), 435–57.

Irénée de Lyon, 'L'empreinte des doigts de Dieu' (Rome, 1979).

Tripp, D. H., 'The original sequence of Irenaeus *Adversus haereses* I: a suggestion', *SecCent* 8 (1991), 157–62.

Tsirpanlis, C. N., 'The Antichrist and the end of the world in Irenaeus, Justin, Hippolytus, and Tertullian', *Patristic and Byzantine Review* 9,1 (1990), 5–17.

Unnik, W. C. van, 'Theological speculation and its limits', in *Early Christian literature and the classical intellectual tradition*, FS for R. M. Grant, ed. W. R. Schoedel and R. M. Wilken, ThH 54 (Paris, 1979), 33–43.

Vallée, G., 'Theological and non-theological motives in Irenaeus' refutation of the Gnostics', in *Jewish and Christian self-definition*, vol. I: *The shaping of Christianity in the second and third centuries*, ed. E. P. Sanders (Philadelphia, 1980).

Verweyen, H., 'Frühchristliche Theologie in der Herausforderung durch die antike Welt, *ZKTh* 109 (1987), 385–99.

Vickers, B., *In defence of rhetoric* (Oxford, 1988).

Vincent, G., 'Le corps de l'hérétique (la critique de la gnose par Irénée)', *RHPhR* 69,4 (1989), 411–21.

Vogt, H. J., 'Die Geltung des Alten Testaments bei Irenäus von Lyon', *ThQ* 160 (1980), 17–28.

'Teilkirchen-Perspektive bei Irenäus?', *ThQ* 164,1 (1984), 52–8.

Werner, J., *Der Paulinismus des Irenaeus. Eine kirchen- und dogmengeschichtliche Untersuchung über das Verhältnis des Irenaeus zu der paulinischen Briefsammlung und Theologie*, TU 6,2 (Leipzig, 1889).

Widmann, M., 'Der Begriff οίκονομία im Werk des Irenäus und seine Vorgeschichte', (Dissertation; Tübingen, 1956).

'Irenaeus und seine theologischen Väter', *ZThK* 54 (1957), 156–73.

Wilken, R. L., 'Early Christian chiliasm, Jewish messianism, and the idea of the holy land', Essays in honor of Krister Stendahl, *HThR* 79, 1–3 (1986), 298–307.

Williams, M. A., *Rethinking 'Gnosticism'. An argument for dismantling a dubious category* (Princeton, 1996).

Wingren, G., *Man and the incarnation. A study in the biblical theology of Irenaeus* (Edinburgh, 1959).

'The doctrine of creation: not an appendix but the first article', *Word & World* 4,4 (1984), 353–71.

Winling, R., 'Le Christ-Didascale et les didascales gnostiques et chrétiens d'après l'oeuvre d'Irénée', *RevSR* 57 (1983), 261–72.

'Une façon de dire le salut: la formule "être avec dieu être avec Jésus-Christ" dans les écrits de Saint Irénée', *RevSR* 58 (1984), 105–35.

Young, F. M., *Biblical exegesis and the formation of Christian culture* (Cambridge, 1997).

Ziegler, H., *Irenäus der Bischof von Lyon* (Berlin, 1871).

Citations from Irenaeus

Citations from the bible

295

Index of classical authors

Index of patristic authors

General index